Strategies for the Digital Customer Experience

NEW HORIZONS IN MARKETING SERIES

Books in the New Horizons in Marketing series make a significant contribution to the study of marketing and contexts in which it operates. As this field has expanded dramatically in recent years, the series will provide an invaluable forum for the publication of high-quality works of scholarship and show the diversity of research on marketing.

Global and pluralistic in its approach, this series includes some of the best theoretical and analytical work with contributions to fundamental principles, rigorous evaluations of existing concepts and competing theories, stimulating debate and future visions.

Titles in the series include:

Social Marketing and Advertising in the Age of Social Media
Edited by Lukas Parker and Linda Brennan

Youth Marketing to Digital Natives
Wided Batat

Strategies for the Digital Customer Experience
Connecting Customers with Brands in the Phygital Age
Wided Batat

Strategies for the Digital Customer Experience

Connecting Customers with Brands in the Phygital Age

Wided Batat

Professor of Marketing, Keynote Speaker, and Entrepreneur

NEW HORIZONS IN MARKETING SERIES

Edward Elgar
PUBLISHING

Cheltenham, UK • Northampton, MA, USA

Published by
Edward Elgar Publishing Limited
The Lypiatts
15 Lansdown Road
Cheltenham
Glos GL50 2JA
UK

Edward Elgar Publishing, Inc.
William Pratt House
9 Dewey Court
Northampton
Massachusetts 01060
USA

A catalogue record for this book
is available from the British Library

Library of Congress Control Number: 2022932883

This book is available electronically in the **Elgar**online
Business subject collection
http://dx.doi.org/10.4337/9781800371897

ISBN 978 1 80037 188 0 (cased)
ISBN 978 1 80037 189 7 (eBook)

Printed and bound by CPI Group (UK) Ltd, Croydon, CR0 4YY

Contents

Figures

Tables

Boxes

About the author

Dr. Wided Batat is the founder of the modern experiential marketing mix and its 7Es tool. She also introduced the concept of "phygital" as an ecosystem for businesses to engage in successful digital transformation strategies. She is a professor and doctor of experiential and digital marketing and one of the best marketing experts in the world: as a university researcher, she carries out important work all over the world. As an entrepreneur and international outstanding keynote speaker, Dr. Batat directs and carries out significant research and consultancy activities in customer experience design and phygital strategies in Europe, the United States, Asia, and the Middle East. With over 17 years of experience in the field, and combining scientific research and business experience, Dr. Batat transforms organizations by providing innovative market research and consumer insights. Her expertise can help businesses gain an enduring perspective of innovation, profitability, progress, and performance. She has also published many books in the field, and her 2019 best-selling title *Experiential Marketing* is invaluable for consumer behavior, marketing experts, and executive teams.

Introduction to *Strategies for the Digital Customer Experience*

This book offers new lenses to understand how companies can implement digital strategies and incorporate various technologies to create compelling customer experiences in the "phygital" (physical + digital) era. Whether you are a researcher, a student, a business professional, or a business journalist, you will find in this book novel frameworks, concepts, and tools that can help you deal with the complexity when it comes to considering a third reality of the customer experience, namely phygital, that combines the characteristics of both physical and digital settings. The objective of this book is to present a critical framework to help companies rethink their digital strategies related to customer experience design by exploring novel approaches to help companies shift from IT strategies based on the identification and incorporation of technologies to embrace phygital. Phygital is an integral holistic ecosystem that goes beyond digital or IT strategy to create satisfying and profitable customer experiences that help customers navigate between online and offline offerings.

The first part of this book, "Customer Experience in Physical, Digital, and Phygital Settings," explores the contributions the concept of customer experience has made to digital marketing and its evolution, shifting from physical and digital spaces to more hybrid and phygital settings. Also, this part illustrates, through three chapters, the main challenges companies are facing in the design and transformation of their brand experiences to create a continuum from physical to digital, and vice versa. Chapter 1 introduces the experiential frameworks (holistic vs. atomistic) and questions why experiential offerings are critical for companies to satisfy the needs of new consumers who are searching for emotional, social, and symbolic experiences rather than merely functional products. Chapter 2 focuses on customer experience design in the digital space. This chapter presents the evolution of digital marketing and its tools and techniques, and explores how digitization shapes the customer experience, usually limited to the physical setting, in digital environments, including multiple touchpoints. Chapter 3 introduces the third realm of the customer experience, namely phygital. In this chapter, I question how phygital can help companies humanize customer experiences and create a continuum linking physical and digital settings.

The second part of this book, "Digital Devices and Tools to Get Phygital with Customers," explores, through five chapters, devices and technologies that businesses can implement to design phygital customer experiences. In Chapter 4, I explain how extended reality technology (ERT), as part of a company's digital strategy, can enable the design of compelling phygital customer experiences. Chapter 5 presents the second technology related to integrating robotics and artificial intelligence (AI) to help companies design highly interactive and humanized phygital experiences. The challenges related to human–robot relationships and interactions are also discussed in this chapter. Chapter 6 focuses on the Internet of Things (IoT) and connected objects and the role of these two technologies in the design of fluid and intuitive phygital experiences that empower consumers and provide companies with valuable insights into the consumption practices of their customers. The benefits and challenges of the IoT and connected objects for companies to transform their relationships with their customers are also discussed in this chapter. In Chapter 7, I introduce the concept of gamification and explain how playfulness and games can help companies create immersive and hedonic phygital experiences. I also define and discuss gamification from a marketing perspective by answering how companies can implement gamification actions to improve the customer experience while dealing with customer journey pain points. Chapter 8 explores the technology of 3-D printing and the online 3-D printing platforms that companies can use in their digital strategies to create highly customized and on-demand phygital experiences. This chapter sheds light on the progress of 3-D printing technology and its role in engaging customers in a co-creation process where they can create their own consumption items, ranging from food to furniture, via different 3-D printing platforms.

The third part of this book, "Strategies for Successful Phygital Customer Experience Design," explores the new tools companies can use to rethink their business practices, including ways of thinking and doing when it comes to designing effective and profitable phygital experiences. This part includes three main chapters. In Chapter 9, I present the limits of the traditional marketing mix in the experiential and phygital era. I also introduce the first challenge that businesses face when designing the ultimate phygital experience and switching to a new experiential marketing mix that goes beyond the traditional use of the mix by addressing the 7Es: Experience, Exchange, Extension, Emphasis, Empathy capital, Emotional touchpoints, and the Emic/etic process. I show how the new experiential marketing mix and its 7Es can help companies meet their strategic objectives and create a solid competitive advantage while creating engaging online and offline experiences for their customers. Chapter 10 focuses on the transition from a big data logic to immersive smart data to develop a digital luxury experience by using alternative market research tools. In this chapter, I introduce "smart data," an immersive and exploratory tool companies should consider beyond the limits of the "big data bang" when it comes to collecting insights about customer experiences in the phygital era. In Chapter 11, I introduce Experiential Design Thinking (EXDT) as a new tool to create innovative phygital experiences for consumer well-being. This chapter examines how the new EXDT model can offer critical insights into new approaches to design innovative and ethical customer experiences in the phygital era. Also, I answer the following questions: What are the limits of the traditional design thinking method? And why should companies consider an "experiential approach" to their innovation process when it comes to creating satisfying, efficient, and profitable phygital experiences? Finally, in Chapter 12, I conclude by presenting a new holistic disruption strategy companies can implement to create innovative customer experiences in the phygital era. In this chapter, I explore the foundations, definitions, and different perspectives related to disruptive innovations. The holistic approach to disruptive innovation in customer experience design is then presented and discussed.

Strategies for the Digital Customer Experience: Connecting Customers with Brands in the Phygital Age, therefore, provides both businesses and academic readers with new horizons for digital marketing strategies to design phygital experiences by using various technologies. This book draws on my professional expertise and my prior work on digital transformation from both sides: company and user/customer across different sectors and industries. This book provides an extensive review of the existing knowledge in this field and examples.

I hope the book will help readers gain an in-depth understanding of the complexities related to the design of compelling customer experiences that create a continuum between online and offline offerings, thanks to embracing phygital as a holistic ecosystem and not only questioning what type of digital device or technology companies should incorporate in their digital strategies.

PART I

Customer experience in physical, digital, and phygital settings

1. Customer experience: the new holy grail for businesses

CHAPTER OVERVIEW

Customer experience is becoming a hot topic for both academics and businesses; yet the definition of the concept remains abstract, and its implementation in practice is somehow limited. This chapter introduces the roots and perspectives on customer experience by examining two main approaches: consumer behavior and marketing. It also explains why experiential offerings are critical for companies to satisfy the needs of new consumers who are searching for emotional, social, and symbolic experiences rather than merely functional products. The four main characteristics of new consumer behaviors through the paradoxical, empowered, emotional, collaborator (PEEC) scheme are presented. Customer experience types and frameworks (holistic vs. atomistic) that can help companies design successful and profitable customer experiences, both online and offline, are also discussed in this chapter.

1   CONCEPTUALIZING THE CUSTOMER EXPERIENCE

This section aims to examine the existing definitions of the concept of customer experience through a multidisciplinary analysis of the literature. It also introduces two main perspectives on customer experience: consumer behavior and marketing.

1.1   Customer Experience: Definitions and Perspectives

Far from only being a concept used in the marketing field, the notion of "experience" made its first appearance in the writings of philosophers and can be situated at the intersection of three fields, including the focus on the philosophy of the mind, knowledge, and science. Etymologically, experience is defined as a feeling of self-enrichment generated by events where a person is more likely to learn about him/herself and develop knowledge about the environment to which he/she belongs. Thus, it is conventional to refer to experience as a mental state, which involves a solid and instant connection of the person's mind with his/her sociocultural environment. Drawing on a cross-disciplinary analysis, five major approaches to the concept of experience have been identified: philosophical, sociological, cultural, management, and business.

1. In philosophy, experience is considered an ambivalent ideological notion. It represents the connection of individuals with material reality and the formation of knowledge and understanding. Nevertheless, at the same time, it is irrational, random, emotional, intangible, and without any connection to the material world. Consequently, the experience can be both a starting point and an endpoint. Either it really has something to teach us or it can confirm our knowledge in a confrontation with reality.

2. From a sociological standpoint, sociologists define experience as multiple and composite. It is embedded in a social context and shaped by the lifeworlds in a particular setting and in contact with social actors, institutions, markets; and is influenced by the macro, meso, and micro factors of the environment.

3. Following a cultural perspective, anthropologists define experience by its subjective, symbolic, and cultural dimensions. Creating an experience is both a process of acting on the natural conditions of one's life and engaging in the self-fulfillment process of one's self-identity. The experience is thus seen as a source of individualization, which conditions and transforms individuals by making them unique and different since they live experiences that are part of their individualization process.

4. From a management perspective, human resource (HR) scholars have recently developed an interest in the concept of experience, and thus contributed to the rise of a new research stream that focuses on the "employee experience" paradigm. From an HR perspective, experience is defined by its cognitive, social, and affective dimensions. Batat (2021a) defines the employee experience as the employee's holistic perceptions of the relationship with his/her employing organization derived from all encounters at touchpoints along the employee's journey. However, while the experiential approach has been heavily used in the marketing literature, the employee experience has not received the same attention in the management literature, where it is considered an emerging research field.

5. Following a business perspective, marketing scholars have provided various approaches to examine shopping and consumption experiences. Although the association of the notion of experience with consumption was introduced in marketing in the 1940s (Holbrook, 2000), few works have considered consumption experience as a field of research. For instance, Holbrook (2000) referred to previous works by Norris (1941), who emphasized the importance given to the moment offered by the

product, considered superior to the product itself, to its technical characteristics or performance. In the same line, Abbott (1955) considered the moment experienced with the product as more significant than the product itself. Why? Because what people really want are not products but satisfying experiences. Current works that contribute to the definition of customer experience follow two leading perspectives: (1) consumer behavior (experiential consumption) and (2) business (experiential marketing). These two perspectives are explained and illustrated by examples in the next section.

1.1.1　Experiential consumption: a consumer behavior perspective

Studies focusing on consumer behavior have evolved over the last few decades. These works highlight the shift from a vision of a "rational" consumer to a more "affective" and "emotional" approach to consumption. This idea was introduced by Alderson (1957), who was the first to consider value from a consumer perspective by focusing on experiences instead of products. This positioning has contributed to the rise of the concept of consumption experience as it is defined nowadays.

The main idea here is that the value a consumer derives from a consumption object does not come from the object itself, understood in its materiality and tangible features, but rather from the use of this product. The notion of *hedonomics*, in contrast to *economicus*, is then introduced by Alderson and used later by Holbrook and Hirschman to emphasize the focus on the hedonic aspect of consumption. Thus, considering consumption as an experience implies a more holistic approach that incorporates, alongside tangible qualities, certain intangible dimensions (e.g., hedonic, social, symbolic, ideological), which have been ignored until now. This idea was first discussed in the seminal article by Holbrook and Hirschman (1982), who proposed a new vision and framework for understanding consumer behavior.

Accordingly, the notion of "experience" was first introduced by these latter two authors, who refer to the hedonic and emotional aspects of consumption as critical components of consumer behavior that marketing scholars often neglected at that time. Thus, following an experiential perspective to consumption and shopping activities makes us reconsider consumers' needs in terms of products and services. These needs are tangible and functional; but they also incorporate intangible, irrational, and emotional expectations—including social, aesthetic, symbolic, ideological, sensorial, and educational.

Consumption is then perceived as a multisensory and subjective experience. This search for pleasure is the basis of hedonic consumption and hence the need to live different types of experiences (Batat, 2019a). Consumers search for unique and memorable shopping and consumption experiences that are lived differently according to the individual's state, personality, and the setting in which the purchase or activity occurs. Considering consumption as a subjective, personal, and emotional state is not a new idea; it has been discussed in previous works focusing on the sociology of consumption since the 1970s. In this research stream, authors argue that consumption is not merely a functional and utilitarian activity where the role of the consumer is limited to "destroying" the product; instead, it is an activity charged with meaning and emotions, and where consumers build value and meanings through their consumption and shopping experiences (Baudrillard, 1970).

This consideration then shifted from sociology to marketing, justified by the fact that researchers had essentially focused on the decision-making process, ignoring the sociological and symbolic dimensions of consumption to understand consumer behavior. The dominant theoretical framework, of a cognitive nature, focused on the consumer's decision-making process studied through its antecedents and consequences (e.g., Willman-Iivarinen, 2017; Engel et al., 1990), considering the consumer as a rational market actor. Thanks to the integration of the sociological perspective into the marketing field since the 1980s, other aspects of consumption (e.g., affective, symbolic, social) were then introduced. This perspective offers a new angle of developing an in-depth understanding of the customer experience as a relevant field of research that can help academics and businesses capture the hidden dimensions and paradoxical aspects behind consumers' adoption and rejection of brands.

In the experiential consumption perspective, the consumer is considered as an individual in search of emotions, feelings, and pleasure. This vision enriches the cognitive and utilitarian approach and emphasizes the core idea that consumers can also access happiness and well-being (Batat, 2019a; Csikszentmihalyi, 1997). This assumption can be explained by consumers' high level of immersion and commitment during a lived experience. This situation refers to the highly popular concept of flow introduced in psychology by Csikszentmihalyi (1997), who considers the experience as a flow when individuals are absorbed by the task they have to perform. They, thus, completely forget the passing of time, which will generate positive emotions and a feeling of plenitude.

Likewise, other authors such as Firat and Venkatesh (1995) consider the consumption experience regarding the phase of "re-enchantment" where consumers are drawn into a magical atmosphere. In so doing, experiential consumption should be enriched by bringing more to the consumer's daily life at all levels and considering various needs, both emotionally and rationally (e.g., Firat and Dholakia, 2006). An analysis of consumption experience conceptualizations underlines the multidimensional aspect of the concept. The most influential definitions can be summarized as follows:

- The consumption experience is defined as a subjective state of conscious-ness conveyed by various symbolic meanings, hedonic responses, and aesthetic criteria. This definition places the individual's subjectivity at the center of consumption activities. This assumption implies that the individual is also an active actor in the experience. Yet this definition has been developed based on leisure activities, characterized by hedonic experiences with a strong, playful dimension and sensory pleasures that should be implemented and discussed in other mundane consumption fields to extend traditional theories of consumer behavior.
- The consumption experience refers to a set of positive or negative out-comes that the consumer derives from the use of a good or service at different lived moments, during and after consumption, but also before, based on the expectations that individuals create for themselves (Arnould and Price, 1993).
- The consumption experience is about transforming ordinary moments into enjoyable lived moments in the form of micro-immersions realized several times, allowing the consumer to develop a feeling of pleasure (Carù and Cova, 2007).
- The consumption experience is a subjective episode in the construction/transformation of the individual, with an emphasis on the emotional and sensitive dimension, beyond the cognitive dimension (Arnould and Thompson, 2005).
- The consumption experience is an internal and subjective response of the consumer to direct (purchase or use of the product) or indirect (word-of-mouth or advertising) contact with the company (Meyer and Schwager, 2007).
- The consumption experience occurs at each interaction with the company, where the experience becomes a "win–win" strategy for the company and its customers since it allows the latter to gain more satisfaction (Grewal et al., 2009).
- The consumption experience is conditioned by the integration of all touchpoints (e.g., product, salespeople, communication) provided by the company to deliver a compelling and accessible experience to customers while being consistent with its corporate values (Dhebar, 2013).
- The consumption experience is a reaction caused by several interactions between the customer and the company. Thus, experience is about creating reactions among consumers through interactions with the brand, along with involving different dimensions, such as sensory, affective, cognitive, behavioral, and social (e.g., Schmitt, 2003; 1999).

A recent holistic and comprehensive definition I have offered previously in my book *Experiential Marketing* defines consumption experience as:

> connected with the lived dimension of the experience, which is embedded within the sociocultural context in which consumers interact with each other and with other social agents, institutions, market actors, family, etc. that constitute their immediate environment. Thus, customer experience is multidimensional, composite, and an evolving construct. It combines a harmonious blend of several factors and actors that directly or indirectly impact successful designing experiences in connection with the marketplace. Further, customer experience can be defined from two main perspectives: consumer and company. Unlike the traditional marketing approach, which focuses on goods (products and services), experiential marketing offers a transformative experience where the consumer engages in the process of self-fulfillment. The impact of the lived experience is global and generates a continuum in the hyperreal world by way of digital means. (Batat, 2019a, p. 61)

From the cited definitions, it should be noted that the consumer behavior perspective on experiential consumption is linked to an individual dimension where the feeling is that of a person. The experience cannot therefore be defined without a connection to the subject who lives it. It also has an evolving dimension: the consumption experience is not static but anchored in the individual's life journey and social interactions. This assumption allows us to understand the consumption phenomenon as an integral part of the individual's life by examining aspects such as the individual's narratives about consumption, the role of consumption in self-development, the social dimension of consumption, and the meanings of consumption items, among others.

Nevertheless, before assessing these dimensions, we need first to distinguish between experiential consumption, defined from the consumer's perspective, and experiential marketing, which refers to the production of experiences delivered by companies. The experiential marketing perspective is discussed in the next section.

1.1.2 Experiential marketing: a business perspective

Experiential marketing has given experience a much more practical and applied aspect while emphasizing the idea that the result should be something significant and unforgettable for the consumer, who will live the experience in contact with the company and its products and services. In the experiential marketing perspective, as I pointed out, an experience represents a new category of offers particularly adapted to the needs of the postmodern consumer (Batat, 2019a). It should be extraordinary, immersive, and memorable. The main idea in the experiential marketing perspective is that companies should create extraordinary experiences by implementing customer-centric strategies through combining different elements and tools. Authors such as Pine and

Gilmore (1998) or Schmitt (1999) consider that the experience must be lived as a total and extraordinary immersion to enrich the product or service offered.

In their article "Welcome to the Experience Economy" (1998), Pine and Gilmore use the metaphor of a birthday cake to enlighten their readers about the progression of value in what they call the "experience economy." The two authors argue that economists typically place experiences in the service domain; yet experiences are economic offerings distinct from services, in the same way that a company's products are.

As goods and services become commoditized, customer experiences are crucial for firms to hold a competitive advantage. An experience occurs when a company intentionally uses services as the stage and goods as props, and engages customers in a way that creates a memorable event. Commodities are fungible, goods are tangible, services are intangible, and *experiences* are memorable. According to Pine and Gilmore, companies aiming to provide experiences to their customers should consider two main dimensions.

The first is the customer's participation, who, from once being a passive customer, now becomes an active customer by being a co-creator of value for a company. The second is that the consumer's connection with the event or the performance he or she attends provides him or her with complete immersion. Thus experiences, like goods and services, should meet the needs of customers. Just as goods and services are the consequences of an iterative process of research, design, and development, experiences are the result of an iterative process of exploration, scripting, and staging that aspiring experience marketers will need to master (Pine and Gilmore, 1998). The question is then: why should companies seriously consider customer experience? We can cite three main reasons.

First, customer experience is considered a new type of offer and not just an additional element. In line with Pine and Gilmore's statement, until now, three types of supply were distinguished: (1) commodities (primary sector); (2) manufactured goods (secondary sector); and (3) services (tertiary sector). Experience appears as a fourth option. The two authors illustrate these four categories with the example of coffee:

- *Coffee as a commodity.* It is directly extracted from nature and traded wholesale in markets at a price determined by supply and demand. At this stage, the cost per cup is less than 10 US cents.
- *Coffee as a manufactured product.* The beans are ground by a manufacturer who packages them for sale in supermarkets. The price depends on the cost of production and the differentiation of the product. The price per cup varies between 40 cents and US$1.
- *Coffee as a service.* When consumed in a coffeehouse, it is an intangible activity, custom-made at the request of a known client. The value that the

customer attributes to this service is much higher than the product's value. For this reason, a cup of coffee can sell for between US$1.5 and US$2.
• *Coffee as an experience*. When it is consumed in a high-end or themed spot such as Starbucks, or in a hotel or restaurant, the price of a cup of coffee can reach more than US$3 or 4. This cup of coffee is very different from the product (the pack of ground coffee) or the service (the cup of coffee served in a bar). The place's atmosphere, the background music, the setting, the design of the cup itself, the friendliness of the waiter, and so forth are elements that surround the simple purchase of a cup of coffee and make it an authentic experience.

This example shows that service quality is not enough to create memorable experiences and remain competitive in the marketplace, as reported by marketing scholars (e.g., Schembri, 2006; Prahalad and Ramaswamy, 2004; Berry, 2002). Indeed, today's customers value experiences, and companies capable of offering unique and memorable experiences can enhance customer loyalty and develop a substantial competitive advantage.

The second reason companies should seriously consider customer experience is related to the company's need to go beyond the value-in-use and the functional attributes of the product or the service. By shifting their questioning from "What products/services do we need to offer?" to "How should products/services be offered to make customers feel good?" companies can create valuable experiences, integrating both the emotional and functional needs of the consumer.

Last but not least, the third reason that leads companies to shift to a more experiential marketing approach is a guarantee of customer loyalty and positive word-of-mouth. Beyond value creation, companies that adopt customer experience, combining functional and emotional benefits in their offerings, expect to increase customer loyalty and transform customers into true brand ambassadors. Therefore, to enhance customer loyalty, a company should take an integrated and strategic approach that focuses on improving the customer's overall experience through different touchpoints that connect customers with the company, both online and offline.

Consequently, in the experiential marketing perspective, authors often use the notion of "customer experience," which is designed and delivered by companies to satisfy both tangible (e.g., functionality, quality, design) and intangible (e.g., symbolic, emotional, social) consumer needs. In so doing, companies must incorporate both the in-store experience and the experience before the point of sale. Customer experiences begin before the purchase phase and continue through to the post-purchase phase, which includes all the customer's attitudes toward a product or service.

Thus, to offer satisfying customer experiences, all of the company's touch-points should be integrated to deliver a compelling experience. These include communication, interactions with employees or via electronic platforms, product or service, point of sale, and architecture (e.g., Dhebar, 2013).

Therefore, the encounter between the customer and the company is a crucial moment. Implementing an effective and all-inclusive marketing strategy is a great challenge for companies to attract and retain customers while differentiating themselves in a highly competitive marketplace. This challenging situation leads companies to shift their focus from a traditional approach to marketing to a more experiential marketing approach that is centered on the customer and his or her tangible and intangible needs. Following this logic, Schmitt (1999) contrasts traditional marketing with a new experiential approach to marketing.

According to Schmitt, experiential marketing focuses on the customer experience that provides sensory, emotional, cognitive, behavioral, and relational values, which replace functional values. Schmitt invites companies to think about their customers more in terms of their emotional rather than their functional needs. Indeed, customers are emotionally and rationally driven. Although they may make rational choices, these are based on their emotions because consumer experiences are often oriented toward the pursuit of happiness and self-fulfillment. For Schmitt, experiential marketing is becoming one of the critical criteria for customer loyalty as the time of customers simply looking to buy products is already over; they want more. Experiential marketing is then an appropriate approach that companies can implement to provide a memorable experience to a customer before, during, and after the purchase. Also, Schmitt distinguishes between in-store experience when buying a product or service and the experience in an advertising or promotional context.

Referring to in-store experiences, experiential marketing is more centered on the quality of the welcome, the environment, and the information given to customers. All these elements should be particularly pleasant for the customer. Salespeople can also rely on sensory or immersive marketing to intensify this aspect of experiential marketing. In advertising or promotion, experiential marketing focuses on offering the most immersive experience possible with the brand, by using storytelling as a tool to enhance positive feelings and thus increase customer loyalty. Therefore, implementing a successful experiential marketing strategy leads companies to shift their focus from the traditional product-centric approach to a more customer-centric logic by placing customers at the center of the firm's strategy and better understanding their tangible and intangible needs.

Following the rise and evolution of an experiential marketing approach that integrates a business perspective, in *Experiential Marketing*, published in 2019, I introduced the tool of the 7Es of the experiential marketing mix:

Experience, Exchange, Extension, Emphasis, Empathy capital, Emotional touchpoints, and Emic/etic process.

This new tool provides companies with a strategic framework for the new experiential marketing mix, and a detailed analysis of the components of the new mix that companies and marketing managers can use to implement effective experiential marketing and communication actions to create and share value and experiences with their customers (see Chapter 9 for more details on the 7Es of the experiential marketing mix). Therefore, a company undertaking an experiential marketing strategy should implement the 7Es tool to position its offer beyond its functional attributes and create memorable and inimitable experiences for the customer, encompassing various forms across different sectors.

Nevertheless, before implementing an experiential marketing mix through the 7Es tool, companies need to better understand the emerging consumer trends and the changes in consumer behavior to offer suitable, enjoyable, and profitable customer experiences. The following section presents the features of new consumer behaviors that companies should consider in their experiential offerings.

2   HOW CAN EXPERIENCE RESPOND TO KEY CHANGES IN CONSUMER BEHAVIOR?

Today's consumers are changing and becoming familiar with instant accessibility, and will expect their consumption and purchase experiences to be immediate, unique, and emotional. Thus, companies need to better understand the key changes in consumer behaviors to create suitable and enjoyable online and offline customer experiences. In my previous research, I highlighted the advent of a new consumer, emphasizing the transformation of the consumer's status, needs, and his/her role in the relationship with the brand or company.

These social changes lead companies to rethink their approach to their customers by implementing not only new communication strategies online and offline but also an experiential strategy, by putting more emphasis on the intangible dimensions of their behaviors and the new emerging consumption trends. Faced with these profound changes, accelerated by the democratization of the Internet and the use of social media, companies must adapt their relational, strategic, marketing, and digital strategies. Two main questions then arise: Who is the new consumer? Moreover, what are the main characteristics of his/her consumption behavior?

Answering these questions helps marketing professionals open the black box of consumer behavior by capturing the key characteristics that can help companies offer satisfying experiences. In this section, I propose to define the main characteristics of the new consumer behavior through four key pillars of the PEEC scheme, referring to the new consumer as Paradoxical, Empowered, Emotional, and Collaborator—as explained in Figure 1.1.

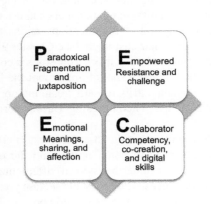

Figure 1.1   The four pillars of the PEEC scheme

2.1   Paradoxical Consumer

This profile emerged due to the postmodern context in which consumer behaviors take place. Thus, the postmodern paradigm can serve as a framework to understand the paradoxical behaviors of today's consumers, which could benefit companies that were initially baffled by the new patterns of postmodern consumption, but at the same time are capable of adapting to these trends by developing creative offerings and integrating technologies to offer customized and satisfying customer experiences. According to Mickey (1997), the postmodern consumer lives in a society filled with doubt, ambiguity, and uncertainty. It is this situation that companies should attempt to understand by identifying the macro sociocultural forces influencing consumer behaviors, attitudes, and motivations to satisfy the needs and expectations of the consumer in terms of brand experiences if they wish to subsist in the postmodern marketplace. For Batat (2019a), the paradoxical consumer demonstrates two key consumption features: fragmentation and juxtaposition of behaviors.

Batat stated that criticism of the modern consumer society has given rise to new forms of consumption underlining the transition phase of the modern era to the postmodern era, and thus the rise of postmodern paradoxes. These consumer behavior paradoxes can be described according to six characteristics: the desire to be alone and together; masculine and feminine; nomadic and sedentary; real and virtual; Kairos and Kronos; and, finally, a quest for old and new (Decrop, 2008, cited in Batat, 2011).

The first characteristic, alone and together, refers to the digital and social media era in which the Internet and smartphones constitute integral parts of the consumer's daily life. These tools enable the consumer to stay permanently connected with friends and colleagues, and at the same time increase his or her isolation and foster the dehumanization of human relations. Therefore, other forms of socialization have emerged, such as online communities with individuals who share the same interests and have common passions for activities (role-playing games, food, etc.) or brands (Apple, Microsoft, Nike, etc.). Here, the individual is willing to reconstruct a family elsewhere with the logic of "Me first, but not alone" (Batat, 2011).

The second characteristic, masculine and feminine, shows that the erosion of boundaries between "masculine" values (e.g., bravery, power) and "feminine" values (e.g., peace, kindness) enhances the paradoxical behavior of the postmodern consumer. Therefore, more and more women are becoming independent and adopting masculine behaviors; men, in turn, are becoming feminized—androgynous, metrosexual (a heterosexual urban man who enjoys shopping, fashion, and similar interests traditionally associated with women or homosexual men), adopting feminine values conveyed by advertising (e.g., cosmetics for male consumers). The third characteristic denotes the need for consumers to be nomadic and sedentary at the same time. Today's consumers are thus facing a paradox: they want to move and to stay, seeking somewhere else but like at home.

The next paradox, real and virtual, reflects the hyperreal dimension of the postmodern consumer society. Hyperreality refers to the attrition of boundaries between the real and the virtual world, such as in video games or dating websites. The fifth paradox refers to the consumer's relationship and perception of time where two dimensions should be distinguished: Kairos (the instant transformed into action) and Kronos (measurable time flowing linearly). This paradox has led to the rise of new consumption trends such as the slow food movement, in contrast to the modern concept of fast-food. The final paradox, old and new, is based on the logic that the paradoxical consumer requires "old" and nostalgic objects, which have to be updated by including "new" options, functionalities, and technologies. In this case, we refer to this consumption behavior as "newstalgic".

BOX 1.1   FOOD CONSUMPTION: A PARADOXICAL RELATIONSHIP BETWEEN CONSUMER AND FOOD

Although eating behaviors are often structured in characteristic food models, it should be acknowledged that food habits are often paradoxical and/or conflicting. For instance, recently the COVID-19 pandemic and lockdowns have raised many questions about food consumption, where food becomes part of the unusual daily life of individuals. Thus, many paradoxes have emerged between pleasure and the necessity to eat healthily.

Eaters are paradoxical beings. There are often discrepancies between the knowledge, convictions, and intentions of eaters, on the one hand, and their actual behavior, on the other. In other words, knowing and even wanting are not always synonymous with doing and acting. This situation can be explained by many factors: a fragmented consumer with multiple facets; an excess of information and contradictory injunctions; a moralization of food; and a context where healthy eating is the dominant discourse within society. The relationship between consumers and their food practices depicts various paradoxical behaviors. These food consumption paradoxes can be classified into five main categories that show how multifaceted consumers can be in their relationship to food:

- *Food quality and saving money: a complex equation to solve?* This paradox shows that, on the one hand, consumers have the injunction to "consume better" and, on the other hand, they need to save money. Price sensitivity is as much linked to economics as to the desire to change someone's philosophy of life about his/her food consumption.
- *Healthy eating and/or indulgence: what are the trade-offs?* Quality is as much about being nutritious and authentic as it is about pleasure, temptation, and gluttony for consumers. The most obvious example is undoubtedly the most popular foods cited by consumers: burgers, pizzas, cookies, or ice-cream, where pleasure is in the spotlight while healthy eating is an increasingly strong concern. In this sense, the consumer chooses between health and pleasure, depending on the time and sometimes the day.
- *Flexitarian behaviors in a society where animal proteins are still dominant.* On the one hand, there is a movement toward flexitarianism (eating more plant-based food and less meat); but at the same time there is a firm increase in sales of animal proteins.
- *Cooking and food delivery.* Although cooking has recently been accelerated, food delivery is still a strong trend as cooking activities can

be limited by intrinsic obstacles such as lack of time and ideas or the pleasure generated by cooking.

- *Food stores and supermarkets: an ambivalent relationship?* The number of food chains responding to mass food consumption has increased since the mid-2010s. Although small stores and farmers' markets are on the rise and very popular among today's consumers who want to control the quality of their food and eat healthily, they still visit supermarkets to purchase food products for two reasons: convenience and cost.

Consequently, when it comes to eating well, consumers behave paradoxically with, on the one hand, a rise in consumer expertise and, on the other, the rise of so-called "healthy" diets and their excesses, such as orthorexia (an unhealthy obsession with "healthy" eating). Characteristics of the postmodern society explain the situation individuals live in, where there is an abundance that makes food immediately available, and yet they restrict themselves—they eat "without." Thus, consumers forget the pleasure of food when healthy eating is the dominant norm; but at the same time, we note that once lockdown was over, many individuals rushed to fast-food chains looking for missed guilty pleasure by consuming pleasurable and unhealthy food.

2.2   Empowered Consumer

As largely documented in the marketing field, consumer empowerment is a multidimensional concept that encompasses multiple cognitive, personal, and social elements. Today's consumers are considered competent and empowered market actors as they have acquired different knowledge skills thanks to information access and consumption experiences.

To become empowered in the digital era, consumers are expected to develop relevant knowledge and skills to help them understand and select the offers that respond to their needs. This state supposes that the new consumer knows how to select, organize, combine, and integrate this knowledge within an environment of constraints and resources. Denegri-Knott et al. (2006) define consumer empowerment as the ability of an individual to control his/her choices and get more control over relationships with companies.

According to Hunter and Garnefeld, consumer empowerment can be defined as the act of giving consumers power through resources, and as a personal and subjective situation produced by perceptions of collective control. These authors define consumer empowerment as "consumers' subjective experiences that they have a greater ability than before to intentionally produce desired outcomes and prevent undesired ones and that they are benefiting from the increased ability" (2008, p. 2). In other words, for consumers, the empowerment experience is two-fold: they want the company to provide them with adequate and transparent information and a relatively controlled process.

Other authors (Arnould and Thompson, 2005) talk about consumer agency, referring to the idea of value creation, which requires competencies and the ability to create a sense of a consumption activity and generate creative knowledge. This creative learning through diversion offers a source of innovation and sustainable competitive advantage. Thus, the empowered consumer is part of today's digital and experiential consumption settings, where the growing use of social and mobile technologies is shifting market power from suppliers to consumers. Hence, creating new consumer profiles raises significant implications for businesses in that they should adapt to this change.

Furthermore, studies show that empowered consumers are more likely to drive innovation and productivity and create a competitive advantage through access to relevant information, which is then shared with other consumers. In so doing, Batat (2019a) identified four pillars of consumer empowerment:

1. consumer competency, which encompasses three key dimensions: cognitive, functional, and social;
2. consumer re(creation), which refers to consumers' ability to use existing brands or company products and/or services to create new items by using two approaches: transgression and reappropriation;
3. consciousness of consumer rights related to the awareness of the consumer, which includes three consumption knowledge domains—the ability to understand prices, the ability regarding complaints, and the ability to understand one's rights as a consumer;
4. consumer resistance, referring to a digital-savvy consumer and his/her overexposure to commercial discourses that leads him/her to be more knowledgeable in terms of decoding advertisement messages.

Thus, companies should focus more on strategies and offers that empower their customers because empowered consumers can drive brand success and new business opportunities. Therefore, companies should stimulate, nurture, inform, respect, and value their customers.

BOX 1.2   YUKA: THE FOOD APP THAT EMPOWERS CONSUMERS AND PROMOTES WELL-BEING

Since customer empowerment, which is correlated to societal and responsible consumption trends, is transforming the role of consumers from passive to active market actors, companies should review their ways of interacting with empowered customers, who have access to information through multi-channel platforms. They can thus influence other consumers positively or negatively; or, even more, they could call for a boycott of a brand or challenge it via online petitions. However, this dialogue is more than simply giving their feedback, it is a channel of communication for empowered consumers to use with brands. They want to understand the company's choices, to know about its evolution and often influence its decisions. One example showing how consumers are gaining power and control over their consumption is Yuka, which provides scores for food and personal care products.

Yuka is a mobile app for iOS and Android, developed by the French start-up Yuca SAS, which allows consumers to scan food and personal care products and obtain detailed information on the impact of a product on their health. The aim is to help consumers choose products that are considered healthy and also to encourage manufacturers to improve the composition of their products. How does it work? The app reads the product's barcode to access details of its composition (ingredients) and returns a note in the form of a color from green to red (healthy to unhealthy choice). If its impact is deemed harmful, the app can recommend similar products that are better for the consumer's health. Users can also access a more detailed analysis, which lists the qualities and defects of the scanned product. If rated "bad" or "mediocre" the app suggests healthier alternatives using a neutral and impartial algorithm. After June 2018, at the request of its subscribers, Yuka expanded its scope by including hygiene products in its database, which enlarged its consumption domains. Since its launch in 2017, the app has become very popular and had 21 million users as of March 2021.

Thus, Yuka aims to improve consumers' health by helping them decipher product labels to make the best choices for their health. This offer is based on the idea that informed consumption leads consumers to force food and cosmetics companies to improve their products.

2.3   Emotional Consumer

According to Batat (2019a), emotion is recognized as a decisive factor in offering memorable customer experiences. Kotler et al. (2010) stated that marketing has moved beyond the age of "messaging" to affecting customers' emotions. Analysis of the literature shows that there are multiple definitions of emotion. The definition by Kleinginna and Kleinginna (1981) highlights three main characteristics of the notion of consumer emotion: physiological, behavioral, and the dyad emotion/rationality. The interactions between these three dimensions have a direct impact on the decision-making process in the customer experience.

Whether positive or negative, consumer emotion is composed of feelings that emerge within consumption experiences, and can be primary or secondary. While primary emotions (e.g., joy, sadness, disgust, anger, fear, surprise) are universal and express visible emotions through facial expressions that each individual is capable of recognizing and decoding in different cultures, secondary emotions are derived from elementary emotions and are influenced by a consumer's background, his/her childhood, consumption experiences, and external environment. They often encompass a mix of two or more primary emotions (e.g., contempt is a mix of fear and anger) or a single emotion, such as fear, that creates anxiety.

Since the 1970s, the predominance of cognitive reactions on the decision-making process and consumer behavior has been discussed and questioned. Thus, many consumer behaviors cannot be explained by individuals' rationality without being affected by their emotions. Nowadays, marketing scholars and companies should focus more on the role of emotions in customer experiences and consumers' reactions and attitudes toward brands.

Today, consumption practices go beyond the maximization of utility and the simple satisfaction of needs expressed by consumers; they integrate an affective dimension that constitutes the heart of the company's strategy to offer more emotionally charged consumption experiences. Studies show that recognizing and considering customers as emotional market actors can help companies create strong bonds with them and enhance their loyalty. To do so, marketing professionals have to rethink their approach by:

- considering the affective dimension of consumer behavior to be just as important as the cognitive one;
- knowing emotions are not necessarily post-cognitive—emotions are used alongside rationality during a purchase in making a decision;
- knowing effective reactions can also be triggered in the absence of cognitive processes;
- recognizing that emotions constitute the primary source of human motivation and can influence the memorization process.

As society has moved into a more experiential consumption era, marketing scholars have started to examine the impact of emotions on consumer decision-making. Thus, creating emotional connections during the experience strongly impacts the decision-making process and consumer satisfaction. Indeed, consumer emotional involvement increases brand loyalty and sales by improving the brand image and its positioning.

Therefore, an emotional experience should be offered by companies in response to changing consumption patterns and the advent of an emotional consumer who favors an affective and reassuring relationship with the company. By focusing on encouraging emotions, companies can then reinforce consumer emotions (positive) which, accordingly, promote action (purchase) and offer a pleasant dimension to the in-store experience (enchantment). Indeed, when customers experience a strong emotion, they tend to act impulsively and spontaneously without using their cognitive abilities.

Offering emotional experiences is then a very effective tool for creating a solid bond between companies and customers. Thus, companies that create an emotional connection with customers can use a wide range of emotions, including perceptions of happiness, sadness, fear, or anger.

Moreover, the role of the company's employees as emotional motivators is critical in creating and offering emotionally charged customer experiences. Companies should transform staff into brand ambassadors by engaging them in building strong and durable emotional connections with customers. Thus, companies should focus more on creating what I call the "emotional capital" of their employees who are in contact with customers.

BOX 1.3   HOW IS COCA-COLA CREATING A POSITIVE EMOTIONAL BOND WITH ITS CONSUMERS?

Brands that create an emotional connection with consumers often seek to be associated with joy (laughter and smiles) and positivity. Coca-Cola is one of many brands that effectively and directly connect with consumers through this positive sentiment. For example, Coca-Cola's "Choose Happiness" campaign is an excellent example of using emotions to connect with the public. This campaign encouraged consumers to share good memories and experiences that made them happy during summer.

Another campaign—"Open a Coke, Open Happiness"—shows that the brand is more than ever found under the symbol of the joy provided by sharing. Coca-Cola is thus becoming an expert in the field of emotional connection that the brand can translate in many creative ways. The latest "Sharing Can" campaign also sends a strong and emotional message to consumers: "From now on, a can is not to be drunk alone, but together!" Also, with its famous "Happiness Machine," Coca-Cola gave people in Sweden a chance to warm up a little while waiting for the bus. To avoid the Swedes getting depressed, Coca-Cola transformed a bus shelter by adding a free vending machine, and recreated a summer atmosphere (if possible). We won't say any more; we'll let you discover for yourself!

Another action implemented by the brand is #Happiness OnlyRealWhenShare, a marketing campaign that Coca-Cola conducted just before Christmas to put some cheer into all hearts. Passers-by could interact with a dispenser installed by Coca-Cola by choosing one of two options: receive a free bottle or #ShareTheGood, which was a very successful marketing campaign just before Christmas.

2.4   Collaborator Consumer

The joint production of goods and services between company and customer is not a new idea; for example, fast-food outlets or supermarkets have gained some of their success through customer participation to reduce production costs. Historically, consumer participation in service production was first studied as a strategy to improve productivity by using the client as free labor, thereby achieving a lower price.

The advent of a new consumer, evolving in a digital and interactive society, requires more and more technologies for playful, relational, interactive, and informative purposes. Consumers are changing their status, and can nowadays collaborate with companies. They are becoming co-producers of online content and information—user-generated content (UGC)—as well as influencers, thanks to blogs and social media platforms, among others. The rise of new-fangled assumption patterns defines a new profile of "prosumer"— PROducer + conSUMER. Batat (2019a) states that the consumers' status as co-producer is a direct consequence of their empowerment in a digital world, which generates growing resistance that rebalances the power in the relationship between customers and companies through engaging in collaboration.

This collaboration has greatly facilitated exchanges between companies and consumers, who are becoming legitimate business partners in the co-design and co-production process with companies. On the one hand, customers consider embracing the role of collaborator to be a rewarding and valuable experience because they feel invested with an essential mission. This involvement allows them to create a direct dialogue and exchange with companies in the co-creation process.

On the other hand, for companies, interest in working with customers is three-fold: (1) taking advantage of the creative potential and ideas of customers; (2) knowing their targets better and building their loyalty in the long term; and (3) developing a positive impression of the company and its products, brands, services, and innovations. In so doing, customers can be involved in the co-creation of the offer or the communication campaign following three main steps: pre-conception, co-creation, and co-production (Figure 1.2). Also, several actions are implemented by companies to involve customers in the collaboration and to benefit from their knowledge and creativity.

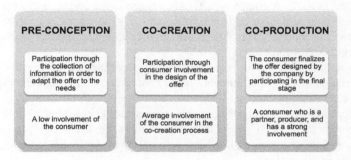

Figure 1.2   Types of consumer–company collaboration

Furthermore, the consumer as a collaborator is the new paradigm that refers to the fantasy of putting consumers to work for free. Indeed, in the postmodern consumer society, consumers are seen as a source of value for companies. Consumers can use technologies and social media in their consumption and purchase activities, which leads to empowerment and skills development. For consumers, product usage requires a dual decision: purchasing a product and using it. The consumer attempts to identify three elements involved in the decision and the usage process in all cases.

The first element is the project, which refers to the anticipation of what he or she will do with the product. It is more or less clear anticipation, more or less assumed, which often changes with use. The second element is the tangible product itself, and the third is the function assigned to the product. This usage shows that new consumers are very active in creating their own culture. They invent their own culture with its codes, practices, and languages. Companies therefore face the development of a collaborative and creative process implemented by the consumer who attempts to escape the consumer experience imposed by producers. Thus, these consumers who are co-producers of content have become more influential and are often seen as relevant sources of information.

This participation in terms of production and dissemination of information is becoming essential for companies, which are implementing actions to enhance the collaboration with today's customers, who can create, disseminate, and influence others thanks to their active role on different social media platforms (e.g., Instagram, TikTok, Facebook). However, the implementation of collaborative work with the customer is conditioned by three key factors:

- Involving customers in the implementation of the company's offer is not an end in itself. A company will only engage in the co-production process if customer participation brings value and if the customer's creative work allows the company to make a return on investment in terms of innovation, image, or customer loyalty.
- Consumer participation requires favorable conditions allowing the transformation of ideas into innovation and conclusively into products responding to existing needs.
- Before involving the consumer, companies should consider the following elements: At which stage should customers be involved—production, conception, or creation? For what type of work? And what is the purpose of the collaboration?

Therefore, it should be noted that customer participation in co-creation with companies can be achieved at different stages of the process—from production to the proposal of ideas, through the testing and validation of products and prototypes, communication, and promotion. However, this collaboration depends on the consumer's profile and his/her knowledge that can guide the company in its choice to involve him/her upstream, downstream, or throughout the creation process.

BOX 1.4   NIKE: CO-CREATION OF VALUE WITH ITS CUSTOMERS

Nike is one of the leading brands that initiated the co-creation process with its customers at different stages of the customer experience and within the Nike+ community. Nike includes its customers in the process of product co-creation through many initiatives. For example, launching a website during the 2006 World Cup encouraged consumers to share videos of their technical prowess at soccer. Moreover, other consumers were invited to comment on and evaluate the videos. Additionally, the NikeID site organized a contest where 20 customers had the chance to design sneakers. Individuals with the most votes from their peers were rewarded each month. Also, the collaboration between Nike and Apple, with the marketing of the Apple Watch Nike, allowed running enthusiasts to accurately track their sessions and share their experiences with a large community of runners while helping them improve their training.

These initiatives have connected millions of consumers to each other and, most importantly, to the firm. Nike receives direct feedback, suggestions, and ideas from its customers. Privileged access to customer data allows the company to know more about its customers' needs, and allows the brand to have a considerable competitive advantage over its competitors. Likewise, by co-creating with its customers, Nike could involve them from the beginning and throughout the project. Co-creation allows numerous hypotheses to be validated from the outset and ensures, at each stage, that the product or service corresponds to customer needs. The company thus makes significant savings on the purchase of marketing studies. Similarly, co-creation considerably reduces the design cycles of innovations and their mortality rate, which makes this type of project more profitable for Nike.

Co-creation is also a tool used by Nike to value its customers and thus develop a strong bond with them. Valuing the client is a prerequisite for the success of the collaborative project, as the client might not be paid. Thus, for Nike, it is critical to keep customers informed of the project's progress: they want to know which ideas have been retained and want an explanation of why this is or is not the case. Moreover, the relationship should be maintained regularly through a collaborative platform accessible on the Web.

3   TYPES OF CUSTOMER EXPERIENCE

Customer experiences are diverse, and their nature depends on various factors to assess customer satisfaction and enjoyment of lived experiences. A positive experience of a brand, depending on its type, has the power to retain and bring the customer back, thanks to an indelible bond with the brand. Yet, the customer experience varies according to the area of consumption. Some areas are, by definition, experiential (such as tourism), while others are somewhat functional (like shops and other outlets). I thus classify customer experiences into three categories: (1) intense vs. moderate; (2) outstanding vs. mundane; and (3) market-free vs. market-related (Figure 1.3). These three customer experience types are explained and illustrated by examples below.

3.1   Intense vs. Moderate Experiences

Customer experience can be related to intense or moderate consumption activities. In domains where the experience is lived intensively, luxury goods, tourism, and hospitality are fields of consumption in which customer experience constitutes a central component of the offer. These domains are part of the service business, which is a highly experiential industry. For example, we do not "consume" a destination or a hotel room; we "live" an experience that incorporates several market actors and factors that can positively or negatively impact the customer experience.

Figure 1.3   Three classifications of customer experience

On the other hand, other domains are characterized by a moderate level of experience. In other words, experience is not the only offer, but rather part of the whole package proposed by the company. For example, Batat (2019b) refers to moderate experiential settings such as retail outlets as fields of consumption where customers do not stay for a long time, for example in a hotel or a restaurant. While the customer experience in the retail sector is then moderate and can be expressed through several forms—a hyper-customization of the service facilitated by customer relationship management (CRM) and digital tools, a streamlined customer journey, offer staging, and experience theming in high-end gastronomic restaurants—the dining experience should be intense by incorporating several elements such as theming, the WOW effect, storytelling, craftsmanship, service, and social connections. These should all be aligned to provide guests with a memorable, enjoyable, and enchanting gastronomic dining experience that is both functional and emotional.

BOX 1.5   INTENSE HIGH-END DINING EXPERIENCES IN MICHELIN-STARRED RESTAURANTS

In my research that examined customer experience in Michelin-starred restaurants, I show that customers perceive the experience as intense.

Customers not only appreciate the quality of products and the know-how of chefs in the kitchen; they also consider the physical place, the service, the overall atmosphere, and the tableware, as well as the chef who expresses him/herself through his/her creative cooking (Batat, 2019b).

The haute cuisine experience is therefore composed of several elements that altogether create balance and offer consumers the ultimate experience. The location and the restaurant's history are two other essential elements that should be emphasized when offering a gastronomic experience; but, above all, if the restaurant lacks excellent service and features ordinary menus, then the experience is interpreted as empty and without meaning for customers. Thus, the experience of the restaurant should match the expectations of customers and what they like.

A historic restaurant with a heritage should then translate the history of the place to the dishes and throughout the menus. Its history can position the restaurant as a unique place that offers a unique experience to its clients. Indeed, other restaurants can copy the concept, the cuisine, and the décor; however, they cannot reproduce the same atmosphere, experience, or history of a restaurant that makes it distinctive. Therefore, the experience of the place and the storytelling go beyond the quality of the cuisine since they are connected to a certain local culture. When people make a booking in a gourmet restaurant, they expect mystery by discovering each stage of their journey: at reception, through the maître d'hôtel, the service, the meal, interaction with the chef, etc. Another important factor in helping customers immerse themselves in an extraordinary culinary experience is the service, including two main aspects: professionalism and kindness. Training that helps staff develop kindness toward the clients is also a critical element in appreciating the gastronomic experience.

3.2 Outstanding vs. Mundane Experiences

The definition of a customer experience from a holistic perspective leads us to define consumption objects as an element of a whole: the whole is the consumer's sphere, including his or her feelings, the meaning of consumption, other objects of consumption, social interactions, and other elements. In this sense, and as stated by Askegaard and Linnet (2011), the customer experience is considered to be embedded in a particular cultural setting, allowing a macro-social vision of the context beyond the unfolding of the moment. Following this logic, which defines the experience in terms of social interactions and consumers' meanings (Holt, 1991; 1995), there is a need to distinguish between what consumers perceive as outstanding vs. mundane experiences. These two types of experience should be seen as complementary rather than opposing; they enrich each other, and thus lead to an in-depth understanding of the concept of customer experience. These two types of customer experience are explained below.

3.2.1   Outstanding consumption experiences

These experiences are referred to as extraordinary; they are defined in relation to consumer self-realization and are considered as strong drivers of community belonging. They are seen as extraordinary for the intense feelings they provide to consumers. These experiences respond to how individuals achieve their self-actualization, a rite of passage in the individual's evolution (Belk, 1989). Yet, extraordinary experiences are not lived every day; rather, they are meant to be one-time experiences to collect, to add to one's record of achievement (Keinan and Kivetz, 2011).

Also, what makes the most sense for consumers is the ephemeral dimension of the moment. The experience is lived for a concise time, and the subject, conscious of its singularity, seeks to invest in it and immerse him/herself entirely. The experience, by its unique character, becomes rich in meaning. The consumer does not seek to understand his or her experience through a cognitive memory of the experience. What is sacred and resonates with consumers are the sensations and emotions that are more in the realm of the experience, the "here and now," rather than in the realm of a past memory. These experiences are often related to the context of leisure activities such as mountain trips (Belk and Costa, 1998), skydiving (Celsi et al., 1993), rafting (Arnould and Price, 1993), or rave parties (Goulding et al., 2002). All these experiences are ways to escape one's self and ordinary life. They also represent an opportunity for the subject to discover new cultures of consumption and "rediscover a sense of self," as stated by Arnould and Price (1993).

Although occasional events, these are interesting to study for both the richness of the meaning they offer to the consumer and the potential business opportunities for companies. From a consumer perspective, extraordinary experiences are lived occasionally and refer to a quest for meaning, sought by consumers as a way to escape their daily life. If they are often linked to extreme activities, it is because the individual is looking for a way to realize him/herself, to push his/her limits, and to reinvent him/herself by looking for new sensations and moments of immersion (Celsi et al., 1993). Additionally, risk-taking is not avoided as it occasionally defines the very essence of the consumption practice. In this risk, the consumer seeks how to evaluate him/herself, motivated by the break of these experiences from the everydayness of consumption activities.

Furthermore, it should be noted that extraordinary experiences have a social dimension created by the interactions among individuals because they share the same exceptional experience. Individuals find themselves in the same new cosmos where each is searching for a different personal meaning. The same rites of passage, the same values of experience, and the same state of mind are shared (Goulding et al., 2002). The shared experience intensifies, for the duration of the experience, the relations of identification and belonging to the community. Arnould and Price (1993) argue that in each person's feelings there is a part of the feelings of the others, in a kind of "communion." Between a quest for personal meaning and a sharing of experience with others, the consumer evolves in his/her own identity construction. The constructed new meaning of the extraordinary experience is then incorporated into the consumer's everyday experience, where other practices are present to give rhythm to the relationship with the consumption system.

3.2.2 Mundane consumption experiences

These refer to consumption experiences rooted in consumers' everyday lives where individuals integrate consumption practices and objects into their life course. The aim here is to understand how these elements allow individuals to construct their identities as consumers. Referring to Thompson and colleagues' (1990) work shows how married women manage their relationships with consumer experiences in their daily lives. The authors identified three main strategies implemented by these women in their daily consumption practices: "being limited vs. being free" refers to constraints and restrictions from the environment; "being controlled vs. being out of control" by the world of consumption, and in particular impulse purchases; and "being captivated vs. being disengaged" from consumption experiences. In this research, the relationship to practices is approached through a cultural reading of consumption based on the values of feminism and motherhood. Consumption experiences are seen as much as everyday practices as sources of meaning.

Other studies have examined the extent to which advertising experiences were embedded in the lives of consumers and how they made sense to them. Mick and Buhl (1992) defined two fundamental notions: life themes and life projects to locate a consumer's experience in a more global framework of his/her life cycle. According to these authors, life themes are existential subjects for the individuals who use them in their daily life to give it meaning. Life themes allow for a better structuring of daily events and experiences to anticipate personal development. These themes evolve through the sociocultural framework but also through the transforming experiences of the consumer. They are specific to each individual according to their experiences, and are linked to the life events of each individual (e.g., they identify freedom, status, and truthfulness as life themes for some consumers).

On the other hand, life projects are defined in relation to the life stages of the subject. They are constantly evolving and changing. McCracken (1987) defines them as developing, refining, and eliminating specific concepts among stable cultural alternatives. They are thus individual projects relative to the self and reflect the different roles that the individual plays throughout his or her life to define, plan, and coordinate his or her life moments (Mick and Buhl, 1992). These projects are therefore not defined in advance and evolve gradually. Four levels are distinguished by Mick and Buhl: national, community, family, and private life projects, relating to the self.

BOX 1.6　COOKING: A MUNDANE SENSORY EXPERIENCE CHARGED WITH MEANING

Cooking, as a consumer experience, can be defined in different ways. Here it is defined as the act of preparing food so that it is suitable for consumption and pleasing to the palate. From this generic definition, two key ideas are underlined. First, cooking implies a thoughtful action since the preparation stage in the definition implies that the individual makes choices: the choice of food to be prepared and how to assemble it.

This action thus calls upon a cognitive and rational dimension as well as an intuitive and emotional dimension. The choices in an activity such as cooking respond to a technical logic and an artistic aspect, which is implied in this definition and retained as a second key element. Second, the sensory and aesthetic dimension is underlined. Here, the focus is on the gustatory sensation of cooking, in that it constitutes a significant aim of this action.

However, the pleasure dimension can be extended to the other sensations of sight, smell, and touch. Cooking experiences refer to the art of preparing food and elaborating dishes and the particular way of preparing food, which suggests that it is specific to an individual, a group of individuals, a culture, a country, a region. Each person, in his/her individuality, conceives it differently. Thus, although viewed as an ordinary activity, cooking experiences are unique and charged by meanings, creativity, and emotions.

Therefore, it should be acknowledged that through consumption experiences, whether they are extraordinary or mundane, consumers produce cultural meaning and memories that are integrated into their relationship with consumption and, by extension, the construction of their own identity.

3.3　Market-Free vs. Market-Related Experiences

Considering consumer subjectivity in terms of consumption experiences leads us to focus more on what is perceived as an experience from a consumer's perspective. This questioning reveals two main types of experience according to how consumers perceive them: experiences that are not in contact with the marketplace, namely market-free experiences; and experiences that are linked to the market and in contact with other market actors and factors, including salespeople, merchandising, and advertising, among others (e.g., going to the mall or visiting a theme park). Indeed, not all experiences necessarily occur within the marketplace; some are private and embedded in the daily lives of consumers, such as welcoming friends to a dinner party or celebrating Christmas at home.

Following this classification, it is relevant to acknowledge the level of the company's control by distinguishing two main features: market-free experiences have a low level of company control compared to those that are connected to the marketplace. Thus, in contrast to market-related experiences, which are centered on the product and structured due to a company-driven approach, in market-free experiences the individual is at the center, and consumption practices are less structured and are oriented toward the consumption object and more toward social interactions.

4   CUSTOMER EXPERIENCE MANAGEMENT MODELS: ATOMISTIC VS. HOLISTIC

Customer experience management (CXM) is an integral part of a company's experiential marketing strategy. It is a strategy that results from a value exchange between the company and its customers. Marketing scholars have proposed several conceptual CXM models to help companies deliver the ultimate customer experience (e.g., Batat, 2019a; Verhoef et al., 2009; Voss et al., 2008). These authors share the idea that customers evaluate their experience with the company holistically, and agree that empirical research has focused on specific elements of that experience in isolation from one another. Analysis of current research shows two critical CXM models: atomistic and holistic (Figure 1.4).

While atomistic models follow a positivist paradigm that views customer experience in terms of its emotional dimension but remains primarily dominated by a cognitive approach (e.g., Mehrabian and Russell, 1974), holistic models are constructivist. They follow a consumer perspective that defines the experience regarding the sociocultural setting in which consumption takes place. Thus, the cultural setting is defined as the very fabric of experiences, meanings, and actions, and thus consumption is understood as the means of experiencing realities (Arnould and Thompson, 2005). These two models are discussed in the following sections.

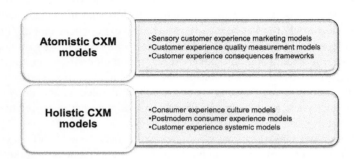

Figure 1.4   Atomistic vs. holistic customer experience management models

4.1   Atomistic CXM Models

The contribution of marketing scholars to the definition of a framework that allows companies to understand and manage their customer experiences underlines the importance of the process related to the consumption and the purchase experience. In this sense, atomistic CXM models involve three streams of research: sensory customer experience marketing; customer experience quality measurement (e.g., Lemke et al., 2011); and customer experience consequences (e.g., Voss et al., 2008). These approaches allow marketing scholars and companies to identify and assess the components that make a customer experience successful.

A *sensory marketing* approach to customer experience was evident in early research by Mehrabian and Russell (1974). This work focuses on the atmospheric aspect of the lived customer experience, and is part of environmental psychology theories, which state that environmental variables influence individuals' behaviors. This causal relationship is based on the Stimulus-Organism-Response (SOR) model of behaviorist inspiration. Introduced by Woodworth (1921) and developed by Brunswik (1955), this model was then used in consumer behavior to assess customer experience. The SOR model allows companies to assess customer experience regarding three aspects: (1) identifying environmental stimuli; (2) explaining their influence on internal consumer states; and (3) predicting their influence on consumer behavior.

To identify environmental stimuli there is first a need to assess what the stimuli are that can affect the customer experience. Bitner (1992) proposed a complete and comprehensive classification of three key stimuli that can influence the lived experience. These stimuli include ambient elements (e.g., light, noise); spatial organization and functionality (e.g., size of equipment or furniture); and signs, symbols, and artifacts (e.g., directional signs). Second, the influence of these stimuli should be assessed. The SOR model suggests that environmental stimuli induce an emotional influence on the consumer that can be measured by an emotion scale (Mehrabian and Russell, 1974). The final stage of the model proposes that these internal states or reactions generate behaviors that are defined according to a dichotomous view of types of behavior: approach behavior and/or avoidance behavior. This dichotomy remains restrictive, however, since the consumer can also adopt adjustment behavior. Besides, consumers can develop paradoxical behaviors, which are more complex, and seek tactics and strategies to cope with consumption situations.

Thus the SOR model, built on a principle of emotional induction, links causal relations that assume a passive consumer—as a receiver of stimuli and with quasi-systematic, even expected, responses. However, this model ignores the characteristics of a postmodern consumer. The latter is defined as a complex and ambivalent being who adopts quasi-opposed values. Environmental variables certainly influence his/her behavior, but the relationship remains interactive. Today's consumers, active in their consumption, influence their environment, and they are willing to co-create the experience as a means of self-actualization. Therefore, companies must focus on the components of the experience from a consumer's perspective to measure the quality of the experiential offering, and thus customer satisfaction.

Regarding works that focused on *experience quality measurement*, studies show that marketing scholars propose multiple scales and models to help companies measure the quality of the customer experience offered, and thus customer satisfaction. For instance, the Cognition-Affect-Behavior-Satisfaction (CABS) model was proposed by experiential marketing scholars Holbrook and Hirschman (1982). These authors renew the explanatory variables of consumer behavior and emphasize that subjects seek out experiences for the pleasure, amusement, and sensations they provide. Later, the same authors proposed a new model, Thought-Emotion-Activity-Value (TEAV). This model features a set of interactions between the consumer's *thoughts*, his/her *emotions*, his/her *activity* (actions and reactions), and the *value* he or she assigns to those interactions. The value is understood as a fundamental element of the experience and not just one of its consequences (Hirschman and Holbrook, 1986). The place of value in the TEAV model recognizes the dual nature of experience as both a lived process and a remembered outcome.

Likewise, other studies suggested unveiling what is inside the black box of the concept of customer experience by identifying its dimensions, which should be measured to guarantee customer satisfaction. Analysis of the literature shows the diversity of the components identified and the weight of the hedonic, utilitarian, and social facets. Scholars often opposed the hedonic component to the utilitarian dimension in the evaluation of a consumption experience. While hedonic consumption refers to aesthetic, experiential, and pleasurable aspects of the experience, utilitarian consumption is related to consumption objects' functional and practical nature (Chitturi et al., 2008). Likewise, the social dimension of the customer experience has also been documented by marketing scholars. This refers to the interaction between a consumer and other consumers or between a consumer and the company's staff (Gentile et al., 2007). Identifying these three components has led to the development of different scales for measuring consumption experiences.

For example, Brakus and colleagues (2009) developed a scale that focuses on consumer responses to brand stimuli related to design, identity, packaging, communication, and environment. Four dimensions form this scale: (1) a dimension assessing the sensory stimulation generated by the brand; (2) a dimension reflecting the affective and emotional charge generated by the brand; (3) a dimension reflecting the action produced by physical interaction; and (4) an intellectual dimension reflecting the consumer's cognitive process.

The logic behind the construction of the scale is not based on the "here and now" of the customer experience. It is instead the idea of evaluating the long-term memory based on multiple exposures to brand stimuli. Therefore, this scale is more likely used in assessing the post-consumption experience phase once it is lived. Table 1.1 summarizes the most relevant dimensions of the customer experience that could be integrated into scales to measure experience quality and customer satisfaction.

When it comes to the models that focused on examining *customer experience consequences*, analysis of the literature reveals two approaches to experience outcomes: value and satisfaction as two main outcomes of the customer experience. On the one hand, the consumer value approach refers to the type of value resulting from a lived experience. Consumer value has been defined by Holbrook (1999) as a comparative, personal, and situational relative preference characterizing the experience of a subject in interaction with an object. Also referred to as consumption value, as opposed to the concept of exchange value, this approach draws upon the logic of subjective value. In other words, the individual's relationship with the object allows him/her to establish the perceived value of the consumption experience. Thus, the perceived value is placed here as a result of the lived consumption or purchase experience.

On the other hand, while the construct of perceived value captures the consumer's enduring relationship with the consumption experience, satisfaction as an outcome of a lived experience is based on a transactional logic. Satisfaction is apprehended as a constructed process, made up of two main components: utilitarian and hedonic. It is part of the post-experience responses. Experiences follow one another, and cumulative satisfaction is presented as a starting point for future experiences (Smith and Bolton, 1998). Significantly, studies show

Table 1.1   Customer experience dimensions

Approach to customer experience	Dimensions	
Customer experience is lived on a positive, engaging, sustainable, and social level and intervenes at different levels of the consumer/company encounter	Level of interaction Emotions Physical setting	Service quality Sensory Cognitive
Customer experience is a subjective mental state experienced by participants in highly experiential and extraordinary settings	Hedonism Escapism	Immersion Recognition
Customer experience is a new and distinct offer of goods and services, with their own characteristics and their own mode of management	Customer participation Customer absorption	Social interaction Customization
Customer experience is a co-creation action between a supplier and a consumer in which the consumer perceives value in the encounter and the memory of this encounter	Perceived value Personal interest Novelty	Learning Commitment
Customer experience is a subjective state of consciousness guided by a variety of consumers' symbolic meanings, hedonistic responses, and aesthetic aspects	Feelings Pleasure Imaginary Utilitarian value Playfulness	Aesthetics Social status Ethics Self-esteem Spirituality

that the affective dimension of a lived experience directly influences consumer satisfaction during a first consumption experience (e.g., Homburg et al., 2006). Likewise, the accumulation of experiences allows the growth of knowledge, leading to overall affective and cognitive satisfaction.

A critical look at this approach shows that what is retained by the consumer in an experience, however unpleasant it may be, is not so much the degree of satisfaction but rather the sense of experience shared with others. This meaning takes priority over a logic of experience satisfaction evaluation: the social keeps a memorable experience that was initially estimated to be negative. In this vein, Fournier and Mick (1999) define satisfaction by its dynamic dimension. It is not perceived here as a response to a specific experience. Instead, this approach takes into account consumption experiences anchored in an unpredictable daily routine. Satisfaction would thus be the result of an active, dynamic process that is prolonged over time. It therefore seems relevant for companies to assess customer satisfaction only for the meaning it brings to the understanding of the consumption experience.

Besides the three cited atomistic customer experience management models—sensory customer experience marketing, experience quality measurement, and customer experience consequences—we can refer to other models with the same approach that marketing scholars have proposed to help companies design and manage customer experiences in different sectors (e.g., retail, service). For instance, Verhoef and colleagues (2009) proposed a model of customer experience creation in the retail sector by identifying seven components of the customer experience: social environment, service interfaces, store atmosphere, product range, price, experiences in other stores, and brand awareness.

However, while Verhoef et al.'s model offers a synthesis of the elements that make up the customer experience, it does not provide insights into how to bring these different elements together. Drawing upon Verhoef et al.'s model, Grewal et al. (2009) introduced the notion of macro factors; in other words, major macroeconomic and political factors such as fluctuations in the price of oil or loss of confidence in the financial markets.

These authors propose an experience management model that starts from the customer's experience at the point of sale and analyzes it through measurements to adjust and correct the different elements of the experience produced by the company to improve it. These models come from quality research approaches where the main objective is to increase customer satisfaction. For example, Voss et al. (2008) proposed a model that introduced the concept of "choreography" to refer to how customer experience is staged in the service industry. According to these authors, there are four main operational elements that firms should consider in staging and managing customer experiences in the servicescape:

- the supply environment and structure (stageware);
- the infrastructure (orgware)—how to organize human resources and create an environment and culture to enhance the customer experience;
- the system for creating and managing all the interactions between the company and the customer, or among customers (customerware);
- the internal communication system (linkware).

Moreover, Prahalad and Ramaswamy's (2004) idea of value co-creation as a core element in customer experiences led to the development of the Dialogue, Access, Risk-Benefits, Transparency (DART) model that organizations can use to implement and manage value co-creation as an integral part of the customer experience. The DART model defines different categories of interaction between the customer and the company in value co-creation:

- *Dialogue* refers to sharing knowledge, but above all to new levels of qualitative understanding between the company and its customers. The latter can thus introduce their vision into the value creation process.
- *Access* challenges the idea that value is only created through the ownership of a good or product. By providing access to experiences through multiple points of interaction, companies can expand their business opportunities.

- *Risk benefit/assessment* assumes that if consumers are co-creators of value with companies, then they demand more information about the potential risks of goods and services. By doing so they can also take greater responsibility for dealing with those risks.
- *Transparency* reaffirms that transparency of information between the company and its customers is necessary to create a climate of trust. Traditionally, the company has had more information about its customers and markets than the customer has about the company, but this asymmetry is rapidly disappearing.

Thus, by combining these four building blocks, the company involves its customers in the co-creation of value alongside risk assessment on both sides. Access and risk assessment are facilitated by a collaborative *dialogue* made possible by a high level of information *transparency*. Also, other authors, such as Payne et al. (2008), proposed a customer experience model that includes three dimensions:

- *Emotion* refers to feelings, moods, and affect-based personality characteristics.
- *Cognition* is borrowed from Holbrook and Hirschman (1982), and refers to both an approach to information processing that emphasizes memory of activities and to processes that are more subconscious.
- *Behavior* refers to the purchase decision and includes the experience the customer has with the product or service.

For these authors, customer processes include the experience linked to the relationship with the company along three axes—emotion, cognition, behavior—and the learning achieved by the customer (customer learning). These elements are critical to assessing the company's interactions with customers, and thus the value co-creation that emerges within different consumption and purchase experiences.

Another model by Lemon and Verhoef (2016), which follows an atomistic perspective, defines customer experience in relation to a consumer journey composed of multiple touchpoints. The authors suggest that the customer experience process shifts from pre-purchase to purchase to post-purchase, following a customer journey that includes past purchase and consumption experiences, external factors, and touchpoints, which are linked to each stage in the journey and can change and evolve from one stage to another.

However, although the customer journey model and experience proposed by Lemon and Verhoef is a successful conceptualization of experience touchpoints, the framework provides a narrow view in thoroughly examining customer experience since it does not integrate perception levels, the distinction between digital, human, and physical touchpoints, and those elements the firm can control and those it cannot control.

Therefore, companies need to go beyond an atomistic approach to customer experience management by embracing a more holistic and integrative approach to design relevant, satisfying, and profitable customer experiences. The holistic perspective on customer experience is explained in the next section.

4.2   Holistic CXM Models

The holistic approach highlights the importance of considering the consumption experience beyond the individual and causal aspects by integrating direct and indirect actors as well as environmental factors while examining the concept of customer experience as a sociocultural construct. In the holistic paradigm, consumption is not seen as an isolated phenomenon but as part of the setting in which it is embedded and by which it is shaped. In other words, a holistic consumption experience indicates that the environment must be considered as a whole rather than through each of its components separately. Customer experience management models considering a holistic perspective have many growth and productivity benefits because they allow companies to manage their businesses centrally, and thus they can gain a comprehensive understanding of where they can improve.

In the holistic approach, the objects of consumption are seen as elements that participate in the construction process of the individual's social life. The consumer experience then goes beyond the simple act of buying to include new dimensions of pleasure and feelings (Holbrook and Hirschman, 1982). Also, in this perspective, consumption is considered a vector of meaning, a type of social action in which individuals use consumption objects in different ways (Holt, 1995). Therefore, analysis of the literature shows that customer experience management models that integrate a holistic perspective follow three main rationales: consumer culture logic, postmodernism, and systemic. These three views of customer experience management models are discussed in the next sections.

4.2.1   Consumer culture view of customer experience
The cultural perspective on customer experience invites marketing scholars and businesses to focus more on emic and etic reasoning by taking into account social and cultural representations and the meanings consumers attribute to their consumption practices and experiences (Batat, 2019a). Consumer Culture Theory (CCT), a growing cultural research stream introduced by Arnould and Thompson (2005), views customer experience as a social representation embedded within a particular cultural context in which consumption meanings are shaped. Thus, CCT conceptualizes consumer experience as a personal

event in a location and a change in the individual with a focus on his or her emotions and sensitivity.

The evolution of the cultural consumption paradigm applied to examine and understand customer experience management has been inspired by works on the sociology of consumption (e.g., Baudrillard, 1970). Since the 1970s, the purely commercial and transactional vision has focused on customer experience, which is more oriented toward the meaning of consumption in individuals' lives. Thus, the value of objects considered solely through their materiality is oriented more toward the meaning of consumption, whether it is public, recognized by others, or private, relating to oneself (Richins, 1994).

By considering the consumer as the unit of study and the market as the place of production of goods, there is a relationship of essence between the two worlds that leads to a redefinition of the way we look at the meaning of consumption, and thus customer experiences. Certainly, between the individuals and the material world of consumption remain communications, conceptions, models, and values that make the world of consumption a socially and culturally constructed universe (Mills, 1963).

Following this logic, the consumption system, analyzed via a cultural framework, is structured through a transfer of meaning between the consumption system and the consumer (McCracken, 1987). The circulation of meaning starts from a culturally constituted world moving toward the individual consumer, passing through consumer goods. Thus, if the trajectory of the transfer of meaning starts from the culturally constituted world to the individual consumer via consumer goods, it is legitimate to ask the following questions: How is this cultural world constituted? And by whom? If the consumption system offers objects and experiences of consumption, the consumer can only be seen as the receiver of this system. Yet, following a consumer perspective underlines the idea that consumers do not choose brands. They choose lives. Similarly, rather than brands, they select meanings that fit with their own values and identities. These meanings are not given; they are co-constructed between the brand that issues its discourse and the cultural meaning emanating from the consumer (e.g., Mick and Buhl, 1992). An individual and subjective interpretation of the consumption objects and practices is then favored. The personal experience takes precedence over a pre-established culture of consumption experiences that are then lived in different ways and take on multiple meanings.

The meaning assigned to the customer experience should then be analyzed through a macro-social analysis of the consumer society. The experience only makes sense for individuals if it allows them to advance in the construction of their life course. The analysis by Belk and Costa (1998) of the experience lived by American city dwellers in a Native American camp shows, for example, that beyond the originality of the experience, this moment is lived by the consumers in a particular and significant way. Here, for the duration of an experience, there is a return to a way of life totally disconnected from urban and contemporary daily life. The authors see in this experience a dimension that is sacred to individuals, as opposed to their daily life, which is symbolized as profane. Consumption experiences are therefore lived by the consumer to different degrees. Some are meaningful to them, depending on the context and the significance of the moment of consumption.

Furthermore, sacredness is seen as a way for consumers to give meaning to their consumption experiences (Belk et al., 1989). This notion qualifies what, in consumption, is seen as more meaningful, significant, powerful, and extraordinary than the self. In other words, the authors oppose the sacred to an experience that would be of the order of routine. Sacredness then allows the consumer to experience moments of intense joy and madness. Taking the example of a soccer match, Belk and colleagues underline the sacred dimension of this experience for consumers, supporters of the team: the team is made up of heroes, the stadium represents a temple, and the objects of the experience are sacred relics. All the elements of the experience are thus vectors of transfer of meaning between consumer culture and an individual in search of cultural consumption. In this relationship between the values of the consumer and the values of the culturally constructed world, it is the individual consumer who attributes the sacred character to the consumer experience. It is therefore not necessary to question what is sacred in the experience, but rather the "process" through which a particular consumption becomes and remains sacred.

4.2.2   Postmodern view of customer experience

The postmodern paradigm emerged in the 1970s and has been the focus of various disciplines, such as sociology (e.g., Turner, 1990), anthropology (e.g., Crapanzano, 1991), psychology (e.g., Gergen, 1991), and recently experiential marketing (Batat, 2019a). Firat and Venkatesh (1995), who imported postmodernism from humanities to marketing and consumer behavior studies, suggest a change of societal paradigm by shifting the focus from a modern to a postmodern consumer society.

Postmodernism refers to the image of a world that does not believe in progress, in the all-powerful science, the tomorrow which sings, and triumphant reason. This definition places postmodernism as a new philosophical and cultural movement, rejecting the ideas of modernism: rational order; material progress; the separation of the productive sphere and the sphere of consumption; and a process of negation without limits.

Considered in a new facet, the system of consumption becomes more liberal, combining opposing dimensions of the real and the imaginary, the rational and the irrational, the individual and the community. The individual is, in turn, a consumer of objects, symbols, and images (Firat and Venkatesh,

1995). Consumption becomes the central moment in the process where symbolic exchanges determine and reproduce a social code. It is an appropriation of signs rather than a destruction of objects. A cultural component is then integrated, offering the possibility of contextualizing consumption practices in a more global and comprehensive customer experience framework.

The rise of a postmodern consumer society is also a consequence of globalization, technology, and sociocultural mutations, and change in the twenty-first century, which led to the emergence of new schemes of production and consumption (e.g., collaborative consumption, sharing, low-cost, online shopping, and so forth) that are replacing the modern approach of mass production of standardized goods. In my book *Experiential Marketing*, I have identified six key characteristics of today's postmodern consumers living within a digital era and their implications for brands and marketing professionals (Batat, 2019a):

1. Postmodernism is based on the idea that society is a social and historical construction, which means that reality and its truth are not objective since they are not only the result of the combination of science and technology, but also include elements such as aesthetics, language, discourses, customs, ideology, narratives, meanings, irrationality, and other factors that marketing scholars should examine to provide brand managers with relevant insights on consumer expectations and needs in terms of their consumption experiences.
2. Postmodernism considers culture and symbolism as integral parts of consumer experiences.
3. In the postmodern era, environmental and social issues are part of what the postmodern ecosystem takes into account, the "lifeworld" in which the individual can find self-expression and acts following his/her own value system through more engaging forms of action, participation, and consumption practices.
4. In the postmodern era, consumers are liberated from the rational scheme, and thus can express their paradoxical behaviors.
5. The postmodern society questions a dichotomous categorization of society that is considered a naïve and unsuccessful approach to examine consumer behaviors and attitudes.
6. Postmodernism defines the act of consumption as equal to production since it is a value-added activity. Postmodern consumers are not only destroyers but also creators of value.

Following the postmodern logic, consumption is then defined as an act of social construction, a moment during which the consumer, in a relationship of co-production with the market, will create his/her own experience and construct him/herself as an individual. He/she is in search of a style of his/

her own. Consumer behavior becomes eclectic, mixing different objects and consumption practices, integrating them as an expression of the individual's personality and as a means of asserting his/her identity and his/her difference.

4.2.3   Systemic view of customer experience

The systemic approach, which has its origins in systems theory (e.g., Rousseau, 2015), is based on the idea of customer experience or any type of phenomenon that should be considered as a system or can be conceptualized according to system logic, as a complex set of interactions. Following this rationale, I introduced a systemic framework of the customer experience, which looks at customer experience design as a process combining a set of systems and processes that include key markers, drivers, and outcomes of the customer experience management model presented in Figure 1.5 (see Batat, 2019a, for more details). The components of the framework are presented and discussed in the following sections.

By framing customer experience marketing as a systemic process, we can note two main categories of drivers: idiocentric (self-oriented) and allocentric (others/environment-oriented).

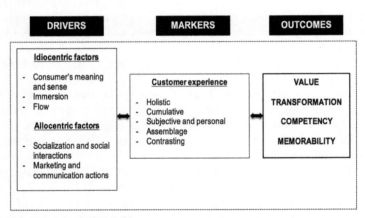

Source: Adapted from Batat (2019a).

Figure 1.5   Customer experience systemic model

Idiocentric drivers of the customer experience

Idiocentric drivers encompass three main factors: consumer meaning, immersion, and the "flow" experience, which are self- or consumer-oriented and generated by an individual's subjectivity within his/her own consumption and purchase experiences. First, the *consumer's meaning* is a relevant driver of the customer experience. Although experiences have a collective dimension, consumption experiences are fundamentally personal, and their meanings belong to the individuals who experienced them. Consumers make sense of their consumption experiences according to the symbolic aspects they assign to them, and how lived experiences will lead to constructing their own personal and social identities.

Symbolic consumption as a construct has been examined since the 1980s in marketing and consumer research following two core perspectives: identity and meaning construction (e.g., McCracken, 1987). By considering idiocentric drivers, companies should go beyond the thinking that focuses on the tangible aspects of their products and consider more the symbolic facets of their goods. Levy (1959) states that "managers must attend to more than the relatively superficial facts with which they usually concern themselves when they do not think of their goods as having symbolic significance" (p. 117). Batat (2019a) gives the example of a wedding ring, which is not only a tangible object defined by its shape, design, color of gold, brand, composition, carat, and so forth but also symbolizes love, commitment, devotion, and faithfulness that two individuals will share. It is then only by giving a meaning to the consumption experience that consumers can memorize it, and thus recall and repeat it if they are satisfied. Elliott and Wattanasuwan (1998) argue that consumers can also use advertising to create meanings based on symbols, icons, texts, and other elements. For example, when creating an advertisement for eco-friendly products, art directors may choose green colors, supposing that they will generate a feeling of nature, color of life, renewal, energy, growth, safety, freshness, environment, harmony, and so forth. The color green is used to induce specific feelings in the consumer experience of the advertisement.

However, the creation of meaning is not only related to the exposure phase; it is also generated and evolves through social interactions and interpersonal communication among consumers capable of creating and sharing a collective meaning. For companies, it is then important to develop a better understanding of the experience, the sense-making process, and the symbolic dimension of consumption. According to Anderson and Meyer (1988), sense-making is a continuing process in which various significances are generated as consequences of the consumer's own interest-focus, the culturally located influence of marketing and advertisement understanding, brand interpretation, product buying, and consumption experience. As brand managers and marketing professionals seek to increase and enhance their knowledge in terms of consumption experiences and consumer emotional and symbolic expectations, semiotics, which refers to the study of signs and meanings embedded within their cultural context, is recommended. Indeed, by using semiotics, companies can decode symbols, identify future trends, and innovate.

Second, when it comes to *consumer immersion*, analysis of the literature shows that immersion originates when a consumer interacts with a firm's experiential atmosphere. Immersion is then defined as a mode of access to a pleasurable and unforgettable consumption experience. Bitner (1992) refers to immersive environments as a servicescape, which comprises three dimensions: ambient conditions (temperature, music, noise, air quality, etc.); spatial layout and functionality (e.g., layout, furnishing); and signs, symbols, and artifacts (e.g., signage, style, décor). The servicescape can have a positive or a negative impact on the quality of customer experience, as well as on consumer behaviors and interpersonal employee relationships and interactions amongst consumers. The servicescape model includes facilitator, functional, and sensory elements that can be classified into two main categories: outdoor (e.g., parking, architecture, signage) and indoor (e.g., décor, fragrance, sounds, layout) elements.

Immersion in consumption experiences is a relevant approach as it is viewed both as a process that allows consumers to access and live intense experiences and as an outcome of a satisfying lived experience. This is particularly interesting for brand managers and marketing professionals since consumer immersion is the key to improving and enhancing consumer satisfaction and loyalty. Consumers who experience immersive consumption and purchase processes will be more eager to develop positive, pleasurable, and memorable feelings, and thus re-experience the same feelings in future experiences. While today's consumers are seeking varied and captivating experiences, marketing scholars argue that future consumers will seek the consumption experience that allows them to escape their ordinary life by driving them into a pre-conceptualized, pre-established, safe, and themed sphere.

Both "ordinary" and "extraordinary" consumption experiences can lead to the creation of intense immersion through exceptional events. Consequently, immersion in consumption experiences—whether they occur within ordinary or extraordinary settings—creates emotions, and thus consumer satisfaction and loyalty. Holt (1995) suggests a need for more multidimensional and holistic consumption frameworks dealing with and emphasizing the concept of immersion in the experience. Immersion is therefore necessary for the experience to be ideal, unique, and ultimate. Companies can consider the integration of five vital factors to help consumers become fully immersed: atmospheric, functional, human and social, cognitive, and symbolic/identity.

Lastly, the *flow experience* is another critical idiocentric factor to consider in consumer experience design and engagement. According to Batat (2019a), the consumer's flow experience can be compared to a peak experience; in other words, an intense experience in which consumers will lose the sense of chronological time and develop consciousness to be entirely in union and fused with the activity in which they engage. The concept of "flow" first appeared in psychology (Csikszentmihalyi, 1991) to refer to the degree of immersion that leads individuals to ignore their immediate setting (including the idea of time), and that the inherent recompense of the activity might lead them to search for experiences, even at high cost, for the simple purpose of doing it. For Csikszentmihalyi (1991), the flow experience refers to an "autotelic" dimension endowed with an intrinsic reward that is oriented toward oneself and which finds its end in itself.

Therefore, Batat (2019a) states that the consumer's flow takes place only during the experience. Activities and behaviors such as attending a concert, watching a movie, practicing tennis or swimming, viewing a captivating natural landscape, falling in love, and so forth allow consumers to experience flow, but only for a limited amount of time as they may disconnect if they are interacting with other social, sensorial, and environmental elements. As the flow experience generates strong feelings, consumers could not experience it without cutouts or breaks. For instance, consumers experience a set of successive immersions that can lead, or not, to flow, depending on the intensity of the immersion for a long encounter of the consumption or a purchase that is, otherwise, a short-term experience in nature. Among the conditions leading to a state of flow within experiences are the similarity between a consumer's activity, his/her level of competence, and the perception of the challenge of the activity. Therefore, companies should design suitable consumer experiences that ease access to an optimal experience and thus lead to the creation of flow.

Furthermore, consumer personality can also create a flow that allows intense consumption and purchase experiences. For instance, certain traits and behaviors could be more motivated by the generation of flow than others; for example, consumers who are curious, not particularly self-centered, or practice activities for essential motives only do not need extrinsic rewards and recognition. For these consumers, the consumption experiences and actions recompense them only intrinsically, and they do not expect flow and intense immersion to fulfill their emotional, autotelic, and functional needs. Using Csikszentmihalyi's definition, Hoffman and Novak (2018) extended the logic of flow and proposed a definition of flow within digital online experiences (see Chapter 2).

Allocentric drivers of the customer experience

These drivers include external factors that are other-oriented and are divided into two main categories: (1) socialization and social interactions; and (2) marketing and communication actions. First, *socialization and social interactions* are relevant allocentric drivers that companies need to evaluate to design attractive and socially enjoyable customer experiences. According to Batat (2019a), socialization is one of the key drivers that contribute to a customer's enhancement during the lived consumption experience. For Batat, there are two perspectives on consumer socialization in the marketing field: the stage perspective and the procedural perspective. While the stage perspective refers to the cognitive learning process and the acquisition of knowledge among individuals within their consumption experiences, the procedural approach of the socialization process as a driver of customer experience formation denotes a social learning process that incorporates different elements from an individual's social environment.

In contrast to a cognitive approach based on stimuli and actions, the procedural perspective that draws upon Bandura's social theory (1986) focuses on the reciprocity of interactions between the individual and the socialization agents involved in consumption learning. Bandura (1980) states that individuals not only respond to stimuli; they also interpret them. This bi-directional influence means that individuals are both the producers and the product of their own environment. Therefore, these two perspectives have lately contributed to the emergence of several consumer socialization models in marketing and consumer studies. These models have two types of socialization outcome: short-term outcomes related to consumption experience, perceptions, and meanings; and long-term outcomes, including the formation of consumption values, ideology, and empowerment. These outcomes allow consumers to give meaning to their consumption experiences and develop new practices and social skills according to the norms and codes of their own consumption culture or subculture where the socialization process takes place.

Second, when to comes to *marketing and communication actions*, Batat (2019a) shows that consumption experiences are also derived from strategies and programs implemented by companies to create engaging experiential offerings, and thus enchant their customers. In this sense, there are four leading marketing and communication strategies aimed at creating experiences: consumer engagement, theming, storytelling, and sensory marketing. *Consumer engagement* encompasses a robust human dimension related to the connection between the consumer and the company. This connection can be created and can evolve throughout the overall customer experience within an actual place or a virtual space.

Likewise, customer engagement enhances customers' interactions and exchanges within their experiences created and designed for them by the firm. When accomplished, a solid customer engagement approach will enhance brand image, positive word-of-mouth, and customer loyalty. Thus, a good product/service alone is not sufficient; and, since it does not guarantee a positive customer experience, companies need to focus on training their staff who are in contact with the clients and who can influence the overall customer experience. Indeed, the human dimension is a primary factor that companies must consider in the design of successful customer experiences that are pleasurable, satisfying, and memorable.

In addition to the human dimension that enhances customer engagement, companies need to focus on *theming* their experiential offerings. Theming refers to the process of creating a specific theme that allows the customer to dive into a deep thematic experience as defined by the company. The objective of the theming process is to create an atmosphere but, above all, to unify the décor of the customer experience. This can be done by ensuring consistency of the theme through diverse elements of the servicescape and the physical environment that give compliance throughout the experience journey. Besides, an uninterrupted themed consumption experience is considered a new way to re-enchant the consumer during his/her purchase and consumption experiences. Mossberg (2008) defines three main factors that contribute to successful theming: an arena (the experiencescape), characters (personal and other customers), and structure (construction of the story).

The third strategy that companies can implement to enhance the customer experience is *storytelling*. This is a strategic tool for narrative communication which consists of telling a story to consumers to promote brand awareness and value by creating a universe, an identity, and an emotionally charged story. As an integral part of customer experience design, storytelling can help companies differentiate their brands, products, and services from their competitors' by sensitizing the customer to the brand's history. Strong storytelling can enhance customer experience by focusing on various components, including communication and brand building, packaging enrichment, staff training (both internal and sales), and so forth.

Lastly, companies can also implement *sensory marketing strategies* in the design of their experiential offerings. Sensory marketing is a form of marketing that appeals to the five senses (sight, sound, touch, smell, and taste) that companies use to connect their brands, products, and services with their customers on an emotional level. It allows companies to create stimulating and memorable customer experiences that can build emotional connections in the customers' minds by appealing to their senses. As stated by Batat (2019a), sensory marketing highlights the idea that a consumer who feels good in a consumption or purchase setting (e.g., retail outlet, restaurant, hotel, museum, gym, etc.) tends to spend more time there, consume more, and have positive word-of-mouth. Therefore, companies should propose multisensory consumption experiences based on the five senses and bring together different types of marketing: olfactory, auditory, tactile, visual, and taste.

Markers of customer experience marketing

The markers of customer experience refer to the core characteristics of the lived experience. As illustrated in Figure 1.5, there are five key customer experience markers: holistic, cumulative, subjective/personal, assemblage, and contrasting. First, customer experience is *holistic* in nature, which means consumers and their activities are interdependent and based on several elements—intellect, emotion, spirituality, society, and external environment—which cannot be isolated. All are connected, related to each other, and embedded within a sociocultural consumption experience that shapes individuals' identities, behaviors, and attitudes. Thus, companies need to consider the holistic aspect when designing customer experiences, which should be embedded in a multidimensional sociocultural context in which the consumer interacts with different social actors to satisfy multiple needs (e.g., functional, social, emotional) within a specific consumption culture and with relation to a specific brand.

Second, the customer is regarded as *cumulative* because past experiences inform the present and build future customer experiences. Cumulative customer experience means everything that follows is based on recent and past consumption experiences. It is thus the accumulation of all consumption experiences in various realms that creates the meanings that consumers release from all these experiences. Through the accumulation of consumption experiences, consumers transform their future experiences; and at the same time they transform themselves, and thus build their own experience.

The third marker refers to the idea that customer experience is *subjective and personal*. According to Batat (2019a), the subjectivity that makes the same experience different from a personal perspective underscores the fact that consumption experiences are constructed from composite inputs related to a consumer's past experiences, present context, and future implications and meanings of the inputs. The way customers live their experiences and view things around them involves personal subjectivity, which defines whether they like or hate the components of their customer experience, such as taste, smell, style, décor, music, atmosphere, social interactions, etc. Therefore, a subjective and personal customer experience is the outcome of the individual's mind. Consumers may have comparable but not the same perceptions.

In addition to subjectivity, customer experience can also be viewed as an *assemblage* of several dimensions: sensorial (five senses), physical (environment), relational (social interactions), emotional, and cognitive (functional benefit). These dimensions can help consumers fully live their experiences. An assemblage is then defined as a key marker of the customer experience since it reflects the dynamic combination of heterogeneous elements, behaviors, and attitudes, which can be individual, subjective, social, economic, environmental, emotional, symbolic, functional, rational, etc., and that capture the heterogeneity of the experience in making and shaping numerous personal consumption experiences. It is certain that without a particular collection of these interconnected yet varied characteristics/elements, it may be challenging to have a whole and satisfying customer experience. Therefore, we cannot separate or isolate one element from the entire assemblage experience.

The last marker is related to the *contrasting* effect of the customer experience, which refers to the existence of a juxtaposition of contrasting elements, attitudes, and behaviors that are part of the same experience and the same individual who can express both hedonic and utilitarian benefits—and can show both cognitive and emotional attitudes within the same consumption experience. In contrast to the atomistic approach to customer experience management, which suggests that products could be viewed as either hedonic or utilitarian, holistic customer experience management models demonstrate that a product/brand experience includes both since these characteristics are reflected and assessed in the decision-making process of consumers who behave in both rational and emotional ways at the same time.

Outcomes of customer experience marketing

Referring to Figure 1.5, we can note that the holistic CXM model encompasses multiple outcomes of the lived customer experience, ranging from value and transformation to competency and memorability. These outcomes should be considered by marketing professionals in the design of experiential offerings that should satisfy both tangible and intangible needs of customers. Indeed, companies should know what kind of outcomes their offerings (products and services) endorse in the eyes of their customers. The first outcome companies have to consider is the *value* expected and perceived by customers. The perception of value is essential to the enjoyment and satisfaction of consumers, and is consequently of massive significance to companies.

I have identified six main categories of consumer values companies should focus on when designing experiences:

1. Value-in-exchange refers to the economic aspect of consumer value, and is the most widespread in the marketing field.
2. Value-in-marketplace describes five forms of consumer values—net value, marketing value, sale value, rational value, and derived value.
3. Value-in-time covers concepts over four stages that correspond to four stages of experience, namely *ex ante* (anticipated) value, transaction (purchase) value, *ex post* (consumption) value, and disposition (remembered).
4. Value-in-use is related to the service-dominant logic of Lusch and Vargo (2006), who emphasize a customer-orientation and the relationships with the service provider.
5. Value-in-possession defines material values as the propensity to place possessions and their purchase as fundamental in a consumer's life.
6. Finally, value-in-experience is related to a consumer's extrinsic/intrinsic perception of self/other-oriented value in relation to his/her active or passive role.

The second outcome of customer experience is *transformation*. Transformative consumption experience refers to the transforming effects that make consumers shift from one behavior to another. Once lived, some intense experiences can lead customers to be fully transformed by developing a new set of beliefs, values, and desires, replacing previously held consumption beliefs, values, and desires in a particular consumption setting. Thus, intense experiences such as getting married, becoming a grandparent, discovering a new faith, immigrating to a new country, or living in a war zone are all transformative experiences that might generate irreversible changes in an individual's social life, and thus his/her future customer experiences.

The third outcome is related to *competency* development. More than learning from past or present consumption experiences, consumers develop creative potential and competencies by living experiences that evolve throughout their childhood, adolescent life cycle, and adulthood. The last outcome of customer experience is *memorability*. Memory is considered an essential personal outcome and a subjective source of information through which consumers decide whether to relive an experience, repurchase a particular product/brand, revisit a place, etc. A memorable customer experience is defined as a significant episode kept in the consumer's memory and recalled after it has happened. If the evaluation is positive, then the experience memorability can strengthen and reinforce the recall of pleasurable happenings experienced by the consumer while engaging in consumption activities, including shopping, visiting a destination, enjoying a film, among other experiences.

KEY TAKEAWAYS

This chapter showed that designing suitable and profitable customer experiences online and offline requires in-depth knowledge of the new behaviors of today's postmodern consumers. Knowing their customers is critical to companies in determining the success of their experiential offerings. Thus, before implementing customer experience strategies, companies must first identify the dimensions that make up the experience, its type, and the model that is suitable for designing and measuring the experience.

2. When customer experience encounters digital technologies

CHAPTER OVERVIEW

The digital transformation is forcing companies to change their business strategy and adapt to the new market reality to satisfy their customers, who are seeking relevant and attractive content while expecting high levels of personalization of their experience. Companies must consider customers' real-time tastes and interests, especially when the customer experience is occurring online. Therefore, the challenge for companies is to adopt suitable technologies, platforms, and devices while implementing digital marketing strategies centered on customers by offering satisfying and effective digital customer experiences across platforms and devices. This chapter presents the evolution of digital marketing and its tools and techniques, followed by an overview of digital transformation impacts on both businesses and societies, and the challenges for companies to successfully integrate technologies and respond to the new needs of the digitized consumer. The last section will explore how digitization is shaping the customer experience, usually limited to the physical setting, in digital environments, including multiple touchpoints.

1 THE HISTORY AND EVOLUTION OF DIGITAL MARKETING

Digital marketing refers to different terms such as electronic marketing, online marketing, webmarketing, e-marketing, or marketing 4.0. Companies implement it by combining traditional marketing techniques with the Internet and digital technologies. The aim is to attract the online market. Figure 2.1 features the technologies and Internet applications relevant to marketing.

Figure 2.1   Levels of technology and Internet incorporation in marketing

1.1   Definition and Development of Digital Marketing

The rise of digital marketing begins with the introduction of the Internet to the general public in the 1990s, a revolution that changed business and marketing practices in many companies across sectors—although the invention of the Internet can be traced back to the end of the 1950s.

- The Internet was launched in 1958 by the US Department of Defense Advanced Research Projects Agency (ARPA), which in 1963 appointed a scientist named Joseph Carl Robnett Licklider as Director of Behavioral Sciences and Command and Control programs to create a network connecting computers at different locations. ARPA has since accelerated the process of connecting computers.
- In 1971, Ray Tomlinson created the first program to send emails, and in 1983 ARPA built the TCP/IP protocol, giving birth to the Internet in its modern form. Since then, this network has continued to grow at a rapid pace.
- Between 1991 and 1997, the Web grew by 850 percent per year (Ryan and Jones, 2012).
- The Internet then evolved from a one-way medium to an interactive medium thanks to the accumulation of technology, which gave birth to Web 2.0.
- In the 2000s, the Internet became a must for companies that started to dedicate budgets for online ads and e-commerce websites. In 2011, Forrester

Research stated that 19 percent of marketing investments in the United States were allocated to digital marketing, predicted to rise to 35 percent in 2016 (VanBoskirk, 2011).

It is therefore interesting to note that it took the Internet a concise period of time (average of three years) to generate US$1 billion in advertising revenue, compared to the length of time it took traditional media such as radio (around 30–40 years) and TV (average of 5–10 years). We can note three significant phases that have marked digital marketing from its beginnings to how we know it today:

1. *Internet supremacy (the 1990s–2000s).* This stage refers to the Web 1.0 era, also called webmarketing. In this period, the first search engines appeared, along with the first file transfer platforms. Companies started to engage in online business activities by promoting their brands and disseminating information without soliciting the intervention of the user, who, at the time, was only browsing the Web to search for information about brands and products. This period is characterized by the rise of the first e-commerce sites and early interest in the opportunities offered by social media, which marked a transition to the marketing 2.0 era and the use of social media.

2. *Social media power (the 2000s–2010s).* This phase indicates the Web 2.0 era, when various platforms connecting people and brands emerged. The terms social media, blogging, and Web appeared at the same time to refer to engaged and interactive online communities. Online social media interactions generate collective and participatory insights, which are beneficial for companies that can use the generated data to create and enhance bonds with their customers both online and offline. As a result, consumers were capable of developing an instant and direct two-way exchange with companies and brands for the first time. Online users could then give their opinions and feedback, share content, and challenge brands' reputation among online communities.

3. *Digital marketing institutionalization (2010–present).* Since 2010, society has become more and more connected. New terms have emerged, for example, semantics, connected objects, big data, and growth marketing; all of them refer to the Web 3.0 and 4.0 eras and the advent of digital marketing as a global marketing strategy. Thus, digital marketing strategy includes all the marketing methods, tools, and practices alongside the marketing mix tools—product, price, place, and promotion (the 4Ps) or these plus people, process, and physical evidence (the 7Ps)—applied to the Internet and mobile phones, as well as extended reality technologies such as virtual and augmented reality for their sensorial dimensions.

However, it should be noted that digital marketing did not evolve in the same way through the three phases outlined above. Its evolution depends on the type of industry and the sector. For instance, in the luxury sector, characterized by inaccessibility and sensory elements, the adoption of digital technologies came later compared with other sectors, the thinking being that luxury is incompatible with digital. In my book, *Digital Luxury* (Batat, 2019b), I identified three major periods of digital marketing evolution and adoption in the luxury sector:

- Static digital luxury, a functional and commercial use of digital luxury. This refers to the first stage, namely the Web 1.0 era, but from 2003 to 2007.
- Social digital luxury, an interactive and social approach that integrated social media platforms. This refers to the Web 2.0 era but from 2007 to 2012.
- Experiential digital luxury reflects a multisensory and emotion-focused usage of digital technologies. It refers to Web 3.0 and 4.0, but from 2007 to the present.

Therefore, digital marketing, as implemented nowadays by different companies across sectors, could be defined as a marketing strategy that encompasses all actions carried out using digital levers to promote a company, a brand, an organization, an institution, or a person; alternatively, it could be used to attract prospects, convert them into actual customers, and build loyalty. Digital marketing relies on clear and measurable objectives to reach specific consumer targets and influence their behaviors.

Digital marketing is also defined as marketing products and services using digital channels to reach the customer through different touchpoints. In this case, digital marketing goes beyond webmarketing because it is related not only to one touchpoint, namely the Internet, but includes multiple touchpoints such as mobile phones through text messaging, social media, apps, interactive television, and connected objects, among others.

All these touchpoints are incorporated as a communication channel that connects the brand with the consumer. Thus, the relational dimension and the connection with customers are core values in digital marketing, and allow companies to personalize their relationships and online content according to online user profiles while promoting their brands and products. Thanks to online audiences and instantly generated insights, digital marketing leads companies to create integrated, targeted, and measurable communication that will contribute to customers' acquisition and retention while building deeper relationships with them.

Furthermore, digital marketing can also be defined as a process of planning and implementing: the development, pricing, communication, and distribution of an idea, product, or service to create exchanges that are carried out in whole or in part using digital technologies, in line with individual and organizational objectives. Thus, this implementation of marketing mix techniques is aimed at acquiring new customers or improving the management of the relationship with existing customers.

1.2 The Marketing Mix in the Digital Era

The Internet has changed the specifics of the so-called traditional marketing mix. This transformation is ongoing, and new trends are always on the horizon. Among the significant changes that affected the 4Ps or 7Ps of the traditional marketing mix, the following should be considered by companies when implementing marketing strategies in digital settings:

- *Product policy in digital marketing.* Within the digital context and on the Internet, the product should more than ever meet customer expectations, and especially keep its promises. A promise not kept could ruin the brand's reputation, given the speed at which dissatisfaction spreads on the Web. Conversely, a product that keeps its promise benefits from the empathy of Internet users and a committed community. Recommendations amplified by social media can thus benefit the brand if it respects its commitments or, in contrast, have long-lasting effects if promises are broken. Consequently, companies should offer their customers, who are also online users, more opportunities to create their own unique product by selecting from many possible combinations. Initially reserved for products whose purchase process is relatively straightforward, this practice has spread to include products where more involvement is vital, such as cars or furniture.
- *Pricing policy in digital marketing.* The Internet makes it easy to compare prices, so the market is evolving into a marketplace of intense competition. To deal with this situation, companies tried at the beginning to differentiate themselves through price. This technique rapidly showed its limits as margins were continually eroded. Therefore, the current trend for companies is to differentiate themselves by value creation, which integrates the service consideration alongside price as consumers are usually more inclined to pay a higher price if the service or product offered and therefore the experience is better. Three main approaches could be distinguished in digital marketing: drip pricing, reference pricing, and bundled offerings. The first approach consists of displaying a price without certain factors. The online customer who is attracted by the price proceeds to the purchase process, which requires several clicks. Before confirming the purchase, the actual price, including all factors such as delivery, is displayed. Having invested time in the process, the prospective buyer is psychologically com-

pelled to continue his/her purchase on the website. This method owes its name to the progressive display of prices. Second, reference pricing refers to the displayed price with the price of the same item before a promotion to create a sense of urgency or competition. Lastly, companies can also apply pricing through bundled offers, which consist of proposing batches of different products, thus making it difficult to determine the actual unit price of any item.

- *Distribution (place) policy in digital marketing.* The Internet has contributed to creating a globalized marketplace that has no geographical barriers for commerce and exchange. The spread of smartphones has also erased the boundaries between online and in-store shopping, and the practice of showrooming is becoming more and more widespread. Companies should therefore ensure that they offer customers a unique shopping experience in their physical stores and find the right balance between online and offline marketing strategies.
- *Promotion policy in digital marketing.* Online promotional strategies should be an extension of offline promotional actions through an integrated marketing strategy. Online promotions benefit from the traceability that this technology ensures and therefore from a higher degree of measurement than traditional methods. Internet communication also offers more creative freedom since it is unrestrained by traditional formats, thus allowing for more creative and interactive formats, such as mini-series or comic strips.

In addition to the 4Ps of the marketing mix, the P of people, which refers to the human dimension, should be reconsidered in digital marketing and online actions. The Internet allows great interactivity between a brand and its customers, who can directly interact with it. Thus, online communities formed around brands/companies allow people to share information, exchange experiences, and post comments, contributing to positive online word-of-mouth (eWOM). Although the interactions are online, the company can create a feeling of human presence that values the online customers. For instance, companies can involve online users in creating the brand's story and being part of it.

1.3   Value Creation and Digital Marketing Strategic Objectives

When implementing the marketing mix on the Internet, value creation in digital marketing involves three key steps: attracting, converting, and enhancing customer loyalty. Companies should consider these steps in their digital strategies to create and share value with their customers.

1. *Customer attraction.* This step refers to a pull marketing strategy that attracts the target audience to the desired digital media. Companies can

implement two strategies: acquisition and generation. While acquisition strategies refer to a set of online levers whose cost is directly correlated to the traffic and value obtained (e.g., an email campaign), generation strategies consider online levers whose cost cannot be directly correlated to the traffic or value obtained, such as natural referencing optimization or creation of a company's Facebook page. Thus, the main difference between these two strategies lies in the way the cost can be calculated.

2. *Customer conversion.* After attracting the target to the desired digital media, companies should implement additional actions to engage online users in various acts designed for them, such as buying something, watching a video, or signing a petition. The steps followed to reach the desired action are part of a conversion path, which is distinguished by its length, defined by the number of steps to follow, and its complexity. To assess the performance of the conversion path, most companies use the conversion rate, which measures how many objectives have been reached given the traffic of the selected digital media. On its own, this indicator does not give an accurate picture of the efforts that should be deployed, which is why companies also use the loyalty rate to measure the performance of their online actions.

3. *Customer loyalty.* Loyalty is often neglected by digital marketing strategies that mostly focus on acquiring or generating new customers, whereas the loyalty of existing customers is often less valued. The indicator used here is the loyalty rate, calculated by dividing the number of stable customers by the total number of customers.

Furthermore, the company's digital strategy implemented through online actions should focus on two main objectives, namely growth and customer experience. To grow its business, a company should focus on digital offerings that can optimize online sales channels through multiple touchpoints (e.g., smartphone, website, tablet, TV, connected objects). Indeed, for companies, online actions and interactions with customers allow them to follow the consumer's purchasing path in real time, and thus collect data about him/her to propose personalized offers and communication. This approach allows the brand to reinforce and customize the customer experience. Therefore, the company's objectives in terms of business growth and customer experience can be achieved by considering customer engagement and online visibility, while offering a satisfying navigation experience. With the development of social media platforms, interactions between customers and brands are now occurring swiftly. Thus, it is easier for companies to encourage customer engagement beyond the simple "like." Nowadays, consumers are no longer passive users of social media; they are becoming empowered co-creators of content through user-generated content (UGC). They can create their own content and even become powerful influencers who can collaborate in a win–win relationship with brands (Batat, 2019a).

Besides this, as consumers are spending more time on the Internet and are increasingly using the Web to search for information, purchase products, or interact through social media platforms, online presence and visibility, as well as e-reputation, become major challenges for companies. Thus, to increase their online visibility and create positive e-reputations, companies should develop efficient e-commerce websites by promoting referencing in search engines or communicating in a targeted way with identified prospective customers. Whether it is an information search on the Web or the geolocation of a store on his/her smartphone, and whatever the touchpoint with the consumer, a positive user experience often leads to customer loyalty and a positive e-reputation. Thus, companies should pay attention to the ergonomics and design of their websites, the loading time of web pages, the quality of their online communications, and the content published on social media.

1.4   Digital Marketing Tools

Companies can leverage different tools to implement successful digital marketing strategies, and thus convert customers. This section presents a selection of tools that constitute an integral part of the digital strategy implementation process. Companies can combine different levers to increase their online visibility, create a positive e-reputation, and engage their customers while offering seamless online and offline customer experiences. These tools are defined as follows:

- *Online advertising* refers to the company's efforts to showcase a website in natural search results, which can take a long time to be visible. Therefore, companies can use online advertising to promote a given website. Of course, online advertising is used to promote websites and any company's service or product. There are two main types of online advertising: display advertising and search advertising. The former refers to an advertisement in the form of a banner that appears on the portals visited by the target. Search advertising, as its name suggests, is an advertisement attached to the results displayed by search engines. It is based on the purchase of keywords that give rise to an advertisement at the top of the results when they appear in a request. Both types of advertising can be specifically targeted because they allow the company to determine the target that will be exposed to the advertisement in advance. This can be achieved by varying parameters such as location, age, or gender. Regarding the advertiser's compensation, two systems can be used: payment by impression, often calculated per 1000 impressions, or payment by click. Display advertising is often considered intrusive, while search advertising is unnoticeable. The current trend is toward interactive ads that engage the consumer and that are playful and less intrusive.

- *Email marketing* is one of the first levers of digital marketing. It refers to direct marketing that uses electronic means to deliver a message to a specific target. Despite its age and poor image because of unsolicited messages, email marketing remains one of the most effective means that a digital marketer can use due to its low-cost, precise targeting, ease of personalization, and highly measurable aspect. Also, email marketing can be used to build and/or retain relationships with existing customers or to attract potential customers, thus contributing to prospective efforts.
- *Website*. The company's website where its products, brands, and services are displayed should be considered a central component in any digital marketing strategy. This is the hub to which the other levers will lead. Efforts should therefore be made to attract as much traffic as possible to this hub. The website should also be well designed to allow the conversion of Internet users who visit it.
- *Natural referencing*. After launching a website, the company should ensure its high visibility on the Web; this is where Search Engine Optimization (SEO) comes into play. SEO aims to optimize the website so that it rises in search results. This is achieved by aligning the site's content on the searches made by the target and by adopting parameters determined by search engines so that they index the site. The optimization of natural referencing intervenes in the acquisition of customers as well as in their retention. Indeed, customer acquisition is enabled by the website's appearance in the search results, which facilitates its discovery and therefore a potential visit.
- *Affiliate marketing*. Affiliation can be defined as a partnership system where associated parties are rewarded for each visit or sale generated from text links on their websites or blogs. Affiliation is particularly effective in generating sales or attracting new consumers. Amazon's affiliate system is the best known and most used because it is easy and efficient.
- *Social media*. This refers to media content that is created to be shared. Social media reflects the ease of collaboration and connection among users and between the company and its customers, thus changing the face of marketing. Social media platforms are diverse, and allow the construction and improvement of company or brand reputation thanks to their sharing function and high degree of posts going viral. The richness of discussions on these networks is a valuable source of information for marketers because of the insights generated through online interactions.
- *Customer relationship management (CRM)*. This is defined as a strategy for managing interactions with current and potential customers. It often relies

on technology. CRM can be implemented by three approaches: a marketing perspective through improving brand awareness; a commercial perspective via increasing sales; and a service perspective by ensuring that people who have interacted with the brand are satisfied. CRM can be used upstream to select the best lever to use for each target thanks to customer insights and the data accumulated.

- *Online public relations or e-PR.* Online PR allows companies to connect directly with their target audience. This tool leads the company to deliver information to unlimited audiences, whereas traditional PR tools are limited to a number of carefully chosen journalists.
- *E-reputation management.* Online reputation management is the process by which a brand/company monitors, measures, and manages discussions on the Internet. It helps acquire, engage, and secure the participation of the target customer audience. Thus, responding to consumer queries and complaints helps improve service levels. By exploiting analyses provided by online reputation management, consumer insights can be generated and deployed to optimize the company's communication and marketing strategies.

These different levers allow companies to create strong relationships with their customers while offering them seamless online and offline experiences. These tools differ from traditional media because they help companies build relationships with their customers over time by offering continuous and pertinent shopping experiences across various devices and platforms. These platforms allow companies to create online experiences, enrich them, and deliver them through multiple touchpoints over time.

To create a successful experience, companies should consider these three aspects: (1) a high quality of online content; (2) setting and times, delivery process; and (3) the purpose of the platform used, which can cover different features such as communication, socialization, purchase, and brand communities. Figure 2.2 presents the characteristics of each platform.

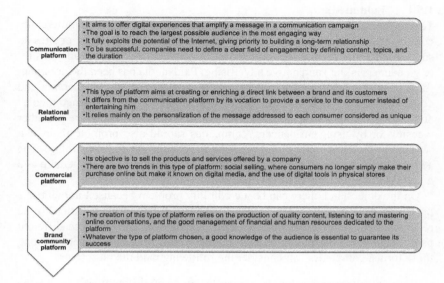

Communication platform
- It aims to offer digital experiences that amplify a message in a communication campaign
- The goal is to reach the largest possible audience in the most engaging way
- It fully exploits the potential of the Internet, giving priority to building a long-term relationship
- To be successful, companies need to define a clear field of engagement by defining content, topics, and the duration

Relational platform
- This type of platform aims at creating or enriching a direct link between a brand and its customers
- It differs from the communication platform by its vocation to provide a service to the consumer instead of entertaining him
- It relies mainly on the personalization of the message addressed to each consumer considered as unique

Commercial platform
- Its objective is to sell the products and services offered by a company
- There are two trends in this type of platform: social selling, where consumers no longer simply make their purchase online but make it known on digital media, and the use of digital tools in physical stores

Brand community platform
- The creation of this type of platform relies on the production of quality content, listening to and mastering online conversations, and the good management of financial and human resources dedicated to the platform
- Whatever the type of platform chosen, a good knowledge of the audience is essential to guarantee its success

Figure 2.2   Platform types and characteristics

1.5   The PESO Model of Digital Marketing

The Paid-Earned-Shared-Owned (PESO) media model was introduced in 2014 by Gini Dietrich, an American public relations professional (Thabit, 2015). It is an advance on the Paid, Earned, and Owned (POEM) model popularized by Forrester Research (Corcoran, 2009). Marketing and PR professionals emphasize the importance of the PESO model in a company's digital strategy.

The four pillars of the PESO model constitute the foundations for a successful digital marketing strategy aimed at using different types of media to gain visibility on the Web. Although we could discuss the innovative aspect of the proposed model compared to its predecessor, POEM, the PESO model has the advantage of distinguishing between earned and shared media. It also emphasizes areas that are shared between two domains. An employee advocacy approach can thus be positioned in the common area between shared and owned media.

Companies can implement the PESO model for different purposes, ranging from increasing brand visibility on the Web and enhancing online user engagement to creating a seamless user experience during the browsing and purchasing process. Thus, digital marketing uses the PESO model's four pillars as main levers to strengthen positive synergies by combining the following types of media: paid, earned, shared, and owned.

1.5.1   Paid media

This refers to traditional advertisements and other forms of commercially contracted content by companies that highlight publications, pages, or sites on social media platforms or search engines. It also includes display ads on sites (e.g., banners, skins) and native advertising. Paid media has been the dominant form of promotional media content for the past century, as Macnamara and colleagues (2016) state. Besides, paid media aims to promote "owned media" and also generate "earned media." In this sense, by buying space on other websites or by using influencers, companies should also promote their own websites, Facebook pages, and Instagram accounts to gain visibility. The advantage of paid media is that it allows the company to get immediate and quantifiable results in real time.

On the other hand, there can be a credibility problem because Internet users no longer trust brand advertisements, and instead pay more attention to the recommendations of other Internet users. Companies can thus use different paid media forms depending on their budgets, objectives, and targets. Among these forms, companies can consider the following paid media actions:

- Display advertising refers to buying locations on different sites where the target of the company is present.
- Paid referencing, also called Search Engine Advertising (SEA), is related to buying advertising links on search engines so that the company's website appears before others that usually emerge in natural referencing.
- Sponsoring can take different forms, either as a partnership with an influencer or as advertising on social networks.

These three forms represent the main paid media actions that the Forrester institute has presented in its model. However, it should be noted that, with the evolution of digital marketing, other forms of paid media have been integrated, such as affiliate links, programmatic marketing, and retargeting.

1.5.2   Earned media

This is media that is "earned" by the company, and results from posts and comments from Internet users. Earned media also refers to editorial publicity generated by organizations in press releases, interviews, and other media relations activities. In other words, earned media refers to all publicity actions related to digital word-of-mouth (eWOM) that allow the company to gain a positive e-reputation. Earned media tools are as follows:

- Word-of-mouth is one of the most influential communication channels because customers perceive it as a credible source of information. For example, customers may publish their opinions and feedback on brands or products. Word-of-mouth can be defined as the process by which an individual influences the actions or attitudes of others. It is also the foundation for two forms of marketing that are considered earned media, namely buzz marketing and viral marketing.

- Buzz marketing is a technique that involves spreading a message to Internet users in a remarkable and memorable way. Thus, buzz marketing is a promotional process focused on maximizing the benefit of word-of-mouth of a product or phenomenon virally via technology, whether through personal conversations or on a larger scale through discussions on social media platforms.
- Viral marketing is an advertising strategy that leverages the word-of-mouth effect among individual relationships to promote a product (Long and Wong, 2014). It is also related to consumer actions to share and spread marketing-relevant information that marketers initially send out to stimulate word-of-mouth behaviors.

1.5.3　Shared media

The term "shared media" is usually used to designate the free audience obtained through social sharing (e.g., Facebook likes, retweets). It can also amplify owned and paid media. Shared media platforms are open to subscribers who can contribute and post comments (Macnamara et al., 2016). In the POEM model, shared media is initially included in earned media, whereas it is distinct in the PESO model. However, a distinction is increasingly being made between earned media obtained on "official" media (e.g., YouTube, Instagram, Facebook, Twitter, Tumblr, Pinterest) and shared media obtained on individuals' "personal" social media accounts. Therefore, shared media platforms such as Facebook allow for brand building and reinforcement, using the network for market research (e.g., opinions, views). For instance, Saravanakumar and Lakshmi (2012) identified five strategies implemented by Facebook that companies can use to attract customers:

- Promoting the company's products and services to the page's "fans." Fans must be privileged over other customers by benefiting from different promotions.
- Crowdsourcing consists of involving the brand's fans in the development of a strategy or an offer.
- Enabling check-in via smartphones whereby the consumer indicates his/her arrival at the store thanks to Facebook's location service, and thus benefits from a discount from the brand.
- Games—companies should use gamification to attract consumers, and thus engage them in the promotion of their products and services.

- Social shopping allows consumers to discuss the company's brands and products and comment on their purchase on the company's page that displays its catalog on, for example, Facebook.

1.5.4   Owned media

This is the content created by the brand, such as articles and podcasts. It refers to the media owned by the company and over which it has the most control. These require more time and resources to set up than other media (Chang et al., 2018). Types of media owned by companies include websites, blogs, social media accounts, and so forth:

- A website is an essential element nowadays for any self-respecting business because consumers tend to do research on the Internet before making a purchase or decision. If a company is not present through its website, it will miss many potential customers.
- Blogs aim to provide brand content and create relationships with consumers.
- Social media accounts reflect the presence of the brand or company on different platforms, such as Facebook, Instagram, TikTok, Twitter, LinkedIn, Vine, or Snapchat.
- Email is also a free element owned by companies. It allows them to create relationships with their actual or potential customers by targeting them with news or current promotions. This is becoming more and more personalized, with brands now emailing promotional codes to customers on their birthday or during holidays.
- Natural referencing or SEO (as presented above) also allows the company to position its website favorably on search engines by choosing the right keywords.

These owned media actions are the most basic that were presented in 2009. With the evolution of digital marketing, companies are developing other forms of owned media, including inbound marketing, webinars, and podcasts. Owned media allows companies to build long-term relationships with existing customers and acquire potential ones while benefiting from the cost-effective and digitally versatile aspects of these media.

2   IMPACTS OF DIGITAL TRANSFORMATION ON BUSINESS AND SOCIETY

This section presents, explains, and discusses the challenges related to digital transformation from two perspectives: the business/company and the consumer.

2.1 Implications of Digital Transformation for Businesses

Digital transformation is not a new phenomenon; it was introduced in the 2000s and examined in different disciplines where authors proposed diverse definitions of the digital transformation process. Thus, the definition of digital transformation depends on the field of study and the sector where digitization is examined. It can be defined as a combination of three phenomena: automation, dematerialization, and reorganization of the business process.

In business and management, the term has been used by authors to examine the drivers of a successful digital transformation strategy, how to digitally transform business models, and what steps and tools companies should consider in their strategies. Moreover, digital transformation lies in using technologies to change the company's structure, production processes, and management system, among others. Digital transformation also refers to the instantaneousness of exchanges between human beings and new opportunities for value creation. Reis et al. (2018) define digital transformation in relation to the use of new digital technologies that allow major improvements in the company's business activities and that influence all aspects of customers' lives. These authors identify three major perspectives to digital transformation: technological, organizational, and social. While the technical definition of digital transformation relies on new digital technologies (e.g., social media, mobile technology, analytical or integrated tools), the organizational refers to a change in the company's operational processes or the creation of new business models. Meanwhile, the social perspective on digital transformation is related to all aspects of human life.

Considering technological perspectives of digital transformation, it should be noted that digital data processing technologies have transformed how companies use data and have profoundly changed consumer behavior and the entire economy to give rise to a digital economy. The digital economy has four specific characteristics: (1) the non-localization of activities; (2) the central role of platforms; (3) the importance of network effects; and (4) the exploitation of mass data. These characteristics distinguish it from the traditional economy, particularly through the change of value creation chains that digital technologies generate. Thus, in the era of the digitalization of companies, one of the main challenges is to ensure that massive investments in modern technologies and collaborative tools are profitable and create wealth for the organization by being effectively used by its staff.

Nevertheless, authors such as Markus and Keil (1994) argue that some technically successful technologies in which millions of dollars have been invested are used little or not at all. This issue related to the acceptance and use of integrated technologies is both complex and multidimensional. Technology acceptance and use by organizations are topics that several authors have widely examined in different disciplines. Many theories have been developed to examine the factors impacting technology's acceptance at the organizational level, which is more related to technology adoption, at the group level through assimilation, or at the individual level by examining factors that impact the use of technology.

At the organizational level, the "adoption perspective" investigates the process by which an organization decides to choose and acquire a technology to make it available to internal actors. This investment decision is often planned and organized. It is framed by return on investment (ROI) issues. However, this decision is not always complete and rational because the adoption of specific technology can be influenced by fashion, lobbying, and emotional elements. Once the technology has been adopted at the organizational level, the issue shifts to its internal assimilation for regular use. The notion of assimilation refers to innovation diffusion and acceptance theories that examine the impact of different environmental, cultural, organizational, social, and individual factors on the adoption of innovation by social actors.

Rogers' (1962) diffusion of innovations theory is one of the most widely used models in the field of technology adoption. This theory focuses on the phenomena of adoption and diffusion of innovations of all kinds. It suggests that elements such as the perception of the innovation's features, type of decision, communication channel, social systems, and agents of change who can promote it can positively or negatively affect the adoption process. According to Rogers, the diffusion of innovation in a social system depends on five attributes. They refer to individual perceptions of relative advantage, namely: the perception of benefits related to adoption; compatibility; low complexity; ease of trial (that is, the possibility of actors giving up technology at low cost if it does not suit them); and the observability of innovation—in other words, whether benefits are visible to end-users.

Drawing on Rogers' theory, the technology acceptance model (TAM) developed by Davis (1989) creates a link between ease of use, perceived usefulness, and intention to use to enhance technology dissemination. The more a technology is perceived as easy to use, the more intention there will be to use it, and thus the more valuable it will be. Therefore, perceived usefulness and perceived ease of use determine people's attitudes toward a system and their intention to use it. Perceived usefulness is also considered to be directly influenced by perceived ease of use. This model relies on characteristics related to the technology (ease of use) and individuals (usefulness and satisfaction of use) to explain the success of the technology through its adoption and diffusion to all stakeholders. Thus, understanding the process of assimilation and implementation makes it possible to explain the conditions of acceptance of a technology by a group of actors in an organization that make it suitable for use.

Consequently, understanding the adoption and diffusion of technologies in the organization to better engage in efficient and profitable digital transformation strategies is a significant challenge for companies, which should rethink the way they operate by integrating digital tools into their actions by covering all functions, ranging from marketing and communication to human resources and accounting. Indeed, the transformation is not only about implementing digital tools; it is also a fundamental transformation of the way of thinking and doing—it is a new mindset. In this new mindset, a company is faced with a change in all known and established practices, new team management, or adaptation to a new business model that generates challenges companies should face and opportunities they should seize.

2.1.1 What are the challenges for companies?

Digital transformation is necessary for a company to adapt to the new uses imposed by the digital on its market, adopt different approaches, and thus optimize its processes to be more efficient and coherent, and to ensure sustainable growth. Companies are thus led to review their organization and governance by embracing a customer-centric approach instead of a product-centric logic. For instance, taking a close look at new business models that have emerged over the last few years and that are disrupting or even endangering well-established, historic companies, we can note that value chains have been reinvented; and one phenomenon that best describes these new trends is "Uberization." Inspired by the Uber ride-hailing company, this model is based on the disintermediation via digital platforms that connect providers to users promptly.

Another new business model referring to "products as services" moves from ownership to use and creates new industries driven by the dematerialization of products such as books, films, and music. An additional trend that is reconfiguring the value chain is the valuing of rental and recycling rather than ownership. Traditional companies are confronted with these new trends, and should respond rapidly to these changes to remain competitive and meet customer demands and new emerging needs.

2.1.2 What are the opportunities and benefits of digital transformation?

Engaging in a digital transformation process allows companies to adapt their strategies in real time. This task goes hand in hand with productivity and, ultimately, overall company performance. In other words, companies that adopt a digital strategy are more profitable and grow faster than those that have not yet begun a digitalization process. The advent of artificial intelligence (AI), big data, robots, and computer systems has allowed companies to automate processes, which saves much time and promotes the quality of these processes. Digital transformation also offers substantial competitive advantage. Using all the new technologies allows companies to be at the forefront of progress and differentiate themselves from their competitors. Every company aims to offer its customers personalization and innovative products and concepts to remain competitive, especially when targeting youth populations such as millennials and post-millennials, who are referred to as "digital natives" (Batat, 2021b). The benefits are considerable because digital transformation allows companies to increase numbers of potential customers while boosting sales. However, successful digital transformation should follow four main criteria:

- *Companies should be able to overcome obstacles to digital transformation.* Within a company that has existed for several years with well-established practices, such a change can sometimes be too complicated to adapt to new market developments. For many companies, the transition to digital is perceived as a constraining necessity. Companies should therefore develop a long-term view at this crucial stage to avoid obstacles—whether human, technical, cultural, institutional, or organizational.
- *Companies should allocate necessary resources.* It is obvious that such a large-scale project as a company's digital transformation not only implies financial costs but also requires human involvement. However, some companies often do not respect this factor (Batat, 2019b).
- *Companies should manage, train, and support their employees.* People play a vital role in the success of digital transformation. Employees should therefore be involved from the beginning of the process by knowing how the new tools work and their benefits, such as improved operations and customer relations. In other words, it is essential to train them and encourage them to accept and become the drivers of change.
- *Companies should collaborate with external experts to support them in the process.* Engaging in a successful digital transformation should be accompanied by an expert who serves as an external eye. This limits the risks and costs, and helps smooth the shift, especially because digital transformation is an ongoing, long-term process aligned with technology development and the rise of new consumer behaviors and consumption trends.

2.2   Impacts on Consumer Behaviors: The Advent of Digitized Consumers

The digital context has contributed to the emergence of a new consumer profile: digitized consumers who are comfortable using digital technologies in their social, consumption, and shopping activities. It is thus critical for companies to identify the characteristics of digitized consumers and develop in-depth knowledge of their social and consumption activities and their shopping behaviors and expectations related to the company's offerings (products and services), both online and offline.

Thanks to the highly technological setting in which they live, digitized consumers are more and more involved in interactive processes, always ready to communicate and react instantly with brands via various tools and discussion platforms (Hoffman and Novak, 1996), using forums, listservs, newsgroups, email, personal web pages, social media, and blogs. The relationship between businesses and consumers has changed significantly. This considerable change has brought about more interactivity, emphasizing online collaboration and communication with users. Among the patterns that characterize the digitized consumer, the following should be considered by companies in their offerings and communication strategies:

- *Interconnectivity and instant responses to requests.* The exchange of information and the creation of communities around a product or a brand directly impact the behavior of the digitized consumer. Also, companies should consider that digitized consumers want to satisfy their needs rapidly.
- *The search for relevance.* With the mass of information that users of digital tools face, the search for relevance is becoming more and more imperative. Marketers should therefore communicate the right message to the right target, or risk being ignored.
- *Accumulation.* Digitized consumers tend to be interested in information related to their interests, and to group themselves in communities sharing those same interests.
- *Personal content publishing.* Digital tools favor self-expression. The levers reserved for this purpose continue to grow and take several forms, such as texts, photos, and videos. Therefore, companies should pay particular attention to the consistency of their messages, the quality of the experience they provide, and the fulfillment of promises they make.

It is evident that the digitized consumer has undergone a significant evolution in his/her role. These new empowered and connected consumers can perform more or less complex operations, sometimes based on the mutualization of needs—for example, carpooling. Sometimes these operations also place the digitized consumer in the role of supplier. Gradually, the digitized consumer is taking on the role of consumer–supplier, and this has emerged in accommodation services such as Airbnb, which shows this dual role. Using this accommodation service, digitized consumers search for satisfaction of their needs while seeking a potential profit. However, this new profile generates some challenges that companies have to face, including unpredictable or unreasonable expectations, influential power, and volatile behavior:

- *Unpredictable expectations.* While companies can implement specific digital tools to adapt to consumer behavior, digitized consumers can develop alternative uses of the same tools to fit their expectations. Moreover, companies and consumers have different interests in aspects such as reviews. While brands use them to collect consumer insights to propose relevant experiences, digitized consumers are aware of their power and can sanction the company by spreading negative feedback, reaching thousands or even millions of Internet users in record time. Thus, this type of consumer is one of the most demanding, and adjusts his/her behaviors according to current trends displayed online through social media platforms.
- *The power of influence.* The digitized consumer has also become a powerful influencer who can collaborate with brands. This new position results from his/her omnipresence in the production chain of his/her favorite products, which gives him/her expert status because of knowledge accumulated and skills developed (e.g., creating and managing a YouTube channel). Moreover, digitized consumers are considered a source of information that can influence other like-minded consumers as much as they influence the company's strategic decisions.
- *Volatile behavior.* The emergence of the multi-channel consumer is challenging for companies that face difficulties defining and implementing effective strategies targeting digitized consumers and thus creating solid bonds with them.

To sum up, we can note that the digitized consumer does not have rigid behavior and adapts to different digital channels. Similarly, the expectations and needs of these digitized consumers are multiple and multiform, and combine both online and offline offerings. Brands and companies should therefore offer a seamless experience that adapts to the consumer's offline and online expectations. The evolution of behaviors and the rise of new consumption trends should not be perceived as risks, but rather as great business opportunities for companies to innovate and anticipate future customer needs.

3   HOW DIGITIZATION IS SHAPING THE CUSTOMER EXPERIENCE

The expansion and dissemination of digital technologies have also affected the customer experience that is now occurring, in addition to the physical setting such as stores, in a digital setting through online shopping, for example. Current digital transformation creates challenges and opportunities for companies, which should design different and satisfying digital experiences, including diverse technologies that respond to diverse digitized consumer needs, whether functional, social, or even emotional.

Customer experience in the digital era refers to customers' use of digital platforms (e.g., social media) and devices (e.g., computer, tablet, smartphone) to search for information about a store or brand, or to purchase items online. The digital customer experience (DCX) reflects all interactions between a brand and its consumers through digital channels (e.g., emails, social networks, online advertising). These digital channels can create value by doing the following:

- improving customer insights thanks to online data and big data generated by online behaviors and searches;
- facilitating the customer journey through identifying the key touchpoints involved in the online purchasing process;
- enriching the connection consumers can have with a brand thanks to the online content published by companies on their websites and social media platforms.

Many brands, such as Intel, are tapping into digital data obtained from public searches or social media databases to enrich their knowledge of customers in Business to Consumer (B2C) or Business to Business (B2B) contexts. Also, brands are engaging consumers by asking them to share their experiences with their online communities, whether fashion products like Burberry or hospitality experiences like Accor. Brands can also decide to launch their own online communities and use the Internet of Things (IoT) to add social value to their products—for example, Nike and its strong connection with its community of joggers, or American Express's connection with its community of entrepreneurs. Finally, brands can create social dynamics and enhance their reputation among their target groups by creating online challenges.

A successful digital customer experience typically rests on two complementary pillars. On the one hand, they are capturing relevant insights and digital data by carefully listening to customers to understand their online journey, and create experiences matching their expectations at each moment of their journey. On the other hand, companies should comprehend and use social dynamics to emphasize the community aspect of online and offline purchasing behaviors, and thus amplify the impact of the proposed customer experience in the digital setting. For example, the L'Oréal group systematically uses digital data to imagine and implement customer journeys; but the group also relies on influencers (e.g., YouTubers) to amplify its brand messages at different points in the customer journey.

BOX 2.1   GOOGLE'S FOCUS ON CONSUMER-CENTRICITY AND INTERNET USER EXPERIENCE TOUCHPOINTS

On search platforms such as Google, the way data are transferred from one application to another to create the ultimate user experience is extraordinary. For example, location data gathered from maps analyzes what kind of restaurants we frequently visit. These data are then used to suggest similar culinary experiences nearby through ads or the search results in our browser. The average human cannot use a mobile phone that does not support Google products. Our contacts, GPS, emails, calendars, searches, cloud storage, phone operating system, and apps are all linked to Google directly or indirectly.

For Google, the experience touchpoint is the user's interaction with a specific product, whether through an ad, a blog post, a click on an ad, a website visit, or the purchase itself. Thus, Google sets up a guide based on five fundamental principles shaping the digital transformation—the five As:

- *Audience*. Based on compiling online data, centralizing, and evaluating it to form a strategy to identify and engage the right people.
- *Assets*. The production of relevant, context-sensitive ads using acquired insights from user data gathered in a fast and straightforward way to create a rich user experience.
- *Access*. With reach as a primary target, the use of cost-effective tools to manage contact frequency without jeopardizing transparency and brand safety standards.
- *Attribution*. Models that account for the dynamics between channels and devices to eliminate errors attributed to the last-click model, which considers that the last click is the interaction that made the user commit to the purchase. Attribution is about measuring the value of each point of contact.
- *Automation*. This is about simplifying and improving performance using machine learning to reduce costs and create a consistent user experience that is fast and efficient.

Furthermore, Google's current primary focus is gathering information from all free products to present relevant and useful ads, eventually generating profits and improving the user experience. This model is now being adapted and used by many online providers, which use free products to gather data to enhance the online experience. Over time, Internet use has become all about efficiency and the intelligent use of data, and, today, Internet users rarely receive irrelevant information or random ads that pop up unexpectedly and trivially.

Therefore, customer experience in the digital setting is related to the company's incorporation of technology, big data, AI, and other connected objects into online offerings. According to Batat (2019b), logic centered on digital experiences has been introduced into advance digital marketing strategies mainly focused on the suitable device or platform the company must consider to promote its products or increase its sales both online and offline.

This traditional approach does not integrate customers' intangible and subjective experiential needs, including emotional, relational, and symbolic expectations. In this sense, a digital customer experience perspective addresses the relationship with the customer from his/her perspective, which evolves and changes according to the purchase stages (both online and offline) and before, during, and after the shopping experience. Therefore, to create the ultimate digital customer experience, companies should consider integrating both human and technological factors in their digital marketing strategies, which can positively or negatively influence online and offline consumer and shopping experiences.

Nevertheless, to offer compelling digital customer experiences, companies must understand what differentiates the customer experience in a digital setting from the experience in a physical context. Among the characteristics that distinguish digital from physical customer experiences, the following should be considered by companies in their digital marketing strategies:

- In digital customer experiences, mobile and social technologies immerse consumers in a sphere where material functioning is different from physical reality. For instance, geographical boundaries are irrelevant, and events from the past can be re-enacted by accessing archived data.
- In digital customer experiences, technological devices, platforms, and online environments allow high levels of interactivity with companies so that consumers can play a proactive role in designing products and services by engaging in co-creation processes with companies.
- In digital customer experiences, companies have to pay attention and capture the new emerging values and trends created and disseminated by online communities.
- In digital customer experiences, customers should circulate between different physical (offline) and digital (online) channels so that they can pass from one to the other with ease.

Integrating other screens giving access to the brand's website in a store or creating an e-commerce website are only minimalist solutions that will barely provide satisfying digital customer experiences. Consequently, the transformation of physical stores by integrating digital tools is not enough; companies should also support the customer throughout his/her experiential journey through different touchpoints online and offline, facilitating consumer navigation between the two spheres.

Furthermore, companies and marketing professionals tend to confuse the digital customer experience (DCX) and the "user experience" (UX), which is one of the complements of the DCX. Batat (2019b) identified the foundations of the DCX that can help companies distinguish between the two concepts. The DCX goes beyond the UX as it incorporates it as a component among others (e.g., CRM, delivery, or loyalty) in addition to all stages of the customer journey, including, for instance, when a customer searches for information, compares prices, tries a product, or contacts an after-sales service. The following example clearly shows the difference between customer experience in a digital setting and the notion of user experience:

> When someone buys an application that modifies photos on his/her smartphone, the customer bought it because he/she likes software, such as Photoshop, and wanted such detailed, adapted, and accessible features on his/her smartphone. However, when using the application (user experience), he/she will realize that the interface is not easy to understand and that he/she does not have the features that were desired on the phone, which generates a frustration and a negative UX. However, with the online service, the consumer finds that one can call the customer service, who responds in a friendly and quick way to explain, step by step, how to access the desired features. In this case, the customer has just had a positive CX (customer experience): his/her problem is solved; he/she had a good time on the phone with a friendly person who created solutions to the problem. In addition, he/she has been offered a gift or a three-month free subscription to the premium service to discover other features and potentially buy them later (ROI efficiency). In this situation, the customer had a bad UX but a good CX. The same example can work in the opposite direction – in other words, in the case where the UX is good and the CX is bad. (Batat, 2019b, p. 30)

Figure 2.3 shows the main differences between user experience and customer experience in a digital setting.

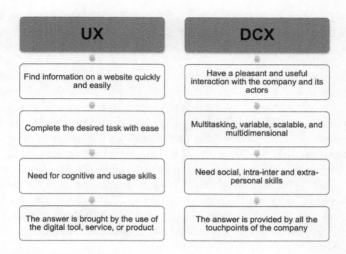

Source: Adapted from Batat (2019b).

Figure 2.3   *User experience (UX) vs. digital customer experience (DCX)*

BOX 2.2   HOW IS APPLE LEVERAGING TECHNOLOGY AND DATA TO OFFER A RELEVANT CUSTOMER EXPERIENCE?

Apple is constantly focused on innovation to improve the user experience. The company believes in simplicity, and fully controls the primary technologies that go into all of its products. Throughout its history, Apple has introduced technologies that quickly became very common across all industries. Apple does not invent the products, but it refines and reinvents them exactly how customers want. Competitors usually follow. Apple is also not afraid to abandon commonly used technological products (like the iPhone's headphone jack), no matter how crazy this may seem at the time. The company sticks to the vision that defines the brand. The most innovative products that make the Apple experience great are the multi-touch screen, the mouse, the laptop trackpad, the sensor for fingerprints, the graphical user interface, USBs, 3-D touch, and so forth.

Another way Apple makes big decisions is by using data analytics. The company might have been slow to adopt data analytics, but it has worked tirelessly to catch up with its competitors. Like everything the company does, Apple is highly secretive about employing data analytics when making technological decisions. However, we know that most of the products are designed to give Apple access to all the data from customers. So, gathering the data is a relatively easy step. It is then up to the company to derive insights from the data and apply these to its strategies to create products needed by its customers.

One area that benefits highly from this approach is application design. Apple has access to how people use apps in their daily lives and modifies its designs accordingly. Similarly, it has an extensive view of how people use its products every day, which gives the company unprecedented insights for improving the design of its products to enhance the customer experience (e.g., from earphones to air pods). Data gathering has also been made easier through wearable technological products like the Apple Watch, which can measure the health and lifestyles of entire populations. The information gathered can then be used to prevent the spread of illnesses, raise awareness about new viruses, and treat sick people. Apple and IBM have entered into a deal to facilitate the development of health apps. This is only the beginning of what Apple can do with the data.

Also, the users' voices that interact with Apple's virtual assistant, Siri, are captured, uploaded to a cloud analytics platform, and compared to other audios from different users. Machine learning is enabling this technology to become better at identifying speech patterns and matching users with their requests. These audios are assigned an indicator that is separate from the ID of each user to ensure privacy. Also, Apple purchased Beats Music, a company that developed an algorithm that pairs users with songs that match their tastes. After tracking your activity and data, the system generates "predictions" of your behavior and customized ads, or suggestions pop up on the screen. Apple might have been slower than its competitors to apply data analytics, but the company quickly realized its importance and the role it will continue to play in the future to help it stay ahead of its rivals.

The shift from customer experience adapted to a physical setting to a digital customer experience should also be achieved by emphasizing what consumers will gain from digital technologies, such as the playful and aesthetic dimensions thanks to the interactive nature of digital technologies and their attractive images and sounds. Furthermore, Mathwick et al. (2002) indicate that social media produces feelings of "we-ness"—that is, feelings of fellowship and togetherness in a group, which creates strong social relationships online and offline. Thus, beyond the functional gain, social media and digital technologies facilitate the emergence of relational values in digital consumption experiences. Therefore, companies can design digital customer experiences by focusing on three main aspects:

- *Functionality*. The digital experience should be as efficient and convenient as possible while providing social interaction and entertainment. A company's website should be technically fluid, allowing rapid loading of available items or immediate shipping information while emphasizing image quality and the sensory element.
- *Sociability*. The digital customer experience should integrate social media platforms that allow the creation of strong connections among different online communities.
- *Emotionality*. The digital experience is also about creating an immersive, complementary, and unique brand experience, in-store or online, that is totally in tune with the image and position of the company.

BOX 2.3   NUTELLA USES DIGITAL TECHNOLOGIES TO OFFER THE ULTIMATE TASTE EXPERIENCE

Technology allowed hazelnut/chocolate spread Nutella to better target its audience through personalization, communication, and the practical usage of data. For instance, when the product was first launched on its website, it allowed interactions among its customers, who could now express their feelings and experiences. These interactions formed a social community of brand admirers, where members felt a sense of belonging.

On this platform, members found a place to share their thoughts about the brand and the added value it brings to their everyday lives. For example, fans share recipes and creative ways to use the spread; but they also publish diaries where they compare their experiences with and without Nutella. The company understood that participation of online brand communities increases consumer commitment to the brand. This online effort to connect with consumers resulted from market research that showed consumers lacked understanding of how Nutella could be used in their daily lives.

Research also showed that the majority of Nutella fans are younger and heavily use social media. The company therefore took advantage of the digital platforms used by consumers to turn them into touchpoints, and later into Nutella's online universe. By increasing its online presence through Facebook, Twitter, and Pinterest, Nutella was able to amplify the passion fans have for the popular spread while simultaneously reaching and inspiring new customers. The company used a paid and organic media mix and increased engagement by collaborating with influencers and celebrities.

Nutella also used technology for other marketing strategies, such as updating its packaging. It partnered with the advertising company Ogilvy & Mather in Italy and used an algorithm to create 7 million jars, each with a unique design. The technology uses software that extracts different colors and patterns from a database to turn every jar into art. The software also provides customization as each consumer receives an original version of the jar. Without this software the project would have needed an impressive team of designers with a massive amount of time. According to Lavinia Francia, creative director of the project at Ogilvy & Mather, the number of unique designs generated by the software is endless. It is programmed to choose one out of four textures available and rotates until it creates a new sleeve. These limited-edition jars were so popular that all 7 million sold out in just one month. This action is not the only time Nutella has used technology for customization purposes; the brand also launched the "Say It With Nutella" campaign, which allowed users to choose words they wanted to add on the jar's label and share them online. The purpose of the campaign was to use the Nutella jar to communicate enthusiasm about the product. However, the campaign prohibited the use of swear words, violent words, and terms such as "cancer," "obesity," and "diabetes."

Nutella extended its portfolio to include the "Hello World" platform, which provides interactive point-of-sale materials that use the most advanced facial recognition technology. The new platform will also be rolled out in the travel shopping market across airports. It will create an enjoyable shopping experience based on the theme of "optimism" because the customer's facial expressions will be detected using facial mapping panels. Once identified, the software will determine whether the person is happy, inspired, or grumpy and will display an ad showcasing the new range of mood-labeled Nutella jars.

If customers do not directly engage with the panels, they will broadcast different content based on the number of people walking by. For instance, if a group passes by, the panel might say "Look at this dynamic duo!" or "You look STUNNING. Did someone say selfie?" Additionally, in a new and original event, in 2019 Nutella collaborated with SoundsOfThings (SOT), a social network based on sound, for the Nutella Café in New York. The event was called "Late Night Bites" and aimed to bring guests a taste of the Nutella Café experience in a new and creative way, through sound and music. The night not only featured a live performance by local DJ Brittany Sky, but also incorporated different sounds usually heard at the venue, like the sizzling of crepes, the sound of the Nutella jar opening, and the café stirring—a mix created by the SOT app.

SOT is used as a marketing platform by companies around the world because it offers, in addition to the iOS and Android app, the Composer

Portal, which can be used by sound designers, musicians, and composers to create their own unique sounds, provided with a limitless database of soundtracks. By attending this event, guests could listen to Nutella's unique music in a heightened experience that would activate all their senses. Event booking took place on Nutella's Facebook page. All in all, Nutella was able to interact with its consumers through the active use of technology and data that increased the engagement between the brand and its audience.

KEY TAKEAWAYS

This chapter has examined the emergence of the digital customer experience (DCX) and the challenges of digital transformation that affect both businesses, which are struggling with the integration of technology, and consumers, who are becoming more digitized. In this chapter, I presented digital marketing tools and strategies companies can use to implement online strategies to connect with their customers while increasing sales. Nevertheless, with the advent of the experiential era, many companies are still struggling to identify the necessary action plans and strategies to create fulfilling digital experiences online that go beyond information search and e-commerce. By differentiating the notion of user experience (UX) from DCX introduced in this chapter, companies can develop customer-focused digital marketing strategies that allow them to offer seamless digital experiences across different platforms and devices, and thus create strong relationships with their customers.

3. How does phygital humanize customer experience and create a continuum linking physical and digital settings?

CHAPTER OVERVIEW

Today, a new set of hybrid consumption experiences, "phygital" (physical + digital), is flourishing that are neither purely physical nor purely digital, but characteristic of both worlds. As a result, understanding and designing valuable phygital consumer experiences have become top priorities for both businesses and marketing scholars. Yet there are some challenges to the implementation of phygital strategies. These challenges are related to the definition of the concept and its confusion with other approaches in the retail sector, including multi-channel, cross-channel, and omni-channel systems. Addressing these issues is a great added value for companies that can rethink their way of working in the new phygital framework. This approach will help businesses create a continuum between physical and digital experiences, and deliver valuable and compelling customer experiences.

1 PHYGITAL CUSTOMER EXPERIENCE: BEYOND CROSS-CHANNEL, MULTI-CHANNEL, AND OMNI-CHANNEL EXPERIENCES

As far as I know, except for my published works and research, there has been no conceptualization specific to the concept of phygital. However, the concept is used by both researchers and businesses. Also, looking at the types of literature together in multi-channel, cross-channel, and omni-channel retailing, we realize that the dichotomous view is present in all of them.

Thus, phygital as a framework can help us look at these experiences through the implementation of a phygital ecosystem that goes beyond introducing technologies in-store as in the multi-channel, cross-channel, and omni-channel logic (Figure 3.1). It requires a new approach to offer the ultimate experience by following multiple stages in the implementation process from the computer science literature (e.g., connection, captivation, contexts, content, collaboration, communication, consistency, and competency).

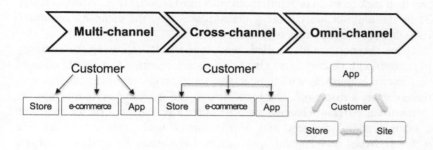

Figure 3.1   Types of channel strategies

This section aims to clarify the concept of phygital by distinguishing it from channel approaches implemented by companies in the retail sector, namely multi-channel, cross-channel, and omni-channel. In this sense, it examines the key differences and similarities among these three channel strategies.

1.1   Multi-Channel Customer Experience

Implementing a multi-channel distribution structure has become a must for retail chains since, in a single-channel mode, a retailer is weakened in the face of companies that, thanks to their presence on several sales fronts, enjoy undeniable competitive advantages. The use of common infrastructures, the implementation of joint operations and marketing policies, and the sharing of customers are all sources of promising synergies between distribution channels.

A multi-channel customer experience strategy uses several communication and distribution channels, real or virtual, to target customers more effectively. This strategy depends on the company's commercial approach and objectives. The parallel use of different distribution channels has increased enormously in recent years, leading retailers to use different channels simultaneously as part of their distribution policy; the fundamental choice is to either combine or separate the alternative channels. Thus, if retailers separate their channels, cross-channel interaction is avoided.

From a consumer perspective, processes and functions will not appear to have a cross-channel connection (Schramm-Klein et al., 2011). For instance, a retailer might operate a traditional store and simultaneously run an online store under a different brand name to allow consumers to examine goods throughout multiple channels separately (Berman and Thelen, 2004). Alternatively, customers can look for information on one channel (e.g., e-commerce website), purchase items through another channel (e.g., catalog), and then pick them up or return them via a third channel (e.g., physical store). Thus, the multi-channel strategy encompasses how the company communicates and sells its offerings to its customers.

These channels are also called "contact channels," allowing the company to connect with its customers via multiple sales channels that should enhance customer relationships with the company while reinforcing the coherence of the company's discourse. The brand image and the company's message are diffused via different channels, which confer a real identity on the structure. Communication, products, and distribution channels such as e-commerce websites, flyers, social media, apps, ads, business cards, physical points of sale (POS), among others; all these spaces should share the same message, helping consumers recognize the identity of the company.

Therefore, the multi-channel customer experience strategy consists of integrating several contact channels into a single system capable of managing their interactions. The contact channels used are based on unidirectional communication, represented by the mass media, or interactive communication, grouping together the traditional channels of direct marketing, including the Internet, text messaging, customer service, or mailing.

The multi-channel customer experience strategy helps companies offer their customers a seamless purchase experience, both online and offline, while responding to marketing objectives such as recruiting new customers and retaining existing customers by maintaining a privileged relationship. A multi-channel strategy also provides the company with an expanded retail presence that represents the chance for a brand to increase the number of opportunities for contact with its customers, provide them with a better level of service, and thus increase customer retention. Other benefits related to the implementation of a multi-channel strategy include:

- attaining the most synergistic combination possible, which should remain coherent from a customer perspective while avoiding cannibalistic competition between channels;
- increasing market penetration by multiplying the points of contact, in particular on target customers who are more sensitive to information and communication technologies and less available to visit physical points of sale;
- offering different companies, both independent retailers and large retail groups, across sectors the possibility of implementing multi-channel customer experience strategies.

Although the multiplication of points of contact with prospects or customers certainly implies certain benefits, it is not without risks. Indeed, if each channel is initially intended for a specific customer segment and managed independently, it is clear that new management constraints will emerge in the form of a customer who has reappropriated the system and no longer hesitates to migrate from one channel to another to solve his or her consumption issues and satisfy his or her needs. Thus, companies should consider two challenges when implementing multi-channel customer experience strategies: customer migration and purchasing orientation.

1.1.1   Customer migration in multi-channel shopping experiences

For companies in the retail industry, analyzing customer migration behaviors between distribution channels is a prerequisite for understanding consumer expectations in terms of multi-channel experiences where customers seek to satisfy their functional, economic, emotional, and social needs. In this sense, the migration of customers from a physical store to an e-commerce website is then a reflection of the evolution of consumer expectations and needs. Consequently, implementing an online store is likely to affect the physical one in three distinct ways:

- First, the e-commerce website proposed by the retailer may have no influence on the multi-channel experience. In this case, customers do not change their purchase behaviors with the actual retailer and remain loyal to its store.
- In a second situation, the website may become part of the customers' purchase habits but does not affect their store visits. In this case, customers mix online and offline behaviors, and buy through the two channels made available to them by the retailer.
- The third situation refers to the inclusion of the e-commerce website in the multi-channel experience preventing customers from visiting the physical store. Likewise, customers abandon the physical store to engage in a prospective new online purchasing experience.

Regarding the latter situation, Dholakia and colleagues (2005) examined how a new channel can become part of customers' shopping habits. They report that customers do not replace their usual channel with the new channel, but instead add it to the set of channels they already use. Their research shows that if the new channel enters the set of customer memories, this entry does not affect the involvement of their original channel in the same set. Moreover, if customers transfer from one channel to another, they tend to do so between similar channels, such as e-commerce sites and catalogs, rather than between distinct channels, including physical and online stores. The most relevant motivation for customers to quit a channel is the risk they perceive when buying from a retailer—their motivations, the product category involved, and the retailer's communication.

1.1.2   Purchasing orientation in multi-channel customer experiences

Studies show that the goals customers pursue when they shop explain their shopping behaviors within the multi-channel space. If their goals evolve, this could explain the evolution of their migration behaviors within the multi-channel customer experience. Indeed, if a retailer's website provides customers with a utility that is more in line with their goals, this site could replace the retailer's store, at least in part. Depending on their goals, some customers would be more inclined than others to abandon the brand's physical store and migrate to its website. Thus, purchasing orientation reveals the potential value of this aspect in explaining customer migration behaviors within multi-channel experiences.

The concept of shopping orientations first appeared in sociology (Stone, 1954), where researchers used it to examine the process of social identification in an urban and impersonal environment. Since then it has been used in retail marketing and has given rise to various applications. Purchasing orientation can be defined as the purchaser's style according to the specific importance he or she places on the shopping activity (Hawkins et al., 1986). In other words, purchasing orientation characterizes the buyer's attitude toward the act of shopping overall, independent of the product category considered. Thus, many types of buyer have been identified in the marketing literature—such as collectors, compulsive buyers, anti-supermarkets shoppers, recreational buyers, apathetic buyers, and social buyers, among others. In this sense, purchasing orientation that can lead to a potential migration in the multi-channel shopping experience depends on the profile of the buyer involved in the shopping activity.

Consequently, following the impulse of a customer who moves or migrates from one channel to another, companies' virtual and real spheres are now gradually coming together, moving toward the era of a hybrid approach reflected in the implementation of a cross-channel customer experience strategy.

1.2   Cross-Channel Customer Experience

The term "cross-channel" here refers to the close relationships that firms need to establish between channels to satisfy their customers. While, as seen previously, multi-channel refers to the use of several channels by the same company without any particular link between them, the cross-channel approach can be defined as a strategy implemented by companies to eliminate breakdowns and discontinuities—whether physical, emotional, economic, operational, or cognitive—when a customer shifts channels during the same shopping experience.

This definition refers to the rise of new shopping behaviors among customers, who switch channels during their decision-making process even though they were previously required to carry out all the stages of this process (e.g., need identification, search for information, evaluation of choice alternatives, or post-purchase assessment) through the only channel available to them. Thus, cross-channel refers to a mixing process that can lead to the emergence of fragmented shopping behaviors and decision-making processes. The cross-channel customer experience therefore reflects a series of interactions between the buyer and the different retailer channels for the same purchasing process, and, like any other experience, can be considered from the consumer's subjective perspective to include aspects such as rationality, emotions, spirituality, sensory, and physical evidence (Gentile et al., 2007; Batat, 2019a).

Furthermore, a cross-channel customer experience strategy not only provides multiple options for consumers to purchase goods; it also involves full mobility between retailers' information channels, as well as complete flexibility with respect to purchase, receipt, and return channels. By combining their channels, companies and retailers can best satisfy customer needs by bridging the gaps between different channels. For instance, the traditional physical store allows consumers to use their five senses when evaluating products, and offers personalized service and different payment options and acquisition immediately. However, to take advantage of these services, consumers must spend time and energy to get to the store, which may not be open at appropriate times.

Therefore, store-less channels, such as online outlets, allow consumers to purchase goods when and where they want to, reduce time and transportation costs; in some cases, they also allow consumers to choose from a wider range of products. As a direct result of increasing customer satisfaction, several studies show that cross-channel retailers can significantly increase their share of the customer service portfolio while benefiting from greater customer loyalty (e.g., Neslin and Shankar, 2009; Zhang et al., 2010; Schramm-Klein et al., 2011).

Nevertheless, to implement a cross-channel customer experience strategy, companies and retailers should overcome some challenges related to such an approach, including organizational structure challenges. Identifying the appropriate organizational structure is considered the biggest challenge most cross-channel retailers have to face (Zhang et al., 2010). This can be explained by the fact that most retailers manage their channels in a decentralized manner; many maintain separate teams for inventory management, product mix, marketing, finance, and analytics within each channel. Cross-channel retailers also struggle when it comes to developing integrated information technology that allows them to analyze data across channels in a holistic manner (Batat, 2019a).

Despite these challenges, retailers are increasingly willing to invest in cross-channel customer experience strategies, services, and retail concepts. This willingness has been enhanced by the considerable innovations and improvements in mobile connectivity and Internet technology. Notably, the rapid spread of smartphones, which can replace computers, is expected to have a continued impact on retail channel structures in the coming years, and contribute to the development of cross-channel customer experience offerings (e.g., Dholakia et al., 2010). Therefore, we can note the motivations of shoppers in terms of adopting cross-channel behaviors: Why do they navigate between channels for the same purchase decision when they have this option? Why do they redistribute their decision process between channels when the entire process could be done through a single channel?

Studies show that since the customer has to spend time and effort to become familiar with the merchandising of each business unit, there are additional costs associated with this behavior. Consequently, this behavior should only be justified if the gain is greater than the cost or if the value is greater than the cost. Understanding what leads to a breakdown in the customer decision-making process is a major challenge for retailers. The goal is to identify the reasons that can push a customer to adopt such behavior. Shoppers assign goals at different stages of their decision-making process and select the channels that best enable them to achieve these goals. There are various goals that are likely to be pursued during shoppers' cross-channel purchasing experience, including:

- search for economic benefit;
- search for symbolic meaning;
- search for social interactions and socialization;
- need for self-actualization;
- search for experiential stimulation.

Therefore, we can see a distinction between the utility derived from the product and the utility derived from the purchasing process, the latter being instrumental or not. The cross-channel experience highlights the fundamental role that the utility derived from the product plays in the customer's decision-making process when choosing a sales channel. Thus, beyond the basic functional utility associated with the acquisition of a product, the cross-channel experience reveals that utility can be intrinsically withdrawn from the decision-making process. The customer will use diverse channels according to the utility he/she is searching for at each stage of the purchase process and the capacity of each of them to respond to his/her functional, cognitive, economic, emotional, social, or ideological expectations.

It should be noted that the shopper is also likely to act in such a way as to circumvent certain difficulties that he/she associates with the use of a channel at one or other of these stages. Thus, consumer motivations to embrace cross-channel experiences aim to generate a higher utility at each stage of the decision process or to circumvent certain challenges, which should generate an overall utility higher than the utility derived from a single-channel behavior. From a consumer perspective, cross-channel behaviors can be classified into two main categories: cross-channel pre-purchase and click & collect.

1.2.1 Cross-channel pre-purchase

This reflects a planned in-store purchase for which the customer needs to engage a cross-channel pre-shopping behavior. It can take two forms: online pre-purchase search and offline pre-purchase search. The online pre-purchase search is when consumers engage in part of their shopping preparations by searching for products online before visiting the physical stores. This is also commonly referred to as Research Online/Purchase Offline (ROPO) behavior, which is part of the cross-channel pre-purchase search, combining both online and offline spheres. For a purchase considered in an online store, consumers perform a cross-channel pre-purchase if they do part of their purchase preparations offline, for example, by going to the store to see or touch the desired product, which is part of the offline pre-purchase search. Although recent studies particularly emphasize the relevance of ROPO behavior, these studies usually only cover a very limited part of the pre-purchase procedure and, in most cases, examine data for a single country, thus limiting the transferability of the findings to other markets.

1.2.2 Click & collect

The best-known example of a click & collect service is the so-called "Drive." This form of cross-channel behavior was initially introduced by food retailers and then became popular among other sectors. The click & collect service works as follows: first, consumers log onto a specific website, place their order, and choose a time to pick it up. They then drive to a predefined loading station and wait for their groceries to be deposited directly into their trunks (car boots) within minutes. Nowadays, click & collect services can take many forms, depending on the retail industry involved. For example, fashion brands such as H&M or Zara allow online consumers to pick up items purchased from the online store at any of their physical stores in the country (e.g., the US or UK). This service allows companies to enhance customer satisfaction and loyalty. Indeed, recent studies showed the growing importance and popularity of click & collect services among consumers, and highlighted its positive effects on customer loyalty and retailer profitability.

Consequently, being attracted by different channels throughout their decision-making process, depending on their goals, more customers are engaging in cross-channel experiences that may start online and extend to in-store, or vice versa. The goals pursued can be utilitarian and multiple, including:

- collecting items purchased on the website from the brand's physical store;
- exchanging or returning a product purchased online;
- navigating between channels to find the desired object or best deals.

During the cross-channel experience, beyond a purchase intention, the buyer can browse between channels simply to examine a product for informational or recreational purposes. This cross-channel shopping sometimes even turns into a hedonic customer experience when the recreational goal is the focus. This behavior can thus reinforce the cross-channel experience that the consumer has throughout the purchasing process. The use of the Internet can also enhance the "economic" aspect of the shopping experience and "gain of time" as well as the "cognitive" dimension, where discovering and learning about the product are the focus, along with the "emotional" dimension, which refers to pleasure. Consequently, navigating between channels during the same purchasing experience to seek information or pleasure is at the heart of cross-channel customer experiences, where the challenge for companies and retailers is to identify the appropriate value associated with such behavior across different channels.

1.3   Omni-Channel Customer Experience

The growth and dissemination of digital technologies has had a considerable impact on purchasing behaviors. Today's customers are demanding, impatient, and willing to give feedback on products and services. Companies should therefore redouble their efforts to offer them optimal shopping experiences. An omni-channel customer experience strategy—which consists of using the company's contact channels, both physical and digital simultaneously and in an interconnected manner—is then a strategic answer in the retail sector. The simplicity and speed of purchase offered nowadays by e-commerce websites, mobile or m-commerce, and social selling have revolutionized the fundamentals of retailing, leading retailers to adopt new forms of commerce in their existing channels through the integration of effective touchpoints at the center of their omni-channel customer experience strategy.

Omni-channel strategies integrate multiple physical and digital channels to create not only transactions but also seamless customer experiences. While multi-channel strategies merely offer consumers several independent channels, without focusing on their incorporation with each other or with the consumer, omni-channel strategies offer all the available and diverse channels fully integrated. Indeed, it is this integration that generates added value and a unique experience from the consumer standpoint. If a multi-channel strategy offers the consumer the possibility of using various channels to make purchases, an omni-channel strategy allows the customer to use various touchpoints during a shopping experience.

These omni-channel strategies aim to offer a seamless experience regardless of the point of contact between the brand and the customer, allowing the latter to use a different point of contact for product selection and pick-up. For example, instead of visiting a store, customers can order items on their smartphone using the brand's app. They can also modify their shopping list by using their computer or tablet to arrange to pick up the product in-store or have it delivered. There are multiple advantages of an omni-channel strategy. First, for companies, it is easier to trace the path of customers because all their data, both online and offline, is gathered and centralized. As a result, companies develop a better knowledge of their customers, purchasing behaviors, and product preferences, which allows them to implement effective targeting and suitable marketing and communication actions while maintaining personalized relationships with their customers.

Also, since all of the company's contact channels are unified, customers are more eager to have seamless shopping experiences through, for example, access to goods in the company's various stores via its website, interactive kiosks in points of sale, or experiencing connected stores. Thus, the omni-channel strategy reinforces the brand image and improves customer satisfaction and the overall shopping experience. Loyal customers often become brand ambassadors, which allows the company to win over new customers and increase its market share. Therefore, the key principles for a successful omni-channel strategy include the following domains:

- *Change management.* The implementation of an omni-channel strategy requires an actual change of management within the company, which implies redefining processes, objectives, and reorganizing teams. The goal is to eliminate silos. Decision-makers should therefore develop the capacity to take up the challenge to embody the project and motivate the stakeholders.
- *Customer relationships.* Unlike the traditional organization, which is often structured in silos with slight interconnectivity between departments, the omni-channel organization favors agility and collaboration. The customer is at the center of the company's actions, and every decision is made with the customer's satisfaction in mind. The company develops a customer-centric way of thinking and doing.

- *The value chain.* An omni-channel distribution strategy integrates the entire value chain. Players should share data in real time related to orders, payments, and stocks.
- *Customer data.* Insights should be centralized on the same tool so that all the company's departments can access the customer database. The database should be analyzed and enriched regularly for better personalization of customer relationships. Various tools allow data to be pooled, and are particularly well suited to omni-channel strategies.
- *Innovation.* It is essential to modernize tools and interfaces to guarantee a seamless customer experience and stand out from the competition.

This omni-channel model therefore presents a multitude of contact points, some physical, others virtual; but, all in all, the innovation comes from their complementarity. Although the omni-channel concept requires new and more experimental touchpoints due to new technologies (e.g., mobile commerce), it also requires the conservation and adaptation of the more traditional ones, namely physical stores.

2   PHYGITAL CUSTOMER EXPERIENCE: A NEW HOLISTIC ECOSYSTEM

Companies have limited knowledge of what makes such experiences valuable for consumers because enabling technologies are novel. Current works do not distinguish between phygital and omni-channel, cross-channel, or multi-channel customer experience. According to Batat (2021c), while omni-channel applies to the retail sector and points of sale, phygital is an ecosystem that applies to different sectors—ranging from education, banking and insurance, and airlines to healthcare, hospitality and restaurants, and entertainment.

Furthermore, phygital uses a combination of both physical elements and digital devices—technologies, extended realities, online platforms, and so forth—to offer unique interactive experiences that should integrate a continuum in terms of consumer value (economic, ideology, symbolic, social) provided from digital to physical, and vice versa. This is why, in contrast to the channel approach that connects touchpoints by using digital with the logic of purchase and e-commerce (economic value in distribution), phygital as a holistic approach can be used in communication, marketing, branding, advertising, product innovation, pricing, and so forth to provide customers with value, not only economic but also symbolic, emotional, and social—thus creating a third realm of customer experience (Figure 3.2).

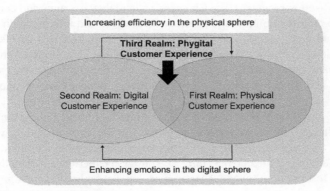

Source: Adapted from Batat (2021c).

Figure 3.2   Phygital: the third realm of customer experience

Phygital, the combination of physical and digital settings, is a term that appeared in 2013 in the business sector as a tagline for a communication agency. Although the term is usually used by business bloggers and journalists, it did not have a reliable definition until 2016, when Batat (2018) proposed the first examination and definition of the concept of "phygital" by focusing on the dynamics between online and offline offerings through the "continuum" paradigm and the logic of a new marketing framework, namely "blue sunflower marketing," which should guide the company's way of doing and thinking to create compelling phygital experiences. According to Batat (2019b, p. 220), phygital refers to

> a physical point of sale that integrates the data and methods of the digital ecosphere to improve turnover. By digitizing the point of sale, companies seek to optimize the effectiveness of their business strategy and attract new customers. The phygital context can be characterized by the installation of touch terminals offering different applications, including real-time price verification, or the perusal of an interactive catalog. Connected interactive terminals allow for more in-depth searches online. They can simplify custom 3-D design or offer new options that are not yet available in stores. Therefore, the phygital sphere puts innovative tools and advanced technologies within the reach of the public. It also improves the marketing experience at the physical point of sale.

Consequently, creating phygital customer experiences will constitute a crucial competitive opportunity for companies in the years to come.

As digital technologies become pervasive, companies should particularly develop an understanding of the influence of digital technology on the customer experience, both online and offline. For example, consumers enjoy quantified-self experiences (see Chapter 6) where they use apps and connected objects to monitor, control, and optimize themselves and improve their health. Augmented reality, digital concierge services, and experiences derived from 3-D printing are a few of the phygital experiences that have attracted attention, among many others. While some consumers find phygital experiences novel, exciting, and valuable, others dismiss them as unnecessary technological gimmicks.

With a phygital approach, companies attempt to understand consumer and brand behaviors in a new environment: the third environment that we need to define, its elements, and how the consumer interacts with the brand in this environment in and outside the store. The phygital experience is then the most complete form of omni-channel experience that can be implemented in different sectors, and is not only limited to retail and sales points.

Companies need first to understand the phygital ecosystem and how to implement a phygital strategy to create engaging and fluid customer experiences that ensure a seamless and barrier-free continuum. In this sense, the use of digital technologies and devices should be well thought out by companies to facilitate the transition of customers from the physical context to the digital, and vice versa, without difficulty and with consistency and fluidity in the lived experience. The customer experience is therefore perceived as manifold and involves the use of various technological tools that are designed to meet specific objectives and are anchored in a definite phygital setting.

Batat (2019b) refers to the phygital setting as a context of consumption that integrates gateways set up by companies between different physical channels (offline and in-store) and digital channels (online) so that customers can switch from one to the other with ease, guaranteeing consistency in the experiential journey from the physical place to the digital space, and vice versa. Thus, companies should create compelling, high-performance phygital customer experiences firmly rooted in consumers' daily habits, profiles, consumption meanings, and paradoxes. This can be achieved by using different technologies one at a time or all together simultaneously—numerous tools and devices are developed in the second part of this book. To develop a better understanding of the concept of phygital and how companies can design seamless and engaging phygital experiences, and thus differentiate themselves, the following section will focus on blue sunflower marketing as a framework that can help companies create successful phygital experiences by rethinking their actual digital strategies. The key success factors for creating successful phygital experiences are also presented.

2.1 "Blue Sunflower Marketing" as a New Framework

I introduced the idea of a new business framework, namely blue sunflower marketing, in 2018 and since then it has been used in different domains, such as for creating phygital luxury experiences. Blue sunflower marketing can thus help companies implement effective phygital, not digital, strategies focused on consumer value by placing their customers at the center and the start of their strategic way of thinking and doing. Blue sunflower marketing can be defined as

> a disruptive strategy combining customer experience, digital marketing, and break-through innovation. It is a hybrid and evolutionary process based on an analytical logic guided by critical and experiential design thinking. The metaphor of [the] "blue sunflower" reflects the complexity and the multidimensional aspect of the phygital customer experience. Furthermore, the characteristics of blue sunflower marketing revolve around three major elements: consumer perspective, uniqueness, and subjective emotion. (Batat, 2019b, p. 71)

Thus, digital marketing strategies should include the consumer perspective and follow the customer in his/her experiential journey online and offline by adapting the tools and devices to customers' diverse needs and values (e.g., functional, economic, emotional, social, spiritual), which can vary throughout the journey including both online and offline navigation channels. Batat's idea of blue sunflower marketing follows the same logic of a sunflower, whose movements and orientation vary throughout the day. The head of the sunflower follows the sun all day long. In the early morning, sunflowers face east; during the day, they follow the sun; and in the late afternoon, they look to the west. Blue sunflower marketing, when implemented by companies to create phygital experiences is therefore not static but rather moving. Companies should then rethink their tools and digital strategies to make them evolve in the direction of the customer in order to offer him/her a suitable and adaptable evolving phygital experience.

The color blue in the metaphor refers to the unique aspects of the phygital experience that should be highly customized, according to the profile and expectations of each customer. Indeed, to offer value to consumers, the phygital experience should be both unique and distinctive compared to dominant digital offerings. In this sense, no one would notice a yellow sunflower, especially in a field where all are alike, all the same yellow color. In contrast, a blue sunflower in a field of yellow sunflowers will be instantly noticed and perceived as fascinating, intriguing, seductive, or disturbing. Like the blue sunflower in a field, the new digital strategies using blue sunflower marketing as a framework can make the phygital experience a pleasant, seductive, or provocative experience.

The third characteristic of the experiential offer in the digital era refers to the creation of positive emotions in the digital world. In order to succeed in their digital customer experience strategy, companies should include components that generate positive emotions for the consumer. This dimension is highly symbolic of the cultural significance of sunflowers in the language of flowers. The sunflower expresses a sincere message of support, a desire to bring some sun to a person in difficulty; this is the goal of the digital customer experience. Therefore, the blue sunflower marketing framework challenges the traditional digital marketing logic that focuses on digital tools by taking into account the disruptive, subjective, and emotional dimensions of digital tools and their impact on consumer behavior according to the context in which the product or service is purchased or consumed.

Furthermore, according to Batat (2019b), implementing blue sunflower marketing to create seamless and successful phygital experiences requires companies to incorporate three main tools: immersive Web 3.0, interactive, and flow tools (Figure 3.3). These tools can convey the company's values and create a strong emotional bond with targets both online and offline.

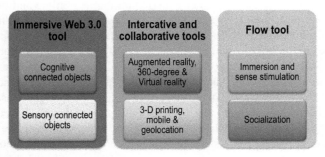

Source: Adapted from Batat (2019b).

Figure 3.3   Tools for designing phygital customer experiences

- *Immersive Web 3.0.* This refers to the Web tools businesses can use to deliver memorable and satisfying customer online experiences. Web 3.0 is an Internet of connected objects in which aggregated data create meanings according to three essential elements: semantics, mobile objects, and connected objects. Web 3.0 marketing enables businesses to use Internet-connected objects, database-enabled devices, intelligent sensors, and instant responsiveness to the real world. In marketing 3.0, there are four main elements: data, objects (connected hardware), social interactions, and software.

- *Interactive and collaborative digital tools.* To create an online experience, it is vital for companies to involve the user/customer in the co-creation process of the product or service. Interactivity and co-creation should be at the heart of things to develop an effective, functional, and emotional phygital customer experience.
- *Flow tools.* Flow refers to a pleasant emotional state that appears during online navigation, characterized by fluid communication, facilitated by interactivity, and accompanied by a loss of self-awareness and self-empowerment. Thus, flow can be facilitated by the characteristics and type of media used during the online experience. In this sense, the consumer experience can be a satisfying cognitive and emotional phygital one, thanks to the rapid evolution of digital technologies and immersive tools that can reach out to the consumer as he/she browses on a commercial website.

2.2 Key Success Factors in the Design of Phygital Customer Experiences

To prevent the negative effects of poor digital experiences on customers in their multi-channel journeys, Batat (2019b) suggests that companies should consider four key success factors to implement an effective global strategy centered on a highly satisfying customer experience characterized by both the functional and emotional needs of customers.

1. Ensure the continuum between the physical experience and the digital journey. To offer a successful phygital customer experience, companies need to guarantee that digital tools complement existing customer journeys in the physical context (in-store experiences). Although the continuum between the physical and digital customer journey is a key element of consumer satisfaction, the majority of companies continue to inappropriately add digital elements to customer journeys that do not directly benefit the quality of the digital customer experience or are useless regarding the value proposed by the company and perceived by the customer.
2. Regularly collect immersive smart data to enhance the digital customer experience. Data collection tools can improve the digital luxury experience by detecting weak points in the experiential journey offline and online. Businesses need to be able to understand how customers feel and perceive a buying experience in order to offer them opportunities for improvement.
3. Focus on the consistency of multi-channel content. The coherence of the content broadcast on a multitude of platforms allows the customer to identify the brand and its values. The multiplication of points of contact

with the brand might give the consumer the impression that the brand offers inconsistent content that varies according to the medium or point of contact through which the consumer has entered. Companies should then optimize the phygital experiences of their customers and offer them a fluid experiential customer journey through various key points.

4. Maintain a regular phygital experience through the visual and the sensory. Providing a consistent digital experience also integrates visual and sensory dimensions into the use of digital tools, interfaces, and products. Consistency is required on many levels. Companies should therefore design websites with identical visual identities, sensory elements, and functional usages on different media, platforms, or devices.

Furthermore, according to Batat (2021c), businesses that are not considering phygital in a holistic way and cannot figure out how phygital will fit into their strategies in the near future should embrace the phygital paradigm by considering the following five aspects before designing customer experiences:

*   Businesses should think human first by placing the customer at the center of their strategies.
*   The use of the five senses and maximization of sensory in the digital space are vital to enhance consumer engagement.
*   Sharing and communicating coherently around the brand's values by enhancing the continuum across different channels.
*   Understanding the accurate and contextualized uses of technology by consumers.
*   Creating phygital experiences that attract customers to the physical store by focusing on complementarity of the experiences to be lived and coherence between channels.

Therefore, the implementation of a phygital transformation strategy requires a holistic and customer-centric approach where the consumer value delivered should remain coherent and consistent throughout the transfer from physical to digital, and vice versa.

KEY TAKEAWAYS

This chapter introduced the concept of phygital as a holistic ecosystem companies should embrace to design compelling customer experiences that allow a continuum from physical to digital settings, and vice versa. Thus, the main idea in this chapter is that companies should go beyond the channel approach—including multi-channel, cross-channel, and omni-channel strategies—and prioritize the phygital aspects of the customer experience in their strategies. The chapter also underscored the necessity for companies across different sectors to merge online and offline experiences to facilitate the buying and browsing processes, thus assisting and guiding the customer/user throughout the consumption and/or purchase journey, from pre-purchase to purchase, after-sales service, and beyond.

PART II

Digital devices and tools to get phygital with customers

4. Phygital customer experience strategy enabled by extended reality technology (ERT)

CHAPTER OVERVIEW

Extended reality technology (ERT) includes various visualization tools such as avatars, virtual models in 3-D, or virtual and augmented reality devices that companies can incorporate in their digital strategies to design immersive and realistic customer experiences. ERT allows companies to offer their customers the possibility of visualizing and personalizing products online, and thus they are more inclined to buy the product as their perception of the displayed image is positive. This chapter aims to answer the following questions: What does ERT mean? What are its devices? And how can companies use ERT to create immersive shopping experiences that connect digital and physical settings, leading customers to experience their online purchase as if it was occurring in a physical store?

1   WHAT DOES EXTENDED REALITY TECHNOLOGY MEAN?

Extended reality technology (ERT), also called cross-reality, refers to technologies that create environments and objects generated by a computer, allowing individuals to immerse themselves within virtual and real settings. ERT can be defined as a technology that integrates the unified connection of real and virtual worlds through the use of augmented reality (AR), virtual reality (VR), and 360-degree video, enabled by computers, smartphones, or other devices, such as smartglasses (e.g., Yim et al., 2017; Dey et al., 2018; Hoyer et al., 2020).

ERT devices are increasingly becoming key to creating special consumption experiences (Sung, 2020). As such, marketers and companies are attempting to enhance their relationships with customers through ERT to achieve a competitive advantage (Batat, 2019a). ERT can be a marketing strategy that enhances brand value by offering customers unique experiences through the use of technology-enabled devices (Denegri-Knott and Molesworth, 2010; Rauschnabel, 2018; Huang and Ha, 2020).

ERT is profoundly changing the landscape of many business sectors (e.g., retail, education, hospitality, service, and banking) and can affect both shopping and consumption experiences in many ways (Rigby, 2011). In the retail sector, ERT such as augmented reality offers customers the option of trying on items such as clothes and make-up before purchasing, and potentially increases their satisfaction with the shopping experience. ERT can also help firms provide a preview to customers of all the services offered; for example, Starbucks uses an AR application that provides access to a virtual tour that connects the physical store with the digital space.

Various forms of immersive technologies (e.g., virtual reality, augmented reality) are used to create phygital experiences, and can be distinguished by the relationship they create between the real and virtual worlds. For instance, while in augmented reality the user observes virtual objects that complement the real world, virtual reality immerses the user in an entirely virtual environment. Currently, companies can implement three ERT forms to design meaningful and highly immersive phygital (physical and digital) experiences: (1) virtual reality (VR); (2) augmented reality (AR); and (3) mixed reality (MR).

These technologies can either immerse users in a virtual setting or make them interact with an environment extended by virtual elements. The virtual contents are thus perceived as very close to reality. Yet, the degree of immersion depends on the likelihood of interaction with the digital environment. The following sections present these technologies and discuss their differences and similarities when it comes to creating phygital customer experiences.

1.1   Virtual Reality (VR)

Virtual reality refers to a realistic and immersive simulation of a three-dimensional (3-D) environment, created using interactive hardware and software, and experienced or controlled by body movement. Thus, VR is a digital simulation where the user can interact in real time with an artificial environment in which he/she is immersed. The key characteristics that define a VR experience include interaction, immersion, digital environment, and real time. Virtual reality is not new; it has been around for several decades and can be dated back to 1957. However, despite its appearance in the mid-twentieth century with the invention of a device capable of reproducing a three-dimensional image, the term "virtual reality" was introduced in 1986 by US computer scientist Jaron Lanier.

Lanier described VR as a technology that uses computers to create synthesized realities that many people can share, that we could apprehend through the five senses, and that we can interact with, all through computerized artifacts

(Curran and Hales, 1995). Nowadays, virtual reality is accessible to the general public thanks to headsets like the Oculus Rift, the HTC Vive, or the PlayStation VR. It took a long time to get to this point, developing from lab technology to an entertainment device used in one's living room. Table 4.1 summarizes the main VR evolution milestones and the associated technologies.

Virtual reality technology creates an entirely computer-generated environment in a 360° setting in which the user is fully immersed and interacts with virtual elements while the real world is completely hidden. Unlike augmented reality, VR requires a dedicated output device such as a video headset, a visual output device worn on the head. Images are displayed on a screen or projected directly onto the user's retina.

With the help of a headset, the user perceives the virtual world; during use, the real world is completely hidden. The degree of immersion is particularly high thanks to this hermetic system and allows users to immerse themselves entirely in the virtual world. Also, these devices require a connection to a computer.

BOX 4.1   MCDONALD'S USES VR TO IMMERSE ITS CUSTOMERS AND BOOST ITS IMAGE CAPITAL

In 2016, McDonald's developed a virtual reality experience to offer users the chance to live an authentic and transparent fast-food experience, from farmer to multi-skilled restaurant team member. To enhance its reputation, the firm decided to create a VR experience, entitled "Follow Our Foodsteps," which allows consumers to go backstage at McDonald's and follow the whole process of making a Big Mac.

Using Oculus Rift or Samsung Gear VR, consumers can discover the work done by the farmers, suppliers, and team members of the chain's restaurants. For example, they can explore a dairy farm, a beef farm, or an egg producer based in Cumbria, northwest England. Users can also explore the working conditions and hygiene in the kitchen. In order to make this experience more fun, two games are included. "Top of the Crop" allows users to drive a tractor to harvest potatoes, with players given scores depending on their speed, precision, and harvest quality. The second game, "Guess My Job," highlights the qualifications of the company's employees. This initiative responds to new consumer demands and emerging needs that characterize a consumer who wants to know more about fast-food.

Table 4.1   *The history and evolution of virtual reality*

Period	Device	Characteristics
1950s	*Sensorama* is the first VR headset concept	In 1957, filmmaker Morton Heilig invented a machine designed to immerse users in an imaginary world, and thus allow viewers to immerse themselves in films by deceiving their senses. The aim was to give a new scope to the cinematic experience by using the Sensorama to simulate smells, produce sound in stereo, vibrations, and even atmospheric effects such as wind in hair. In 1960, he patented his idea as a VR helmet with a stereoscopic screen, a field of vision comparable to that of humans and stereo sound
1960s	*Sword of Damocles* is the first operational VR headset	Created in 1968 by Ivan Sutherland and presented as "the ultimate screen," this headset embeds a stereoscopic screen displaying simple shapes, changing the perspective according to the user's head movements. As the screen is not obscuring the person's view, these shapes are superimposed on images of the real world, which is why this device can be considered the first AR headset. However, it remained at the experimental stage because of its heavy weight; hence its nickname, "the Sword of Damocles," in reference to the famous Roman tale by Cicero
Early 1970s	*The Super Cockpit* is the first VR flight simulator	This is a training cockpit capable of displaying computer-generated 3-D maps, infrared and radar images, and real-time flight data in 3-D space. According to its creator, military engineer Thomas Furness, this project cost several hundred million dollars. Before the advent of VR flight simulators, this project allowed pilots to train using gestures, speech, and even eye movements
Late 1970s	*Aspen Movie Map* is the ancestor of Google Earth VR	This project was developed in 1978 by Massachusetts Institute of Technology (MIT) in collaboration with the US Defense Advanced Research Projects Agency (DARPA). Based on photographs captured by cars in Aspen, Colorado, the software allowed the user to visit the city in the first-person view—a principle that Google Earth VR would take up many years later, in 2017
1990s	The *Sega VR* is the first VR headset for gaming	Sega was one of the first companies to market a VR headset dedicated to gaming, and more generally aimed at the general public. The Sega VR was conceived as an accessory for the Sega Genesis console. Its development began in 1991 and continued for two years
2010s	*Oculus*	In 2010, US entrepreneur Palmer Luckey created the prototype VR headset, Oculus Rift. The device offers a 90° field of view
2017 onwards	*Oculus Rift* and *HTC Vive*	A year after the Oculus Rift and HTC Vive, hundreds of companies started working on their own VR headsets, including Oculus, HTC, Samsung, Sony, and Google

Source: Adapted from The-VR-Headset (2018).

Since its introduction, VR has been defined in several ways. It can be defined by its outcomes, applications, functions, or even the techniques it includes. Indeed, VR lies at the crossroads of several disciplines such as computer graphics, computer-aided design (CAD), simulation, remote operation, audio-visual, or collaborative work. It uses many hardware devices and software techniques for each application area. Nowadays, VR can be referred to by several terms: virtual environment, virtual space, artificial world, or synthetic reality. Although VR can be defined in different ways, most authors agree that this new technology extends human–computer interfaces.

VR can be defined as an advanced human–computer interface that simu-lates a realistic environment and allows participants to interact with it (Ellis, 1994). The different definitions led to the rise of different research streams that examine what virtuality is. Paul Milgram proposed a unification of concepts by considering a linear continuum that runs from real to virtual, including mixed reality (MR) as the interval between the real and the virtual, augmented reality (AR), augmented virtuality (AV), and virtual reality (VR) (Milgram and Kishino, 1994).

Nowadays, VR is already transforming how we see, perceive, and analyze the world around us. Imagine traveling inside the human body and its organs or interacting with entities that do not exist, touching them, picking them up, moving them, and/or deforming them. VR technology allows us to do all this and more by immersing individuals in a virtual environment, a term introduced by MIT researchers in the early 1990s (Heim, 1995).

The virtual environment uses a 3-D model of real or imaginary data that can be visualized and interacted with in real time, creating a place to host one or more users and allow them to perform tasks with the impression of being in a specific setting. According to Kalawsky (1996), there are different types of virtual environments according to the degree of immersion they provide to the user: non-immersive virtual environment (NIVE), semi-immersive virtual environment (SIVE), or fully immersive virtual environment (FIVE). Moreover, to create a highly virtual setting, companies should consider the main components specific to VR: immersion, autonomy, and interaction.

1.1.1 Immersion

Immersion in a VR can be defined as the exposure of a user to a virtual environment using devices that obstruct all or part of the real world, displaying instead a digitally simulated world. Immersion is directly related to the user's percep-tion of his/her virtual world. It is achieved by replacing as many natural sensa-tions as possible with their equivalents in the virtual world. For Bowman et al. (1999), immersion refers to the sensation of being present, which is provided by certain virtual settings. In other words, a user is considered "immersed" when he or she feels that the virtual world around him or her has replaced the physical world to a certain degree. The presence of a user in a virtual world is another factor that plays a vital role in a better sensation of immersion. Indeed, presence gives the user a feeling of being "inside" the virtual environment. When talking about presence, it is essential to distinguish between the virtual presence and social presence (Slater et al., 1996). Virtual presence denotes the sensation provided to the user to be part of the virtual world and that the objects surrounding him/her are really present; social presence, on the other hand, characterizes collaborative virtual environments. It refers to the user's awareness of other participants and their activities within the shared universe. Thus, to enhance users' sense of presence in a virtual environment, individuals are frequently represented by virtual entities called avatars.

1.1.2 Autonomy

In VR, the notion of autonomy is related to the different components of the virtual environment. The user is one of these components, and is considered the most active entity in this space. The place of the user in VR is related to the interactive level of the simulation. In the case of a VR application, the user is exposed to an autonomous digital environment that provides him/her with a certain level of freedom to evolve, change the properties of the virtual environment, and interact with its entities without fixing any parameters before or during the experience. The user is often represented by an avatar, who can be a spectator, actor, and creator of the digital universe all at once. The user's autonomy lies in his/her ability to coordinate his/her perceptions and actions during interaction with the other virtual entities.

1.1.3 Interaction

Since the emergence of VR, researchers have been particularly interested in interaction, which can be considered the driver of any interactive system. Interaction can be defined as a language of communication between human and machine. This language corresponds to reciprocal actions/reactions between the human and the computer through sensory interfaces, motor interfaces, and interaction techniques. In a VR setting, 3-D interaction, a system that uses software as input to connect different hardware devices and software techniques, can be used to create interactions in virtual environments.

Therefore, thanks to its highly immersive and interactive aspects, VR allows companies to engage and interact with their customers through various devices. Thus, companies can use VR by implementing different tools and hardware depending on the domains in which VR is used and its outcome.

1.2   Augmented Reality (AR)

Augmented reality refers to technology that adds virtual objects and information to the real world, and thus creates an extension of it. The virtual elements created can encompass images, text, or animations. With AR, the real environment remains the central point of perception. User interaction with the virtual objects is limited or even non-existent. Initially derived from the notion of virtual reality, the term "augmented reality" is, however, debatable as, technically, it is not reality that is augmented, but the user's perception.

As outlined in Table 4.1, AR was conceptualized by Morton Heilig, who in 1962 created the "Sensorama," a helmet equipped with sensors to simulate a scene, for example riding a motorcycle. In 1968, Ivan Sutherland invented the first heads-up display (HUD) helmet with a transparent vision that reacted to head movements, nicknamed the "Sword of Damocles." Then, in the 1980s, Canadian engineer Steve Mann invented the EyeTap, a headset that displays virtual information in front of the user's eyes. This was the first accurate AR headset.

So far, AR is the most common form of extended reality. The main reason for its success lies in its low technical requirements. Augmented reality works with a simple smartphone, tablet, or PC and therefore is easily accessible for users. In addition, there are special AR glasses (smartglasses) that project virtual objects directly in front of the eyes. In this case, the real world remains visible beyond. A very well-known example of AR is *Pokémon Go*, an application available for iOS and Apple in which the device displays digital characters (Pokémon) in the real world. It is one of the most popular games for mobile devices, and the most successful AR game to date.

Computers equipped with webcams are the most convenient equipment to work with because companies do not have to worry about computing power constraints as on mobile devices. They can do almost anything related to 2-D and 3-D projection. Also, with advances in mobile technologies, especially in phones, more and more possibilities are offered to users, thanks to the use of smartphones and the integration of GPS positioning and other advanced apps. Companies can also use video consoles such as the Xbox 360 to create virtual settings. In addition, virtual glasses allow users to visualize virtual elements while being in the real context. Moreover, AR has entered our daily lives through social media platforms; for example, filters enable users to supplement their photos with virtual objects such as hats, sunglasses, or make-up.

Augmented reality requires a set of sensors to locate the user (e.g., GPS, camera, accelerometer, hygrometer, hydrometer), a computer to interpret the environment and mix it with the virtual elements, and a screen to display the result of this mix. Initially, the first AR software was based on a camera, a computer, and a screen. Since 2009, following the rise of smartphones and the 3G/4G network, the phone has become the principal interface for viewing augmented reality. This feature distinguishes augmented reality from virtual reality, which is mainly based on VR headsets like the Oculus Rift. The main advantage of the smartphone is that it allows the exploitation of geolocation data thanks to its portability. In addition, these high-tech devices can handle calculations, just like a computer.

In recent years, however, other AR tools have appeared. Google Glass was introduced in 2012, released in 2013, but taken off the market the following year. However, since then, other AR glasses have proliferated. These devices are particularly convenient for sports enthusiasts as they display useful information on the visor while leaving the user's hands free. Overall, AR is the emerging technology that bridges the gap between the digital and the real world, and can be defined by three characteristics: (1) it combines real and virtual objects; (2) it records information in three dimensions (3-D); and (3) it allows users to interact in real time (Azwna, 1997). In other words, AR offers a real-time, direct, or indirect view of a physical environment that has been augmented by the addition of virtual and computerized content. Thus, it enhances and enriches the user's perception of and interaction with the real world.

Regarding the domains of VR application, they differ depending on whether VR is used for medical, professional, educational, tourism, commerce, or entertainment purposes. In the medical field, AR can help better visualize different aspects of a patient by superimposing information directly on the patient. There are already several systems that have integrated it, especially in surgery. For example, there is a 3-D reconstruction service of the subject in real time during an operation. This allows better precision than with a simple camera and reduces risks during complex operations. Another service has been developed that improves hygiene in the operating room. It uses the Kinect peripheral to direct the computers or other electronic devices present in the room but does not touch them. Thus, the guarantee of hygiene is better preserved.

When it comes to education, AR can be used to explain a complex system using a 3-D model and interact with it to see how it is constituted and functions. For example, teachers can illustrate how a turbine works. Children's books are beginning to incorporate AR experiences so that the child gains a better understanding of the concept. In addition, AR can give a visual of the situation which is well remembered. This makes it easier for the child to recall it and learn. In architecture, AR allows the creation of virtual models that are more ecological and economical because there is no need to purchase materials to make actual models. Models of this kind are much more interactive, and one can immediately change any aspect that is not appreciated; there is no need to redo everything.

On the other hand, in tourism the main function of an AR application is guidance on the various tourist places (e.g., in a city) thanks to GPS. Also, with apps that project objects in 3-D, one can reconstruct a historical scene in a specific place; for example, AR in a ruined castle would allow visitors to see a reconstruction of the castle. Companies can also use AR to enhance the user experience and immerse customers in an interactive setting where they can test and touch the product virtually.

BOX 4.2   COCA-COLA USES AN AR IMMERSIVE APP TO INVITE USERS TO VIRTUAL LIVE STORIES

Several scenarios have been created to tell the Coca-Cola story. Timber, a company based in Santa Monica, California, collaborated with marketing agency Ogilvy to create 3-D elements for Coca-Cola's interactive AR experience where users point their smartphone at a can of Coke. From there, they can access 12 stories that come to life in the real setting. Each story begins with an animated exchange between two characters, who come to an understanding by having a glass of Coca-Cola together. One story shows two children having their beach ball punctured by an umbrella, while another shows a young couple watching a movie dropping their popcorn because they are scared. Another playful video shows two rival soccer fans battling it out by beating their own team's drum. As things heat up, a ball pops out of the can and the two rivals become friends and start playing together. All the activities revolve around the Coke can, which becomes a means of bringing people together and reconciling them.

Although AR is an easy and highly immersive technology, it still faces some issues. AR apps that are used outdoors have to deal with the sun as outdoor temperatures interfere with perception. For example, in the case of AR tourism apps, which require going to a tourist location to enjoy virtual elements superimposed on reality, this inconvenience can ruin the experience.

Augmented reality can also pose safety issues. For example, a cyclist or skier wearing AR spectacles may be confused by the information displayed on the screen and risk causing an accident. Another problem is privacy as AR glasses require a camera to function. However, this camera can allow people to be filmed without their knowledge. This is one of the issues that caused the failure of Google Glass, for example.

1.3   Mixed Reality (MR): A New and Complex Reality

Mixed reality combines the practical elements of AR and VR, and is considered the most complex immersive technology. Paul Milgram and Fumio Kishino (1994) defined MR as any place between the extremes of the virtuality continuum. Thus, between the real environment and the virtual environment, there would be a continuum of intermediate states that these authors encompass under the term mixed reality. In contrast to AR and VR, MR does not refer to a specific state or device but to a set of possibilities. Milgram and Kishino admit to having focused mainly on the display modalities and the subject's relationship to immersion. MR also refers to specific properties around the human experience and the possibilities of seeing, feeling, and acting in the real setting.

This form of extended reality mixes the real world with virtual environments to create a new reality. Users can interact with their real and virtual environments simultaneously. This technology requires an MR headset and an ultra-high-performance processor. An example of a mixed reality headset is Microsoft's HoloLens, introduced in 2015. Thanks to a transparent screen, these glasses represent objects in 3-D in the user's immediate environment. The headset video embeds sensors, speakers, and its own computing unit, so no additional equipment is required for its use.

Although different devices can be involved, mixed reality does not respond to a specific technology; it is realized in the intercrossing of existing worlds. When we talk about virtual reality or augmented reality, we directly associate specific devices (e.g., glasses, headsets, 3-D). For mixed reality, we can make the link with projection and video capture systems, but this material is not specific to it.

BOX 4.3   WHEN THE NATIONAL FOOTBALL LEAGUE (NFL) USES MIXED REALITY: THE CAROLINA PANTHERS CASE

In September 2021 in the Bank of America Stadium, home of the Carolina Panthers American football team, the team's fierce mascot comes to life in mixed reality. Created by the specialist company The Famous Group, the video, which mixes VR and AR, features a giant panther that leaps into the stadium and snatches the pennant of the opposing team, the New York Jets, at the kick-off of their NFL game. The spectators did not imagine it. The "animal" suddenly appeared in the stadium, and then roamed around before virtually "attacking" the players on the field as if it were real.

The rest of the world was also able to enjoy this immersive experience through a video posted online. We can see the animal climbing the scoreboard, tearing off the rival flag, jumping on the field, and mingling with the players. The video went viral and generated a huge reaction on Twitter.

2 ERT FOR BUSINESS: OPPORTUNITIES AND CHALLENGES

The use of ERT in the business sector is continually developing. So far it has mostly been implemented in the entertainment industry that has expertise in this technology. However, extended reality and its multiple potential applications are gaining ground in other sectors, including medicine, the military, industry, and tourism.

Video games are the best-known application of ERT in the entertainment industry, partly because this industry adopted VR technology relatively early, and quickly made it available to end-users. The new technologies offer many possibilities for events such as concerts or sport. ERT allows fans to watch events at home with an Internet connection and experience them as if they were attending a concert or play in person through extended reality and virtual environments. This new offering allows event professionals to considerably increase their ticketing ranges.

Furthermore, ERT offers great opportunities in terms of product launch, display, and sales by helping companies create actual interactions with their customers. Thanks to the immersive nature of ERT, customers can experience and try a product in a virtual environment before they buy. Moreover, ERT opens new avenues for companies to interact with their customers remotely. For example, the real estate sector can implement ERT to involve clients in the visitor experience, thus offering great advantages to professionals in this field. Potential clients interested in a property can visit it from the comfort of their own home, making it easier for agents and owners alike; and, in planning new buildings, immersive technologies allow architects and designers to materialize their visions.

ERT can also be used in the retail sector to create the fusion and continuum between in-store and online e-commerce because immersive technologies offer great added value to online stores: when customers make online purchases, before finishing the sale, they do not usually have the opportunity to see or touch the product live. ERT allows companies to implement AR e-commerce websites that allow online customers to visualize virtual replicas of the product and to project themselves with it, virtually, before they purchase.

Although ERT offers countless opportunities for companies to increase sales and engage customers in a highly immersive experience, these technologies are still in their infancy and not yet integrated into our daily lives. Thus, there are many challenges related to the interaction of ERT that prevent its diffusion and adoption in both business and society. These challenges involve three main aspects: economic, regulatory, and technical.

- *Economic challenges* are related to the high cost of the development, implementation, and maintenance of ERT. For instance, unlike AR technologies used for games and entertainment purposes such as *Pokémon Go* or social media filters, which are accessible to all smartphone users, virtual reality and mixed reality requires relatively more expensive equipment. Therefore, these immersive technologies are primarily aimed at companies, specific user groups, or technophiles.
- *Regulatory challenges* refer to data privacy and protection issues related to the use of ERT that is supposed to collect much more detailed, sometimes personal, data, especially regarding the user's immediate environment. Respecting all the rules on data protection is therefore a real challenge for any developers who want to make their extended reality products accessible to a large number of users.
- *Technical challenges* include technology development and design issues. The diffusion and adoption of ERT requires not only ergonomic and fancy designs but also IT infrastructure development and technically reliable and comfortable devices. For example, VR headsets are often too heavy and uncomfortable for extended use.

3   ERT IN THE DESIGN OF IMMERSIVE AND SENSORY PHYGITAL EXPERIENCES

Immersion in a virtual environment is the perception of being physically present in a non-physical world. This perception is created by incorporating extended reality technologies that can simulate the five senses with images, sounds, or other stimuli, offering an enchanting and highly immersive setting. ERT can also create different types of immersion, including technical, cognitive, and narrative. While technical immersion refers to users' ability to interact with virtual elements through devices such as smartglasses or VR headsets, cognitive immersion is associated with users' mental challenge and decision-making processes to project themselves into the virtual environment by selecting suitable options.

On the other hand, narrative immersion occurs when users are captivated by the story, and thus immerse themselves in the virtual environment in the way one used to be immersed when reading a novel or watching a movie. This is what Batat (2019b) calls the power of "digital storytelling" that leads users to be involved in the action and thus become part of the "digital storydoing" with the brand. In this case, virtual immersion is created with or without extended reality technologies.

Companies face many challenges when it comes to incorporating ERT to design a highly immersive phygital experience by encompassing the five senses—sight, touch, sound, taste, and smell. As stated by Batat (2019b), nowadays, only two senses can be integrated by companies when using ERT. For example, companies have tested haptic technologies to simulate the sense of touch, but this is still in its early stages; and, although some technology does exist to help companies reproduce taste and smell in the virtual environment, simulation of these senses remains very limited.

Nevertheless, the future is promising as the way we see, touch, and feel the world may not be the same in the future. Many tech companies and start-ups are becoming particularly innovative in terms of creating sensory devices that can help companies design sensory and highly immersive customer experiences involving all five senses. These technologies and tools include:

- *sight*—3-D displays, full-dome, headsets, and holograms;
- *sound*—3-D audio effects and high-resolution sound;
- *touch*—haptic technology and gloves with sensors;
- *smell and taste*—olfactory diffuser devices and artificial aromas.

Nowadays, companies can use various technological tools and devices to enhance the sensory immersion of their customers in a virtual environment where they can interact with products and brands. For example, visual, sound, haptic, tactile, and olfactory ERT devices allow companies to recreate the five senses of the experience virtually. Regarding sight and sound, we can note that over the last years, most headset-based virtual reality experiences could offer users the possibility of experiencing high-quality visuals and sounds thanks to the second- and third-generation helmets that are more powerful, ergonomic, and accessible than the first generation of VR and AR headsets and helmets. The latest such devices have also been improved when it comes to their immersive features. In addition to the visual and audio features already proven in the early headsets, there are now sensory sensor devices and haptic accessories with many features similar to those of the gamepads used in video games.

Other functionalities are under development, such as joysticks, triggers, or motion sensors to increase user immersion in the scenario and the action while interacting with virtual elements. For instance, the Leap Motion controller can capture the user's hand movements without contact; and Oculus Touch (improved joysticks) can be used along with the Oculus Rift and the Perception Neuron sensors placed on the body.

The absence of touch in a virtual world removes a valuable source of information, resulting in limiting the interaction and thus the immersive experience. If companies manage to recreate a tactile reaction in virtual environments, they will not only be able to make virtual experiences more realistic but will also allow customers to perform more difficult tasks. The sense of touch is a vital element in the immersion process and the generation of emotions in different domains. For example, the porn industry has recently initiated several experiments in virtual reality, and some producers in the sector imagine that VR could eventually replace real sex thanks to the development of connected haptic technologies and other devices to release scents during virtual experiences.

BOX 4.4   THE "PLACE IMMERSIVE" CONCEPT: A RESTAURANT EXPERIENCE INVOLVING THE FIVE SENSES

Many businesses are now using extended reality technologies to offer customers immersive and unique experiences. The ultimate goal is to stimulate senses other than vision to add a greater degree of realism. Gastronomy, a field that already uses sight, smell, and taste, has seized this opportunity to offer an innovative concept that has given rise to the "Place Immersive" in Madrid, Spain—a combination of technology and gastronomy for an immersive experience.

The Place Immersive is a space for innovations about immersive experiences. This unique project aims to offer an environment of 360° sensory experiences where it is possible to organize business meetings, workshops, or other activities in a setting where technological innovation and gastronomy are combined to perfection. A condensed version of state-of-the-art technologies is proposed to materialize another universe: projections, virtual and augmented reality, image walls, holograms, and tactile and interactive surfaces, among others. All this is ingeniously arranged in an experimental space of 30m² to offer new disruptive forms of entertainment, but also of education, discovery, and consumption.

The objective was to imagine a space that would make the awakening of the five senses tangible through digital technology in order to offer users a personal and unique experience. They can move through remote places and landscapes via different projections, transported to another dimension by means of sounds, smells, sensations, and movement. This multitude of technologies deployed on the four walls of the room composes unique and innovative environments while allowing customers to fully live 360°

experiences using their five senses. While the audiovisual projections fill the room with immersive images, the smell simulator activates feelings of well-being, happiness, and comfort. State-of-the-art audio equipment provides crisp and optimal surround sound and synchronized music, a true backbone accompanying the projections. Interactive tables offer various AR possibilities to trigger creativity and the sense of touch. All these experiences are accompanied by gastronomic discoveries to stimulate, in turn, the sense of taste.

Digital technology makes the restaurant industry ideal for discovery as gastronomy is a field par excellence for stimulating the senses and discovering new sensations. Indeed, even when we go to a traditional restaurant, the atmosphere, the smells, the music, and of course the dishes constantly stimulate our senses. As each individual has different sensibilities, digital technologies are a real complement to the immersion of the customer and contribute to the creation of a unique and personal experience. Only the sense of touch is not really mobilized. It is in this sense that the project is particularly innovative. In addition to being immersed in a new environment, the tactile and interactive technologies encourage the user to interact and complete the stimulation of his or her five senses for optimal immersion. In this way, digital technologies can only enhance the pleasure of taste and offer the customer the opportunity to discover tastes and food from a completely different perspective.

From a consumer perspective, companies should consider the impact of ERT on behaviors, attitudes, and expectations in terms of shopping experiences. Research shows that users' expectations are multiple and influenced by a multitude of elements, including the proactivity of the application, the relevance and sensitivity to the context, the social aspect, and immersion, among others (Olsson et al., 2013). However, although user interactions with ERT devices are still at the prototype stage and have a high risk of failure (Barba et al., 2010), integration of immersive technologies can enhance shopping experiences and attract customers by offering service personalization. An essential element of ERT applications, such as AR and VR, includes personal and immersive dimensions (Olsson et al., 2013). ERT can also offer relevant and contextualized information about the user's exact location, along with a new multisensory shopping experience through high-quality visual and sound elements.

Although the online experience brings multiple benefits to consumers' daily lives, it has some limitations compared to the traditional physical store experience (Batat, 2019b). Indeed, customers cannot evaluate the store's atmosphere, interact with salespeople, or seek a sensory experience when shopping on an e-commerce website (Daugherty et al., 2008). Instead, with the integration of ERT they can interact with 3-D visual products through a virtual experience. Thanks to its interactive nature, product visualization in 3-D triggers the user's mental processes when placed in an environment enriched by sensory elements (Daugherty et al., 2008). The main advantage of using ERT to create a virtual shopping experience is therefore to allow the consumer to evaluate the product before purchase, where online buyers can compare products in 3-D from different angles and perspectives in the same way they interact with products in physical stores.

Regarding the impact of ERT on the shopping process, most studies examined shoppers' behaviors in the retail industry. For example, a study by Pachoulakis and Kapetanakis (2012) found that virtual fitting rooms with augmented reality make the shopping experience more attractive to the customer. Moreover, the implementation of ERT included different types of products (ranging from furniture to cosmetics) that used different technical devices in physical and digital settings. Below are some examples of how different immersive technologies can be incorporated into the customer's purchase process, including various consumption items:

- *In the eyewear industry*, 3-D apps are used by many companies for users to virtually try on pairs of spectacles. How does it work? Users have to upload their images to the website or take a picture of themselves directly from their webcam to view the available models. Although design costs were relatively low for the retailer, this solution was still limited to a front view, without considering the user's movements. Therefore, the experience had some limits because it did not allow a full view of the selected product. Alternatives proposed are to film a short video sequence and then superimpose the glasses onto a 3-D model that faithfully reproduces the user's face. However, these 3-D tools did not offer a real-time fitting mode. Other, more interactive technologies have now been developed on mobile apps with augmented reality including a real-time virtual fitting tool.
- *In the cosmetics industry*, L'Oréal's MakeUp Genius was the first app to emerge. The principle is simple: users hold their smartphone as a mirror and try the beauty products available on the mobile store. Thanks to the app's integrated motion capture system and the phone's front camera, the buyer can switch from lipstick to eyeliner in an interactive way and in real time. The success of this initiative shows that visualization tools constitute added value as a shopping assistant for beauty consumers.
- *In the furniture retail sector*, IKEA's mobile app, launched in 2013, offers users the possibility of discovering the catalog of products by visualizing their future decoration objects in real time. The added value of this app lies in the calculation of dimensions at real scales. Users can thus evaluate

several furnishing solutions in their own living room before purchasing the product.

Therefore, as illustrated in the above examples, the expansion of e-commerce is conditional on improving the online shopping experience because the main challenge of online shopping is to match the in-store shopping experience. For some specific products, such as clothing, in-store shopping remains the preferred choice of consumers. It is obvious that shoppers prefer to try the product on directly or maybe ask for help from the salespeople in the store. Thus, lack of direct information or interaction with the product leads to higher risk and lower trust in online sites (Lu and Smith, 2007).

Additionally, research shows that some product categories require a higher level of consumer involvement, especially when the consumer's self-esteem may be involved. For example, for clothing, shoes, jewelry, and home furnishings the buyer will need to see and touch the product (Citrin et al., 2003). As a result, the development of new immersive technologies and the integration of ERT can help retailers narrow the boundary between physical and online channels because these new visualization tools have a positive influence on purchase attention (Schlosser, 2003) while using the affective factors during the shopping experience, and decrease the consumer's perceived risk (Lee et al., 2010) by using immersive tools such as avatars, 3-D/4-D models, magic mirrors, and VR headsets, among others. Furthermore, ERT presents opportunities in terms of branding (e.g., augmented reality brochures), advertising (Yang et al., 2020), and viral marketing to promote consumer engagement. The most challenging aspect of ERT is the quality of interactivity, which is often hampered by availability and not-so-easy-to-use technology. Flawless interactivity is necessary to guarantee an enjoyable and emotionally engaged shopping and consumption experience (Bonetti et al., 2018).

Although companies and marketing scholars are showing more interest in ERT, most studies to date lack knowledge in this area in terms of examining how ERT can enhance customer and shopping experiences and advance marketing strategies. There is a need then to expand understanding of various facets of ERT and their impacts on marketing practices, consumption experiences, and the consumer journey.

KEY TAKEAWAYS

In this chapter, I introduced the concept of extended reality technology (ERT) that companies can incorporate in their digital marketing strategies to create experiences capable of immersing customers in phygital settings where in-store and online shopping experiences are connected and complementary. By distinguishing three types of immersive technology—virtual reality, augmented reality, and mixed reality—I identified various innovations and devices companies could use to improve customer immersion by creating highly sensory experiences that replicate the five senses in virtual contexts. This chapter also examined consumers' perceptions of ERT and their attitudes toward integrating these technologies in the purchase process, both online and offline.

5. Phygital customer experience strategy enabled by robotics and artificial intelligence (AI)

CHAPTER OVERVIEW

The growth and democratization of the use of robots across different sectors represents an excellent opportunity for companies to rethink their relationship with their customers, their marketing strategies, and to reflect on how the incorporation of different forms of intelligent robots, equipped with artificial intelligence (AI), can help them improve the customer experience within digital and physical (phygital) settings. This chapter explores the evolution of robotics and its integration into the commercial sector. It answers questions related to the types of intelligent robot companies can use to design effective and adapted phygital experiences that allow customers to easily navigate between real and virtual components. Challenges related to human–robot relationships and interactions will also be discussed.

1 ROBOTICS AND ARTIFICIAL INTELLIGENCE: DEFINITION AND EVOLUTION

The introduction of robots is related to the development of artificial intelligence (AI), and its use across different industries, ranging from the medical sector to hospitality and education, is a major technological disruption that is still in its early stages. AI, introduced by US computer scientists John McCarthy and Marvin Minsky in 1956, refers to the set of sciences and technologies that imitate, extend, or increase human intelligence with the help of machines.

AI includes all the techniques that allow machines to perform actions or solve problems usually reserved for humans, which may seem very simple, such as recognizing objects in an image, but whose resolution may be very complex to model. AI is not about endowing the machine with real intelligence; it is about enabling it to perform complex tasks that equal or even exceed the performance of a human being in well-defined domains that can be very varied, such as optimizing a journey or calculating travel time.

Since the 1950s, AI research has focused on creating "thinking machines." More recently, tech companies have started to invest heavily in robot personality development systems and humanoid robotics as many experts suggest that, within the next few decades, artificial intelligence will be fully conscious and instant. However, while AI is not necessarily physically embodied beyond a computer terminal in which it can demonstrate its capabilities, robots can and do implement their abilities in the physical world. They are, first of all, objects. We can define a robot as a mechatronic device combining mechanics, electronics, and computing. It includes numerous components: sensors (e.g., cameras), which the robot uses to recognize its environment; actuators, which give the robot the ability to act (e.g., move); a source of energy (battery) to allow it to move, or at least to activate its actuators; and an information processing system, giving the robot the ability to use its actuators according to the perceived environment.

Humanoid robotics can be defined in various ways because there is a great diversity of robots, both in terms of appearance and functionality. Accordingly, many definitions exist across different disciplines where humanoid robots can be defined as automatic devices capable of manipulating objects or performing operations according to a fixed, modifiable, or adaptable program.

The International Organization for Standardization (ISO) defines robots as programmable mechanisms operating on at least two axes with a degree of autonomy, moving in their environment to perform planned tasks. Meanwhile the Institute of Electrical and Electronics Engineers (IEEE) defines robots as autonomous machines capable of sensing their environment, performing calculations to make decisions, and performing actions in the real world. While an attempt to legally define the robot was undertaken in 2017 at the European level, the European Union (EU) did not manage to give it special legal status, even when focusing on autonomous and intelligent robots. The four criteria proposed by the EU to define robots were:

- the acquisition of autonomy through sensors and/or data exchange with the environment (interconnectivity) allowing data exchange and analysis;
- the capacity for self-learning (optional criterion);
- the presence of a physical covering;
- the adaptation of behavior and actions to the environment (autonomously, without human intervention).

These approaches, although they contribute to clarifying the concept of humanoid robots, underline the lack of consensus within the global scientific community on the definition of what an intelligent and autonomous robot is. Therefore, instead of providing a comprehensive definition of robots, we need to focus on the fundamental elements characterizing them, such as mobility in space, the ability to perform multiple tasks or actions, autonomy, and automaticity. Regarding their evolution, robotics and AI are not technologies of the future: they already exist in our society and are implemented across different industries and within societies, where they have started to transform our daily lives, sometimes without us even realizing. Indeed, this is happening not only at the industrial level but also at consumption levels, leading individuals to interact more frequently with AI systems, such as asking for directions, calculating a distance, or searching for an item to purchase.

These devices act on our behalf. They allow us to perform actions that were previously the responsibility of physical people; for example, personal digital assistants (PDAs) perform tasks previously done by secretaries, e-commerce algorithms replace sales advisors, and facial recognition software replaces security guards in charge of identity checks. The adoption of these new technologies produces a displacement of tasks, with some being automated for a multitude of reasons, including: greater efficiency; lower operating costs; better service availability; reduction of the risks linked to human work; giving the decision back to the end-user.

Thus, robots are increasingly present in our daily lives, including the most popular—connected voice assistants (e.g., Alexa)—which have recently been developed and allow us to give voice commands to control a whole series of everyday objects: play a song, close the shutters, lock a door, search the Internet, etc. Since the introduction of the first robots in the automotive industry, robotics has thus evolved a lot. In addition to the industrial sector, robots are now used in many sectors. For example, one of the best known in the medical field, the Da Vinci Surgical System, is used to perform surgery; it reduces operating times and improves the results of surgical tasks (Hamedani et al., 2019).

The hospitality sector is also witnessing the rise of robot receptionists, waiters, or butlers. Robots in hotels, for example, can hand over keys, accompany guests to their room, or order them a cab. In social care services for the elderly, care robots provide physical, cognitive, or emotional support. There are also domestic robots that are used to perform daily tasks such as mowing lawns or vacuuming. Scholars argue that the emergence of humanoid robots with artificial intelligence will have profound implications for society and business, where companies should focus on consumer–robot interactions in the marketplace.

Industrial robots are capable of adapting to inaccurately defined tasks—for example, picking up objects of different sizes and weights from a conveyor belt or composing batches of packages in warehouses (as with Amazon's robots). Conversely, however, following the logic of productivity, repetition, and limited interactions with humans, service robots have high degrees of interaction with humans and require great adaptability. Human–machine interaction is thus truly at the heart of the development of humanoid service robots.

BOX 5.1   ADVANTAGES AND DISADVANTAGES OF INTELLIGENT ROBOTICS

Robots are objects and, as such, devoid of affect—unlike human beings and animals. But robots have developed affective capacities that allow them to simulate emotions. Analysis of the literature reveals some affective dimensions of intelligent robots, such as their ability to recognize human emotional expressions, their capacity to simulate what in humans would correspond to emotions, and their ability to reason with emotion-related information.

Scholars note that the ability of humans to develop an emotional relationship with an object is not new. In her work in the military field, Julie Carpenter (2013), a researcher at the University of Washington, showed that American soldiers could become attached to their demining robots, give them a name and refuse to replace them, or suffer when they were destroyed, even though they did not look human or even pet-like.

Modern robots can be endowed with attractive physical envelopes (skins), making them resemble animals or even humans, and increasing the natural tendency to anthropomorphism (attributing human attributes to animals or things). Moreover, progress in recognizing emotions by machines and in the simulation of human behavior now allows social interactions with robots, something that seemed impossible only a few years ago.

Conversational robots or chatbots are thus capable of sustaining a discussion according to pre-established parameters, and are proving to be very efficient. These robots have considerable advantages: they are endowed with unlimited patience and give precise answers to many questions. The applications of affective and intelligent robots are potentially very broad and can be developed in the domestic universe: companion robots could thus complement pets in the home, but provide many more services to family members. However, emotional robots also have their dark side. The capacities of affective robots could be used to manipulate humans by playing on their emotions and eliciting specific emotional states: more fragile audiences, such as children or the elderly, who forget or do not realize that their speaker is an object, are more sensitive to indirect incentives or nudging intended by the owners or managers of robots. Humans, by becoming emotionally dependent on robots, could thus lose part of their free will. These fears lead us to question the ethical rules in the robotics industry that should be enacted to prevent abuses.

2 DIVERSE FORMS OF INTELLIGENT ROBOTICS

There are different forms and types of intelligent robot; they can include both physical and virtual robots. Multitasking robots can also be very specialized and meet only very limited needs. Nowadays, the robotic landscape is marked by fragmentation and is very fluid due to continuous technological innovations and the fertile imagination of tech companies and start-ups. Thus, intelligent robots can be classified into three main forms that companies can use to enhance customer experiences and interactions, both online and offline. These include humanoid robots, voice assistants, and chatbots or conversational robots.

2.1 Humanoid Robots

As its name suggests, a humanoid robot has the appearance of a human—it usually consists of a head, torso, two arms, and two legs—and its behavior is inspired by humans. However robots with only one body part, for example, from the waist down, are also considered humanoid. Humanoid robots are capable of performing many actions as their mechanical properties are particularly advanced: they can move and act autonomously, reproducing as many actions as possible made by humans. This category includes robots whose aesthetic rendering can be very different. For example, Nao is a small, childlike robot measuring 58 cm, while Rashmi is human-sized and strongly resembles a person. Robots such as Rashmi are called android robots. This term refers to humanoid robots designed to resemble humans aesthetically. They have the features of human faces (eyes, ears, mouth) and will often be covered in a material resembling human skin.

In contrast to these are machine robots, which are machine-like in appearance; they do not have overtly human characteristics (Walters et al., 2008), and their configuration maximizes the dedicated functions of the robot (e.g., vacuuming robots). They are used to provide commercial reception functions or for educational applications (interactions with children). Humanoid robots can also be used as social robots to autonomously interact with humans in a socially meaningful way (Lee et al., 2005). To do so, these robots must be capable of recognizing the emotions of others and/or expressing their own emotions; communicating; establishing/maintaining social relationships; using natural cues (e.g., gaze, gesture); learning/developing social skills; and they must have a unique personality. They can take different forms, such as humanoid, animal, machine, etc. However, intelligent and humanoid robots have limited capabilities. If programmed, they are not capable of an infinite number of tasks, and can only perform those assigned to them. For example, a reception robot will be able to recognize the emotions of customers and engage in conversation to give them information but will be unable to shout "fire" if a fire breaks out nearby unless it has been programmed specifically for that purpose.

BOX 5.2   PEPPER: A POPULAR HUMANOID ROBOT WITH MULTIPLE USES

Pepper, available for sale since 2014, is the most famous humanoid commercial service robot on the market today. According to various sources, there are now about 10,000 Pepper robots in operation around the world. The utility of this robot is primarily commercial. It can guide, advise, take orders, and chat with customers in stores where it is installed. Although Pepper is a commercial success in Japan, its implementation in Europe and the United States remains marginal. Pepper is less anthropomorphic but still has human characteristics such as arms, eyes, and a smile. It is able to memorize its name, show humor, and express some emotions.

Pepper was initially designed by the French company Aldebaran, which was acquired by SoftBank Robotics in 2012. Pepper measures 120 cm and weighs 29 kg, and its main colors are white and gray. Its large eyes have pupils that light up in blue, white or red, depending on the interaction in progress, and it has a small mouth which hides a microphone. Pepper has no legs but moves thanks to three wheels hidden below a "skirt" (at the maximum speed of a human). Despite having some female attributes, the robot is considered more asexual. Pepper also has two arms with three joints at the "shoulders," "elbows," and "wrists," and hands consisting of five fingers. In addition, Pepper has a voice with a rather metallic tone. These characteristics were selected to maximize acceptance by users.

Furthermore, Pepper is the first humanoid robot capable of identifying faces and major human emotions. Among other things, it can interpret a smile, a head movement, the intonation of the voice, or even the lexical fields used, thanks to numerous microphones and cameras. It was designed to interact with humans in the most natural way possible through dialogue in 15 languages and the touch screen on its chest, which represents a physical interface facilitating interaction. Connected to the Internet, this screen allows Pepper to display maps, images, and videos, or propose games, quizzes, or educational content. Given its interactive capabilities, Pepper is used in many fields, mostly for social tasks. Thus, its main role is usually to welcome customers in settings such as supermarkets, banks, train stations, and hospitals, among others. For example, Pepper is present in various hotels, where it is used as a receptionist. It can also accomplish some tasks following guests' requests, such as booking a table in a restaurant, proceeding to check-in and check-out, or informing guests about the facilities available in the hotel. It is also used as an educational tool in schools and universities.

2.2   Voice Assistants

Robot voice assistants are possibly more accessible and easier to use than humanoid robots. These involve software that performs tasks for a user through voice or text commands. Users can interact with them through a chat interface or simply by speaking a command out loud. Voice assistants are available on different terminals. Initially, they were integrated into smartphones and tablets, and, in a second phase, into other everyday tools such as cars, televisions, and connected speakers. These voice assistants have been developed thanks to the progress of digital voice recognition technologies. They were first integrated into smartphones to allow actions to be controlled by voice (e.g., Apple's Siri was installed in its products in 2011). The market for virtual assistants has gradually diversified, with numerous products and technical platforms available today besides Siri: Google Assistant (Google), Alexa (Amazon), Cortana (Microsoft), Bixby (Samsung). Recently, domestic voice assistants (e.g., Amazon Echo, Google Home) have been launched to help users with domestic tasks such as searching the Internet, controlling domestic appliances (e.g., lights, electric shutters), and playing music, among others. Moreover, these voice assistants become more sophisticated with use: equipped with AI, they identify user preferences and adapt to them. They also enhance human/object interactivity in everyday life and have been rapidly adopted by users.

BOX 5.3   ALEXA: AMAZON'S VOICE ASSISTANT ENHANCING THE CUSTOMER AND EMPLOYEE EXPERIENCE

Alexa is an artificial intelligence that acts as a personal assistant. It is able to listen to any voice command from users, interpret it, and act accordingly. In 2014, Amazon released the first version of its Echo voice speaker with Alexa, whose name refers to the Library of Alexandria, a temple of human knowledge. When integrated into its speaker (the Amazon Echo), Alexa can safely control various connected devices and/or answer certain questions from users. Alexa is thus available on Amazon's voice speakers as well as devices from other brands. It works with a dedicated smartphone app to set it up and install new features. The app also allows access to a history of interactions with Alexa and rates the quality of those interactions. Connection via a web browser is also possible. On iOS, the app allows users to interact with Alexa directly without a speaker.

Additionally, several basic commands allow Alexa to answer questions, play audio content, set tasks and alarms, provide forecast information on the day's news, sports scores, traffic conditions, nearby businesses, or even make online purchases. These can be extended by installing skills, similar to apps that can be added to a smartphone. Since everything is hosted in the cloud, the skills are updated automatically and the number that can be activated is unlimited. Far more skills are available in English than other languages, but the number is constantly rising. The Internet of Things (IoT) also allows Alexa users to control smart home appliances (e.g., switches, thermostats, microwaves).

Essentially, using Alexa means choosing to control everything simply by voice. Indeed, it is about using one's voice to address this AI and ask it to perform a number of tasks. No more manual work or tapping the screen of a tablet or smartphone. The benefits of Alexa that are most appreciated by users are as follows:

- *Home automation control.* Alexa allows users to remotely control various devices and gadgets in their homes, the devices are connected to its speaker. This is one of the main features greatly appreciated by both businesses and customers as it is quick and saves time.
- *A large number of connected devices.* Various speakers allow the control of about 4,000 connected devices, which is very practical because it saves invaluable time and offers speed of execution.
- *Communication in several languages.* Alexa integrates various languages, so is very practical in international environments where many languages are spoken, such as airports.

2.3   Chatbots or Conversational Robots

Chatbots are machines designed to converse with humans by giving the latter the impression they are talking to physical people and not a machine. Chatbots do not understand the conversation but aim to imitate a human interaction in a conversation. This is why they are classified as "low AI" applications. Programming chatbots requires entering a considerable amount of data to respond to the diversity of possible conversations. They can be used in various applications, including telemarketing, to guide travelers in their geolocation, or to finalize e-commerce transactions. Overall, chatbots are specialized in a particular domain and cannot support all types of conversation. They have the advantage of being fast, available all the time (including outside the usual opening hours of service), and are relatively easy to use. However, they can also be limited in their responses and not able to answer all questions. This is why a transfer to human speakers may be necessary at the second level.

Although chatbots have some conversational limits, they represent a growing trend in society, and their use by companies across different sectors seems promising. As stated by the American Marketing Association (AMA, 2020), the global chatbot market is expected to reach more than $1.3 billion by 2024, representing an annual growth rate of 24.3 percent. Companies therefore need to incorporate chatbots to strengthen relations with their customers and develop highly personalized, interactive, and instant automated interactions because chatbots are accessible 24/7.

Most studies on chatbots have mainly focused on the key factors determining their acceptance in customer service and retail. To enhance users' acceptability of chatbots, Batat (2019b) underlined the importance for companies to give the chatbot the ability to respond in a relevant way to the identified request. This means that a well-thought-out and well-designed process and interface should be set up by companies in order to build, maintain, and control the knowledge base. Chatbots can also be used for promotional purposes. For example, National Geographic created and used a chatbot to promote its series *Genius*, centered on Albert Einstein. The chatbot allowed users or viewers to chat with the famous scientist, thus entering the intimacy of the character endorsed by the chatbot, which reacts in a friendly way and with humor, so that the user will want to watch the series to get to know Einstein even better.

BOX 5.4   TACOBOT, THE TACO BELL CHATBOT

Chatbots are an innovative and efficient way for brands/companies to interact with their customers, and the mass use of messaging tools like Facebook Messenger makes them increasingly essential. These automatic conversation bots can be very efficient if used wisely, and, on top of that, they can be created without writing a line of code. TacoBot, from US fast-food chain Taco Bell, is an excellent example of chatbot implementation to enhance customer relations and increase sales.

Early adopters of conversational commerce include such striking examples as fast-food chain Taco Bell's TacoBot, which allows customers to order via text message. The benefits of conversational commerce via AI-based chatbots in the buying and selling experience are multiple, viewed from the perspective of both customers and companies. Benefits for customers include convenience and speed: the chatbot can verify everything for the user; advise on purchases; give personalized recommendations and offers; secure payment; and provide real-time, 24/7 responses with no waiting, among others. Chatbots have various advantages for companies: improved customer service; buyer loyalty is encouraged; online reviews are boosted; feedback is collected immediately; cross-selling and upselling opportunities are available; more accurate recording of information and conversations; analysis of user behavior; processes are automated; and no salary or days off are needed, thus saving money.

3 CHALLENGES OF INTELLIGENT ROBOTS IN CUSTOMER EXPERIENCES

While advances in intelligent robotics are exceptional, understanding the factors that influence a consumer's decision to accept or reject a technology is critical; the same is true for robotics. As promising as the technology is, it will only reach its full potential and successful diffusion if accepted and adopted by users (e.g., Savela et al., 2018; Latikka et al., 2019). Acceptance of different forms of intelligent robot also influences users' behaviors when interacting with them (especially in the case of social robots). That is why it is important for companies to examine how intelligent robots can positively or negatively affect customer attitudes and experiences and identify the key challenges and opportunities generated by the integration of such technology.

The main challenges related to the integration of intelligent robots in customer experiences are related to user perceptions and acceptance of these technologies, which are mostly related to five main factors: (1) the robot's socio-demographic criteria; (2) the robot's sector of activity; (3) the robot's personality; (4) the robot's appearance; and (5) the user's profile.

3.1 Robot's Socio-Demographic Criteria

Overall, several studies have highlighted that new technologies are generally more accepted by males, educated people, and younger people (Scopelliti et al., 2005; Heerink, 2011). Regarding robotic acceptance and gender creation, research shows that males have a more positive appreciation of intelligent robots compared to females, and are more willing to use them in their daily lives (Gnambs and Appel, 2019). On the other hand, highly educated individuals appear to be more open to robotics than people without a tertiary education. This assumption is in line with Gnambs and Appel's research, which revealed that office workers (or white-collar workers) hold more positive attitudes about robots compared to manual (blue-collar) workers. This is probably due to the latter's fear of losing their jobs and being replaced by industrial robots. Indeed, manual jobs with routine tasks are at the greatest risk of being replaced by robotization. On the other hand, age does not seem to be a primary variable in explaining the acceptance of robots, unlike what is usually the case for new technologies (e.g., de Graaf and Allouch, 2013; Gnambs and Appel, 2019). Moreover, most European populations perceive intelligent robots positively; and it is noted that citizens in northern countries have significantly more positive attitudes toward robots than southern countries.

3.2   Robot's Sector of Activity

The adoption of robots also depends on the sector where they are introduced. For instance, robots are well accepted in the industrial sector as well as the military and search and rescue operations. However outside of these technical fields of use, individuals are much more reluctant to use them in more social areas, such as child care or assistance for elderly people or those with disabilities (Taipale et al., 2015). In recent years, the main concerns have been about robots working in sectors involving social interactions. Different studies have pointed out that these concerns are, among others, due to the misconception that social robots are intended to replace human beings or human tasks, when their most common purpose is to support their users or help professionals in these sectors (e.g., nurses) with demanding tasks.

3.3   Robot's Personality

Personality, initially defined for human beings, is also applicable to robots, and is defined in terms of a person's characteristics that account for consistent patterns of feeling, thinking, and behaving. Studies on personality underline five main traits to be considered in the definition of personality: openness, conscientiousness, extraversion, agreeableness, and neuroticism. When it comes to robotics, scholars have mostly used these five human traits to explore the robot personality (Robert, 2018). Most researchers have focused on extraversion, which is the easiest observable feature of the five traits (Lippa and Dietz, 2000), and the impact this has on individuals' perception of robots. The conclusions of these studies show that human beings tend to prefer a robot personality that is different from their own (e.g., introverted people prefer robots with an extrovert personality) as well as robots with a personality they consider as complementary to their own. Also, social robots should use both verbal and non-verbal cues to make their personality easily understandable from a human perspective (Nass and Lee, 2000). In contrast, other studies have emphasized that individuals prefer to interact with a robot with the same personality as theirs. Since various studies on the same subject obtain different or even opposite results, it is difficult to conclude what kind of robot is best suited to a person.

3.4   Robot's Appearance

Research shows that individuals' acceptance of intelligent robots is closely related to the robot's appearance, which has evolved over the years, impacting the perception and acceptance of robots among users (e.g., Saygin et al., 2012; Ferrey et al., 2015). Overall, studies have highlighted some aspects related to robots' appearance that can affect people's perceptions. For example, people interacting with robots can find the experience much more comfortable when the robot is wearing glasses (Geller, 2008) or when human and non-human elements are mixed (Ho et al., 2008). Yet, despite the prevailing uncertainties in this field, many studies state that it is risky for manufacturers to create intelligent robots that resemble humans in appearance. But they still decide to design android robots, so some precautions have to be considered, such as the robot's face, as it seems that the eyes can cause discomfort if they are poorly designed.

Research into the acceptance of robots has been dominated by the theory of the "uncanny valley," one of the first examining the impact of robot forms and appearance on human beings. The theory was developed by the Japanese roboticist Masahiro Mori in 1970 and has been cited in numerous articles. It emphasizes the idea that the more similar the appearance and movements of robots are to those of humans, the more they create a feeling of familiarity. However, this phenomenon is not linear. When the robot's appearance gets too close to the appearance of humans and becomes an android, it generates a sense of strangeness and repulsion (Mori, 1970). In other words, this theory suggests that as robots become humanoid, people feel more comfortable. However, when the robot becomes *too* humanoid in its appearance and behavioral characteristics, such as its voice or the way it moves, people end up feeling negative emotions for this robot or even reject it. Although this theory was developed in the 1970s, researchers are still not unanimous on what causes robots to be rejected when they get too human. Analysis of the literature reveals three main reasons to explain this rejection:

• The first explanation, by Saygin et al. (2012), underlines the idea that when the robot resembles a human enough, the human's brain triggers a "mental shift" and will perceive the robot as a potential human, which generates confusion as the individual no longer knows how to react to the non-human aspects of the robot. It would then be seen as a human failing to act properly.

- For Mori (1970), human rejection of overly humanized robots is related to the discomfort caused by the perception of anomalies related to the robot's appearance and behavior. Humans associate these anomalies with anomalies present in seriously mentally or physically sick people. This assimilation causes a negative feeling since humans naturally fear mental illness and death.
- Another reason is related to the difficulty of categorizing what human beings perceive as familiar objects but which are not, which ends up being a cognitively and emotionally demanding task to achieve.

Furthermore, studies show that the perception of robots' appearance is also influenced by the cultural context. The study by Haring et al. (2014) indicates that the Japanese have a stronger preference for humanoid robots with human traits than their European counterparts. However, this cultural effect remains ambiguous, especially between Americans and Asians, as different studies have found opposite results, depending on how sample differences and concepts have been measured.

3.5 User's Profile

The user's personality is a vital criterion in the acceptance or rejection of intelligent robots. As stated by Walters and colleagues (2008), introverted people with low emotional stability seem to prefer machine robots more than the average population. The degree of extraversion of the user also appears to influence robot personality preference, although more research is needed to clarify the nature of this impact. In addition to these criteria, there are other person-specific characteristics that can affect robot perception and acceptance. First, many scholars highlighted the importance of personal innovativeness in the acceptance or rejection of robots (e.g., Hur et al., 2012; de Graaf and Allouch, 2013). Thus, individuals' willingness to try any new technology is related to their personality traits. In other words, people are labeled innovators if they quickly adopt the innovation. Innovators are usually early adopters who actively seek information with minor proscriptions. Therefore, this personality trait influences the acceptance of many technologies and has an impact on robot acceptance. Indeed, research shows that the more innovative people are, the more likely they are to admit robots into their homes. Highly innovative people are also more affected by the emotional value of the robot, while less innovative people focus on functional values.

The second factor refers to self-efficacy, which is essential in increasing acceptance of intelligent robots among users. Self-efficacy refers to an individual's confidence in his or her ability to manage a particular situation or task. What matters is not someone's actual abilities but his/her degree of confidence in his/her own abilities. Also, since this concept is related to the specific activity of an individual, its measurement must be related to a particular situation and task. Technological self-efficacy can be defined as individuals' estimation of their ability to use technological devices such as a computer. Compeau and Higgins (1995) examined computer self-efficacy as perceived by individuals. Their results show that individuals with a high measure of self-efficacy enjoy using computers more and have experienced less anxiety about them. Regarding robots, a study by Latikka et al. (2019) that focused on robot self-efficacy and acceptance was conducted in the healthcare sector. The authors distinguished between social and non-social robots, and used three forms of social robot—humanoid (robots with human features), zoomorphic (robots with animal features), and telepresence (a medium using transducers such as video cameras and microphones)—to examine the self-efficacy of healthcare staff's beliefs about their ability to use them. Their results show that self-efficacy positively influences acceptance of all three types of social robot but not of the non-social robot. Among the social robot assistants, the strongest relationship was found between self-efficacy of robot use and acceptance of the humanoid robot. This seems to emphasize that the role of self-efficacy of robot use becomes more important as their human aspects increase.

In addition to the challenges related to the features of robots and users cited above, studies show that the integration of intelligent robots can also negatively impact the customer experience, especially in the retail sector, where robots can replace or coexist with salespeople.

Primarily, the implementation of robots in stores could threaten many sales jobs. However, it is challenging to accurately anticipate the impact that retail automation will have on the structure and functioning of workplaces across different sectors. On the one hand, some studies claim that it will drastically reduce the number of employees needed to run a store. On the other hand, the management of these robots requires qualified personnel and will therefore generate new jobs. Some scholars even claim that creating jobs linked to the appearance of service robots will be more significant than the loss of jobs generated.

Various studies have also shown that contact with robots generates "compensatory responses" in customer reactions. These compensatory responses refer to behaviors that are caused by a feeling of discomfort or even insecurity in customers when interacting with robots, especially when the robot is anthropomorphic with a high resemblance to a human in appearance and attitudes. Thus, for retailers, the integration of robots should not be imposed; they should instead allow customers to choose between human and robot interactions (Mende et al., 2019). Another challenge related to the integration of robots is that customers are more demanding when interacting with intelligent robots than when dealing with human beings. Indeed, customers expect intelligent robots to be fast and efficient, and have effective AI that allows them to instantly respond to various requests. This means that customers are more unforgiving of mistakes made by robots than of those made by humans, due to the lack of empathy present in human–robot interactions.

The human–robot relationship underlines the vital role of empathy, which can lead us to imagine programming actions resembling empathy in a robot, as is found in some voice assistants such as Alexa that can generate answers that are fluent and attentive. Although robots do not allow empathic interactions with humans, a recent study by Chen et al. (2021) revealed "primitive forms of empathy" in AI installed in robots by showing that two robots can have the ability to anticipate each other's actions following an observational phase.

Therefore, questioning the potential existence of human empathy toward robots is a central element in the design of satisfying customer experiences. Chen et al. (2020) also examined why consumers seem to be less satisfied when facing a machine rather than a human in the context of various services. The findings of this study show that if there is no malfunction, customers are just as satisfied with the service provided by a self-service kiosk as they are with a human. On the other hand, when an error occurs, the dissatisfaction of people who have to deal with an automatic kiosk is significantly higher. This is true even when the error is actually due to user mishandling. This difference could be explained by the fact that robots or machines are perceived by humans as being "less human," and thus the absence of empathy leads people to extreme negative reactions.

KEY TAKEAWAYS

In this chapter, I introduced the rise and evolution of intelligent robotics in both the business sector and society, and the challenges related to their incorporation into the customer experience, especially in human–robot interactions. The chapter emphasizes the most significant challenge for companies: rethinking their relationships with their customers and their marketing strategies due to the arrival of artificial intelligence, chatbots, robots, virtual assistants, and so forth. This chapter underscores the idea that using robotics and AI to humanize the customer experience holds great promise for enhancing customer relations in the future. It is no longer a matter of whether or not companies should implement these new technologies; instead, the more pressing concern is "How should they implement these technologies successfully?" to offer the ultimate customer experience by merging physical and digital spaces.

6. Phygital customer experience strategy enabled by the Internet of Things (IoT) and connected objects

CHAPTER OVERVIEW

The Internet of Things (IoT) refers to objects and systems connected to each other and to humans. This chapter introduces the IoT and connected objects as a new step in this technological evolution. This technology transforms the simplest and the most complex everyday objects into connected objects to provide in-depth knowledge of consumers and thus offer highly customized and seamless customer experiences online and offline. These technologies support applications and services in many domains: medicine, wellness, home automation, agriculture, manufacturing industry, transport, logistics, or even ready-to-wear. This chapter first discusses the articulation between connected objects and the IoT. Then, the impacts of these technologies on customer experience and consumer behaviors are presented. This is followed by the opportunities, benefits, and challenges of the IoT and connected objects for companies to transform their relationships with customers.

1 THE RISE OF THE IOT AND CONNECTED OBJECTS

The emergence of the Internet of Things (IoT) is due to the diversification of access media to the Internet and the Web since the 1990s. This was the first indication of the large-scale development of connected objects, designed with the rise of the Internet and the Web. O'Brien (2016) refers to IoT dissemination as the Fourth Industrial Revolution and considers it as an opportunity to make everyday objects intelligent, leading to economic growth across different sectors.

The development of the IoT and connected objects also refers to the technical revolution linked to the connectivity between objects and systems. Technical objects have acquired the particularity of exchanging data with each other and with one or more power plants to meet economic objectives such as saving cost, time, and human resources. A second technical revolution is the link between electronics and biology. As soon as connected objects are designed and programmed to measure a wearer's biological data it becomes possible to monitor and analyze the wearer's daily activities in real time. Likewise, companies can use these technologies to enhance and renew the customer experience of their offer because the IoT can lead to high levels of customer engagement and value co-creation (Prahalad and Ramaswamy, 2004; Batat, 2019b).

The development of the IoT is related to the expansion of Web 3.0. This is also called the Web of objects as objects now can use Web technologies to develop services and applications related to networks of connected objects. IoT use has risen since 2009–2010 due to the multiplication of connected objects such as bracelets, tablets, watches, thermostats, and televisions.

However, the idea of connecting objects can be traced back to the 1960s in the computing science field. In 1966, Karl Steinbuch, a pioneer in computer science, expressed his vision of the future of the computer, stating that in a few decades computers would be integrated into almost all industrial products. The first connected objects appeared a few years later with the development of connected computing. The underlying idea of interweaving digital technologies with physical objects in the environment is reflected through several concepts, such as machine-to-machine communication.

One of the first known connected objects was a soda machine at Carnegie Mellon University in Pittsburgh, Pennsylvania. In 1982, computer science students Mike Kazar, John Zsarnay, and Ivor Durham connected their soda machine to the first network for data transfer—the Advanced Research Projects Agency Network (ARPANET)—to avoid unnecessary trips to an empty machine. They did so by installing micro-switches to detect the number of bottles in the machine and writing a server program that, when queried, indicated the number of bottles and the time. Later, in the 1990s, students used World Wide Web (WWW) protocol to connect their machines. Another connected object was a toaster connected to the Internet by John Romkey and Simon Hackett in 1989. The toaster could be turned on and off remotely, which determined how long the bread would take to toast via Simple Network Management Protocol (SNMP). The following year, a robotic arm was added to the toaster to pick up slices of bread and insert them into the machine.

No doubt other connected objects were conceived at this time, but the examples presented here indicate the current interest in connected objects. These are physical objects of everyday life that integrate communication technology such as Wi-Fi and a computer system to create new automated tasks, including turning appliances on and off, reading emails, quantifying activities, listening to music, and ordering goods, among others. Thus, the IoT has been visible since 2009–2010 through the multiplication of connected objects used in various fields: e-health, connected homes, social media, energy management, smart cities. This growth in recent years is due to favorable technological conditions that allow the IoT to be implemented on a large scale. The main technological levers include the following:

- the growth of wireless communication technologies, which vary in energy consumption, throughput, and range;
- the improvement of battery autonomy;
- the miniaturization and low production cost of components such as sensors and actuators;
- the use of cloud computing for storage, database, messaging, and data analysis over the Internet.

These factors have reduced the technological and economic barriers to the integration of technologies into everyday objects and led to their widespread commercialization. However, the hype and the diversity of players create confusion around the concepts of the IoT and connected objects, which refer to real or virtual objects equipped with data sensors and algorithmic instructions that allow them to communicate with each other and carry out concrete actions without human intervention. Authors have distinguished several categories of connected objects, including connected homes, mobility objects, and health-care devices or wearables (Hoffman and Novak, 2018). Connected objects can be classified as follows:

- personal mobile objects, such as smartphones or tablets;
- portable objects, such as watches, bracelets, or glasses;
- environmental objects, such as toasters or dishwashers;
- passive objects, such as equipment with Radio Frequency Identification (RFID) chips.

Therefore, we can state that connected objects achieve a physical/digital connection that has one or more means of communication and data storage, processing, and analysis. They maintain a close relationship with the environment—physically with sensors and actuators, and virtually by manipulating data corresponding to environmental parameters. Also, the design of the object is constrained by its context of use and requires adapted resources in terms of memory, bandwidth, energy consumption, and computing power.

Consequently, connected objects are the visible supports for the applications and services supported by IoT technologies. Thus, the IoT, which is the extension of the Internet to objects, is made possible by the existence of connected objects, which means that these two concepts are linked. One does not work without the other. The starting point is the connected object. The second phase is the Internet that allows connection of this object to another (the IoT).

To summarize, the main points of difference and convergence between the IoT and connected objects is that connected objects are objects that incorporate three elements: (1) sensors that identify and measure data; (2) actuators that perform actions based on the data captured; and (3) a system for transmitting these data. In contrast, the notion of the Internet of Things refers to the networked interconnection of objects. However, the use of the Internet is not systematic for all connected objects; other types of connection exist (e.g., machine-to-machine, RFID).

2   THE INTERNET OF THINGS: A DEFINITION

The IoT is part of ongoing technological trends and generates interest for debate, news, investigation, and research. As a result, the concept is difficult to pin down as there are so many different definitions, which sometimes merge with those of machine-to-machine communication or Web 3.0. This conceptual blurring also stems from the ideas underlying the IoT that have been present since the emergence of connected computing, the Internet, and the World Wide Web.

The term initially appeared in 2002 in an article in *Forbes* magazine in which Kevin Ashton, who was at the time head of the MIT Auto-ID Center—whose aim was to make RFID a standard for tracking and identifying products— called for the creation of an "Internet of Things" to digitally identify, describe, and track physical objects (Ashton, 2009). The IoT vision is focused on "dataizing" the environment through sensors and RFID tags.

According to Ashton, machines only receive data about the environment through humans when they write documents, enter data into a spreadsheet, or upload photos. However, he notes that humans lack the time, accuracy, and attention to describe the environment in a systematic way. The IoT will then deploy technologies for machines to observe, collect, and process data from the environment themselves through sensors, actuators, and radio tags.

This vision emphasizes the "dataization" of the environment by machines, from industrial facilities to public spaces and consumer demand. Yet, some authors have proposed different conceptualizations of the IoT. Although different, these definitions converge on the following points: it is an ecosystem of physical and virtual objects, interconnected via the Internet and Web communication protocols, identifiable, equipped with sensors and actuators, and programmable.

A comprehensive definition has been provided by the Institute of Electrical and Electronics Engineers (IEEE), the world's largest technical professional organization for the advancement of technology. In 2015, the IEEE referred to the IoT as a complex, adaptive, self-configuring network that connects "objects" to the Internet using standard communication protocols. The interconnected objects have a physical or virtual representation in the digital world, a detection/actuation capability, a programmability characteristic, and are uniquely identifiable.

The representation contains information such as the object's identity, status, location, or other relevant business, social, or private information. Objects provide services, with or without human intervention. The service is operated through intelligent interfaces and is made available anywhere, anytime, and for anything that considers security.

As a result, nowadays, the IoT is making technologies ubiquitous (e.g., Bluetooth, RFID, Wi-Fi) and provides contextual services, with or without human intervention, depending on events taking place in the physical environment. Likewise, connected objects can be considered providers and/or consumers of data related to the physical world (Miorandi et al., 2012). This means that, with the IoT, organizations are changing the way data are produced and processed, whereby data production, information extraction, and knowledge model building become fully machine-operable.

Thus, the IoT combined with connected objects, can help both companies and users achieve four main tasks, as stated by Porter and Heppelmann (2014): (1) monitoring through sensors and external data; (2) control, thanks to embedded software; (3) optimization via better use; and (4) more efficiency, and autonomy in operation and coordination with other objects.

3   IMPACTS OF THE IOT AND CONNECTED OBJECTS ON THE CUSTOMER EXPERIENCE

Nowadays, in the digitally infused consumer society, more and more everyday objects are connected (Batat, 2019a). Marketing scholars agree that these connected objects will become increasingly central to consumers' lives, and their use will impact consumer behaviors—whether in shopping experiences or in highly experiential fields of consumption such as leisure, tourism, food, culture, and art (Batat, 2020a). Therefore, faced with a rapidly growing market of connected objects used by consumers, companies need to identify the impacts of these new ways of consuming that involve these technologies.

Studies show that the introduction of connected objects can positively or negatively impact the customer experience (Kourouthanassis et al., 2007; Batat, 2019b). Marketing scholars suggest that connected objects positively impact the purchase experience, which can affect customer satisfaction and then, indirectly, loyalty. Technologies such as RFID can also improve the consumer shopping experience. For instance, interactive mirrors and fitting rooms equipped with RFID positively affect the shopping experience and provide retail professionals with a better understanding of customer behaviors and expectations.

Another study by Ngai and colleagues (2008), which focused on the implementation of an RFID system named personal shopping assistant (PSA) in a point of sale, suggests a positive impact on the consumer's shopping experience, thanks to access to additional information on products. Other studies have also highlighted that near-field communication (NFC) technology, combined with other technologies, could positively contribute to the consumer's overall shopping experience. Similarly, the incorporation of connected objects at the point of sale also increases the perceived degree of technology, improves the store's image, and positively impacts the perceived value.

Beyond efficiency, which is provided by the integration of the IoT in customer and shopping experiences, some studies show that the use of these technologies is driven more by hedonic than utilitarian motivation (e.g., Kim and Forsythe, 2007). Also, the integration of connected objects and other technologies is gradually breaking down physical and virtual barriers, represented by the dichotomy between traditional commerce and e-commerce, to allow connected consumers to navigate between online and offline offerings. Yet, the integration of IoT and connected objects can have different impacts on consumer behaviors. On the one hand, consumers can develop quantified-self activities to empower themselves; on the other hand, they can display resistance to these technologies, which can be explained by various factors. The following section will discuss these two perspectives.

3.1 A Quantified-Self Experience for Consumer (Dis)Empowerment

IoT dissemination has led to the rise of quantified-self connected objects, whose data are produced by individuals themselves, for themselves. The quantified-self trend can be defined as an approach of continuous quantification, in real time, contributing to the social production of standards of behavior, performance and health, continually evolving and allowing the visualization and, possibly, the comparison of their progress by users connected directly to the Internet through the sensors that quantify them. These objects work through connected body sensors such as a watch and apps on a smartphone.

Quantified-self objects allow consumers to continuously analyze and compare themselves, and to share the analysis and personal data on social media or with communities of other users of the same system or app. Users are then endowed with a new power to understand and modulate their behaviors to improve their well-being, and regain control and autonomy. Most quantified-self experiences reflect different forms of self-monitoring related to health goals, such as stopping smoking, losing weight, improving sleep, and others. Various devices can be used for quantified-self activities:

- *Sensors.* There are different types of sensor, which are becoming less expensive, more powerful, and increasingly specialized: accelerometer, gyroscope, proximity detector, altimeter, light detector, etc. Smartphones integrate several sensors. They are also integrated into objects such as watches, bracelets, helmets, sports accessories, clothing, or in the form of patches applied directly to the skin.
- *Biosensors.* In the medical field, biosensors can record biological parameters such as temperature, heart rate, blood pressure, and others.
- *Smartphone peripherals.* These refer to devices usually reserved for healthcare professionals, but which are becoming available to the general public (subject to approval). These include medical devices such as blood pressure monitors, whose legislative framework differs from country to country.
- *Wearable technologies.* In the sport and wellness fields, numerous companies are developing connected objects dedicated to health. For example, the Fitbit pedometer, equipped with an accelerometer and an altimeter, calculates the number of calories burned according to distance traveled, and can monitor the duration and quality of sleep by recording the number of awakenings during the night. Also, OMsignal84 has developed connected clothing: a t-shirt equipped with sensors allows multiple measurements, such as physical activity, pulse, heart rate, humidity, and skin temperature in relation to the outside temperature. A women's version also offers pregnancy monitoring.
- *Mobile applications and services.* In the last few years, ubiquitous computing has allowed the development of context-sensitive apps that consider the user's context. Mobile apps are the preferred interface for users as they provide both data collection services that rely on the user's environment and contextual support, interactions, and summary data visualization services.
- *Data processing platforms.* The processing of data from sensors has given birth to a new generation of data-driven platforms. Most platforms offer a set of personalized services in the form of dashboards and data visualization for personalized coaching services proposing goals to reach (e.g., Fitbit, Nike+). The data visualization varies significantly from one platform to another: for example, using counters or even 3-D avatars to show bodily changes.

Thus, quantified-self experiences allow users to meet their self-knowledge objectives. This desire for knowledge of self leads to the goal of self-improvement; self-knowledge is not sought for its own sake but as a means of changing and improving one's practices. For some users of connected objects to quantify their consumption practices and activities, improvement of behaviors is based on relatively simple measures, on a single type of data that will allow them to discipline themselves. Other quantified-self users employ more complex data, based on the initial assumption that collecting a large amount of information will allow them to identify correlations between various aspects of their daily lives, consumption practices, mood, and allow them to look for explanatory factors for some of their behaviors. Whether the data are used in a more or less complex way, they always serve a two-fold objective: developing and enhancing users' knowledge of themselves, and self-improvement of daily life.

The novelty of the quantified-self trend among today's consumers is its collective dimension: if the description of the objectives and practices may seem very individualistic, the quantified-self users define themselves as a "community." For these users, personal data are not meant to remain private but to be disseminated and shared with their communities, on social media platforms, websites, and blogs. Group members will thus be able to compare their experiences and results to confront their quantified-self data. Although the quantified-self trend allows consumers to regain power over their lives and improve themselves, some scholars have questioned whether the role of the quantified-self is an empowering or disempowering practice for users.

On the one hand, the quantified-self can be seen as an empowering practice that enhances consumer emancipation, driven by the idea that the quantification of oneself allows a form of empowerment thanks to control of the production of one's data. In a society where our digital tracks are recorded without our consent, becoming a producer and analyst of our own data would also be a form of resistance against submissive data collection intended to make us consume, or even to monitor us, but not to improve our existence.

This logic refers to psychological empowerment (e.g., Denegri-Knott et al., 2006), which designates improvement in skills, autonomy, and control of the consumer thanks to the quantified-self movement that transforms consumers by promoting a feeling of autonomy and control in their decision-making. This is made possible by the perception of a gain in skills thanks to the use of technologies. Indeed, technological development has given rise to a new profile of customers who are tech-savvy and knowledgeable, and becoming more informed and demanding. They are also becoming actors of their consumption using different kinds of digital devices, including the IoT and connected objects, to strengthen their capacity, their power to act, and their autonomy.

For example, in the field of connected healthcare, quantified-self devices allow users to distinguish between the lived body and the cared and measured body. By giving access to knowledge of one's body, the quantified-self favors the change from an intuitive approach to the body to an apprehension mediated by its objective data, reserved until now for doctors. The relationship between caregivers and the medical community has changed, taking advantage of the knowledge gained, including self-measurement and the search for information to interpret it. Patients are more knowledgeable, more demanding of their doctors, and are seeking to play a more active role in their diagnosis and choice of treatment.

On the other hand, the quantified-self is considered a disempowering practice for its users. Thus, a critical view of self-measurement practices questions the capacity of the quantified-self to be a source of empowerment. Some scholars have pointed to the fetishization of data, which is beyond the claim of regaining the power of self-appropriation, presented as the aim of self-quantified activities.

According to this criticism, self-quantified users may internalize social and well-being norms without sufficient insight, leading to an unlimited search for performance. Indeed, as one's evaluation is based on inter-individual comparison, the standard always is moving, and the person potentially never produces enough "normal" or worthy data. By altering the capacity to rely on the intuitive perception of one's performance, which is likely to foster critical distance to norms that cannot be applied uniformly to all, the objective apprehension of oneself or one's activities by applications with studied ergonomics, which individuals blindly rely upon, is more alienating than emancipating.

Moreover, the data produced by the applications and connected objects can be recovered by the manufacturers for commercial purposes—that is, the privacy of the user is eroded. The quantified-self is also criticized as a movement that promotes individualism, where the emphasis on performance, responsibility, and self-improvement weakens the individual and, potentially, collective unity. These criticisms tend to consider self-quantified users as relatively passive and unreflective actors of a technological system, and give a unifying vision of the phenomenon.

However, the question of the reflexivity of self-quantifiers requires examination of their practices and the meaning they give to them, which also reveals the diversity of uses of self-quantification. In this sense, other scholars reject the idea that self-quantifiers are passive, and distinguish three main attitudes toward quantified-self practice outcomes:

1. "full awareness," which refers to the strong presence of oneself that the quantified-self allows one to access;
2. "resistance," by becoming involved actors and regaining control;
3. a "narrative" practice, by posting stories about one's performance on social media and other online communities.

Other studies based on a description of self-quantifiers' practices highlight a more nuanced view due to the ambiguities of measurement. These ambiguities can turn some people off the practice or lead to subjectification of the measurements, even though this is supposed to objectify the practice or the body, with the consequence of focusing on certain measurements that are more amenable to interpretation, which can lead to the loss of a global vision of the self.

Ambiguous in its capacity to emancipate the individual, the practice of quantified-self is also ambiguous in its collective dimension. The sharing of personal data is often perceived as a manifestation of the desire to expose oneself, and those others involved in the measurement process would be spectators of a staging of one's identity.

BOX 6.1   THE DARK SIDE OF SLEEP TRACKERS

Sleep trackers in the form of connected watches, headbands, and devices placed on the bed or the bedside table are now fashionable devices used by various user groups to monitor/track and improve their sleep. These objects, all linked to apps downloaded on the user's phone, are selling like hotcakes. However, specialists and doctors believe that the data collected by these devices are not always reliable and can exacerbate symptoms related to insomnia. The explanation is simple: worrying about meeting one's "sleep goals" can worsen the user's anxiety and cause them to lose sleep.

In 2017, researchers at Northwestern University School of Medicine and Rush University School of Medicine coined the term "orthosomnia" to refer to this unhealthy obsession with getting perfect sleep. They noticed that many patients complained about the data recorded, such as rapid eye movement (REM) sleep duration. The vast amount of data generated after each night, accompanied by complex-sounding terms such as percentage of sleep deprivation, sleep patterns, and graphs that compare the individual's sleep to other people's sleep only creates confusion.

Many patients spend more time measuring and understanding their sleep when in bed, ultimately worsening the insomnia they already suffer. Moreover, doctors have a hard time convincing patients to switch off their phone and put the data on their screens into perspective. Yet, researchers at consumer electronics and fitness company Fitbit believe that few people suffer from severe anxiety insomnia. For them, monitoring sleep is primarily a reminder of the importance of bedtime and wake-up times, as well as the effects of sports or alcohol consumption on sleep. It is therefore relatively complex to estimate how reliable these apps and devices to monitor sleep are, since the discourses of the companies involved and the medical profession are very different.

3.2   Consumer Resistance to Connected Objects

While it is true that connected objects can offer consumers many advantages—such as convenience, time and energy savings, and new services (e.g., health, energy, diet)—there are still major challenges to be met. Indeed, the advent of connected objects implies new modes of regulation concerning safety and privacy, two critical issues for adopting these objects.

Moreover, studies show that many consumers question their usefulness, raise concerns about their intrusive aspects, and reject the dominant discourse that emphasizes the potential of this market and the revolutionary aspect of these objects (e.g., Hsu and Lin, 2016). In this sense, consumers can show resistance to innovation in general (and connected objects in particular). This resistance should meet three conditions: (1) a force must be exerted on the subject; (2) it must be perceived; and (3) the subject must seek to eliminate it.

Regarding consumer resistance to connected objects, we can note that various actors, such as companies and governments, are part of this ecosystem and thus can be a pressing force, collecting sensitive insights and data about consumers without their knowledge. This is the surveillance society. The aversion can be due to the objects themselves as they are likely to reinforce human dependence on machines, since any everyday object is likely to become a connected object (e.g., refrigerator, vacuum, TV, curtains).

On the other hand, consumers perceive pressure on them as they are aware of this power and believe that connected objects make them more dependent on machines. Regarding the third condition of resistance, the subject must seek to eliminate it, it should be noted that this condition is reflected via the activism of some online communities calling on consumers to be aware of the dangers of connected objects and to put in place strategies to deal with them.

Therefore, companies need to examine the main factors that prevent consumers from adopting connected objects and recognize what the forms of resistance might be. Exploring these two subjects allows companies to understand and anticipate the factors that could hinder the development of connected objects that should respond to consumers' needs while providing them with assurance in terms of privacy and safety.

Several studies have examined the forms of resistance expressed by consumers toward innovations, new products, and technological devices to understand why products fail (e.g., Kerr et al., 2012). Marketing scholars define resistance as a set of negative responses that consumers have to the functioning of the market and the behaviors of firms that they consider conflicting. These forms of resistance have multiple impacts on the company's business, including tainting its image, increasing the failure rate of its new products, and slowing the adoption of its innovations.

Numerous forms of resistance have been identified. For example, while Fournier (1998) analyzed resistance according to intensity—avoidance, reduction of consumption, and active rebellion—Peñaloza and Price (1993) defined consumer resistance as individual versus collective, radical versus reformist, targeting products versus signs, using the marketing system as an instrument of resistance versus other means of change outside of that system. When it comes to consumer resistance to connected objects that are perceived as innovations and new products, the literature shows three main factors explaining resistance: human, innovation, and market factors.

3.2.1   Human factors

These are related to the consumer's personality and perceived vulnerability. Faced with an increasingly connected world and increasingly complex technologies, the issue of user vulnerability is becoming more acute. Vulnerability refers to notions of powerlessness, loss of control, and dependency, and may be imposed or deliberate (Batat and Tanner, 2021). By adopting connected objects, users can potentially express different forms of vulnerability due to exposure to risks related to data management, health (physical and psychological), and expectations of the technology. Thus, perceived risks can be potential sources of opposition to the adoption of connected objects. Studies show that perceived risks enhance consumer resistance to innovation. These perceived risks can be categorized into six typologies:

- Safety risk is related to the security of the communication between connected objects and refers to the hacking of data and the taking control of the object by unauthorized third parties.
- Physical risk is linked to the consumer's health due to the significant volume of waves emitted, especially as some connected objects are in direct contact with the body (e.g., bracelets, chips).
- Performance risk is associated with connected objects' reliability in terms of functioning, measurement, quality of data, or expected performance and value.
- Financial risk includes losses in terms of investing in unsuitable connected objects and consumer expectations.
- Privacy risk is related to the collection and use of sensitive personal information by connected objects without the consumer's knowledge.
- Psychological risk refers to the risk of technological dependence and of isolation caused by the substitution of communication with humans.

3.2.2   Innovation factors

These are related to the characteristics of connected objects, which include three aspects: connectivity, intelligence, and ubiquity. Connectivity refers to the ability of connected objects to integrate communication protocols, allowing the exchange of information with their environment, other objects, or servers. This characteristic can increase consumer resistance as users have no control over the information communicated. Likewise, users may be against the idea of sensitive data being communicated without their consent or knowledge. Resistance can also be explained by the fact that the consumer is not necessarily aware of the nature of the data collected and their later use. The intelligence aspect of connected objects allows them to make decisions autonomously based on data previously captured. This aspect can lead the consumer to lose control of the object's functioning. In addition, reliability issues and/ or security flaws can lead the object to endanger the consumer (e.g., hacking), which thus prevents consumers from adopting connected objects in their daily life. Ubiquity, which reflects the omnipresence of connected objects, anytime and from any support, can represent another obstacle to adopting connected objects. Fear of a generalized surveillance system and the health risks due to the high volume of waves emitted everywhere are among factors that lead consumers to resist the adoption of these technologies.

3.2.3   Market factors

These are related to the mechanisms of innovation diffusion on the market. Resistance can be linked to companies' advertising communication and their actions on the connected object market, such as customized commercial offerings based on data collected without the consumer's knowledge. Thus, resistance reactions may appear against a dominant discourse that is both promotional and prescriptive. Connected objects are often presented as a positive revolution that everyone will want to accept. The market then exercises a dominant power with a discourse mainly highlighting the advantages of connected objects without alerting consumers to their possible dangers. Consumers can then express a desire to escape this dominant system and thus reject connected objects as a form of expression of freedom.

4   HOW CAN COMPANIES USE THE IOT AND CONNECTED OBJECTS TO CREATE PHYGITAL EXPERIENCES?

The IoT represents an essential growth lever for companies to create seamless and engaging customer experiences in the phygital setting, where both physical and digital consumption and shopping activities are aligned. The IoT and connected objects have various benefits as they allow companies to develop a better understanding and knowledge of customers' consumption patterns thanks to the data collected by the connected objects in their homes and in real time. Indeed, faced with increased consumer versatility, it is crucial for companies to reposition the customer at the heart of their strategy by embracing a customer-centric culture. This requires them to rethink their marketing and communication actions by using the IoT and the insights generated by connected objects to strengthen their customer relationship, and thus increase customer and brand loyalty.

The IoT can provide a powerful lever allowing companies to meet the challenges related to developing an effective retention plan and increase customer satisfaction in different settings and in real time across various sectors. Whether in the field of healthcare (e.g., optimized patient care), transportation (e.g., intelligent traffic management), or urban planning (e.g., smart homes and cities), the IoT market continues to expand by combining physical and digital objects to offer new interactions with the customer and provide a powerful marketing lever, generating opportunities through different actions as outlined below.

4.1   Offering a Highly Customized and Seamless Customer Experience

The IoT and connected objects allow companies to deliver an enriched customer experience in physical and digital settings. The customer is at the center of any marketing strategy. The key question for companies is how to stand out from the competition and offer a unique experience. This customer experience needs to be more sophisticated and highly personalized. Thanks to the IoT and connected objects, brands can, in real time, communicate information and propose offers (products and services) adapted to customers' consumption habits or their latest online search. Knowing the consumer better allows companies to be redirected in a very straightforward way to their interests and needs, and thus optimize their purchasing path, sometimes even in real time. For example, the connected and geolocatable MagicBand bracelet set up in Disney parks, coupled with the My Disney Experience app, offers visitors an outstanding experience. It highlights the most relevant activities according to visitor profile; it also offers guests the ability to unlock their hotel rooms, to benefit from a personalized itinerary, avoid queues, and pay without physically taking out their wallets. In addition to improving the fluidity of the customer's journey in the resort, the bracelet creates an environment conducive to prolonging the visit or, better yet, renewing it.

4.2   Improving the Company's Targeting and Segmentation Strategies

Customer segmentation is an essential step in adapting communication actions to the different profiles of defined groups. However, this conventional "one-to-many" approach has its limits today: for example, it forces the company to deliver messages that do not always correspond to the needs of all targeted users. Therefore, companies need to be capable of identifying customers' consumption habits and placing them in the context of their lives to address them better. In this sense, the IoT and its collected data reflect the accurate and unbiased use of the product/service: information that proves to be valuable for companies. It allows them to design experiences capable of adapting to customers' real expectations. For example, many car insurance companies are using the IoT and collected data on drivers to re-segment their customers and thus propose suitable offerings and tailor-made policies that fit more with customer profiles (e.g., rates based on the driver's actual behavior).

4.3   Identifying Pain Points that Can Harm the Experience

Identifying pain points to reduce their occurrence is another objective behind the implementation of IoT devices. Companies can act in two ways: intervening in the product or in the service. If a product shows early signs of failure, the agent responsible is contacted in real time by the mechanism connected to this object (e.g., a sensor) and can fix the problem, even before the customer has experienced this failure. Thus, by analyzing data collected through the IoT, companies can anticipate customer behavior by detecting potential risks. For example, a drop in the use of a service or product, such as an alarm system, can enhance the risk of unsubscribing. Thanks to this information, companies can implement the necessary actions to avoid the loss of these users by identifying the pain points and proposing an adapted service that considers actual consumption habits. The IoT is therefore considered a means of providing the customer with an extended or even enhanced service, allowing for cost optimization, greater efficiency in processing requests, and optimal customer retention.

4.4   Enhancing Customer Support and Anticipating Future Requirements

The implementation of IoT devices connected to a customer relationship management (CRM) database is an opportunity for any customer service to obtain much more accurate and valuable insights on the context of customer needs. These technologies allow companies to better understand and identify customer requests and issues and therefore better qualify them, assign them directly to the right contact person, and thus put an end to multiple redirections to different agents. They then process them more quickly and efficiently, resulting in a smoother customer experience and saving time and therefore productivity for support teams. Regarding the anticipation of upcoming consumer requirements, the IoT and connected objects allow companies to implement relevant, personalized, and fast incentives. When users interact with brands through smart objects, personalized actions can be triggered automatically when required indicators are reached. Deployed at the right time, these rewards will reinforce customer satisfaction and maintain a perceived "value" interaction. Through the IoT, companies can know and even anchor themselves in the daily habits of their customers, which allows them to guarantee and even increase their attachment to the brand.

Although the IoT and connected objects can have multiple benefits for companies in terms of knowing their customers better and improving their online and offline experiences, there are some challenges related to the use of these technologies that companies have to consider in their implementation processes. Indeed, the gains of the IoT rely on the data of many users, provided by customers themselves, that need to be protected. Building a relationship of trust while using connected objects to share customer data with companies requires the companies to be transparent and develop ethical practices regarding data safety, confidentiality, storage, and further use.

Companies should therefore provide information about how customer data are collected and processed. They also should provide customers with control over their data to ensure that they can control their use at all times. The IoT and connected objects represent a powerful lever for companies to transform and customize the customer experience. It is therefore vital to implement a robust and rigorous data protection system throughout the entire life cycle (offers/customer) and across the entire production line (e.g., manufacturers, service providers, partners).

KEY TAKEAWAYS

This chapter emphasized the most significant challenges for both companies and consumers in terms of integrating and using the IoT and connected objects. In this chapter, I identified the impacts of these technologies on consumer behaviors and the company's design of suitable and satisfying customer experiences. The chapter revealed different factors (personal, market, and innovation characteristics) that can lead consumers to adopt or resist using connected objects. Additionally, the chapter highlighted the idea of consumer (dis)empowerment related to the IoT and connected objects to allow users to retain control of their consumption and monitor their daily practices to achieve well-being. This chapter sheds light on the benefits and challenges companies should consider while implementing the IoT and connected objects to learn more about their customers and create seamless and highly personalized customer experiences.

7. Phygital customer experience strategy enabled by gamification

CHAPTER OVERVIEW

This chapter introduces gamification as a strategy enabling the creation of enjoyable, playful, and immersive phygital experiences. Gamification is not a new concept; it has been discussed in the game design field, but its introduction into the marketing arena is recent and can cover different fields, ranging from communication and marketing to customer experience and loyalty programs. This chapter defines and discusses gamification from a marketing perspective by answering the question: How can companies implement gamification actions to improve the customer experience while dealing with customer journey pain points? Opportunities and challenges related to the use of gamification as a marketing approach and illustrative examples will also be presented in this chapter.

1 THE ADVANCE OF GAMIFICATION: FROM GAME DESIGN TO MARKETING

The term "gamification" was coined in the video game and design fields. The first referenced usage was in 2008 (Reeves and Read, 2009), but the term was not fully adopted until the second half of the 2010s. Competing terms continue to be used, and new ones are still being introduced. However, gamification has gradually become institutionalized as the most common term. It is also a highly contested term, especially within the games industry and game studies community. Dissatisfaction with how the concept has been implemented, oversimplifications, and interpretations have led to different conceptualizations.

Conceptualization of the term "gamification" was proposed as early as 2002 by Nick Pelling, a games designer who introduced gamification as a globally recognized trend on his blog post, written several years after he coined the term (Pelling, 2011). The current development of gamification focused on explaining the process examined through the well-established mechanics, dynamics, and aesthetics (MDE) framework (Hunicke et al., 2004), developed in the game design field, and covers three main areas related to games: mechanics, dynamics, and emotions.

• Game mechanics refer to instructions, goals, rules, settings, interaction types, and situational boundaries. These elements are exclusively related to the designers' decisions and do not change from one user to another across time.
• Game dynamics include the behaviors and interactions that emerge when people begin to play, when they participate in a gamified experience. These constructed dynamics are more difficult to predict as they are player-dependent and can change over time.
• Emotions reflect the positive or negative affective states that occur when people participate in the game experience, whether alone or with others.

These three components are interrelated and work together to create an engaging gamified experience that considers two perspectives: the designers' and the players'. Thus, the challenge lies in implementing adequate mechanisms that will engage users in a highly interactive dynamic, and consequently generate both positive emotions from the user perspective and desired outcomes from the game designer or company perspective.

In the marketing field, gamification appeared with the first airline loyalty programs, offering Air Miles to reward frequent fliers (Batat, 2019b). Depending on their objectives, companies have implemented different strategies to provide a positive experience to their customers. Gamification is one of those facilitating mechanisms that have been instituted to enhance the customer experience and, in the long run, engage the consumer. Gamification is a concept that has been around for many years; but it was only in 2010 that it gained popularity with companies interested in engaging their customers and employees.

While professionals in the field of game design and video games proposed the first clarification of the concept of gamification, its adoption by marketing professionals seems confusing because of its limited conceptualization. Although gamification is mainly associated with the world of economics, this notion is, in fact, much broader and covers many contexts and meanings. When it comes to implementing gamification in marketing, Coll (2013) states the example of loyalty cards and bonus points, such as Air Miles; this is an excellent one, which demonstrates that this gamification strategy is not a game at all, but rather a mode of surveillance, social control, and biopower.

2   CONCEPTUALIZATIONS AND CHARACTERISTICS OF GAMIFICATION

Deterding and colleagues (2011) define gamification as the application of design, psychological elements, and the mechanisms of video games in other contexts and fields. Other scholars who specialized in the gaming field have defined it as the mobilization of collective human intelligence through games to solve problems that computers cannot yet solve or that cannot be solved by overly limited groups of humans (e.g., Von Ahn, 2006; Quinn and Bederson, 2011). In this sense, the idea of "games with a purpose" (GWAP) has emerged, and designates gamification as games with a useful and productive purpose that result from human–computer interactions. This section examines the diverse definitions of gamification provided by different authors across disciplines and analyzes the characteristics of a gamified user experience.

2.1   What Is Gamification?

Essentially, gamification refers to games, not to "play," which can be understood as a broader and more flexible concept. In research that focused on games and their relationship to playfulness, scholars distinguished "gaming" from "playing" by stating that while playfulness designates a freer, more expressive, and even more unrestrained recombination of attitudes and meanings, gaming takes over playing by structuring it with rules and a goal-oriented competitive principle (Salen and Zimmerman, 2004). In this sense, classic definitions in games studies establish that gaming and games, as opposed to playing and toys, are characterized by explicit rule systems driven by competition or struggle in which actors pursue their own goals and achieve distinct outcomes (Juul, 2005). Thus, most of these definitions focus on the common system of PBL—points, badges, leaderboards—with additional rewards (e.g., bonuses). The gamified system defines a goal and steps to reach it, with varying levels of difficulty.

Other research underlined the distinction between game and play by emphasizing the crucial role of values and state of mind generated while playing a video game (e.g., Juul, 2010). However, some scholars (e.g., Deterding, 2012) have criticized the gamified aspect of applications—for example, created by different brands that almost exclusively focus on promoting goal-oriented play (the gaming-focused approach), leaving rare options for open-ended, exploratory, and free play (the playing-focused approach). By combining both playful (free play) and "gameful" (rule-based) aspects, companies can offer successful, engaging experiences in which gamification can be implemented in a game universe characterized by three factors: (1) gamefulness, which refers to the experiential and behavioral aspects of gamification; (2) gameful interactions, reflecting the artifacts that give access to these aspects; and (3) gameful design using game design elements and purposes.

Another definition by Petkov and colleagues (2011) focuses on the psychological dimension of gamification. It introduces the notion of player motivation by referring to gamification as a persuasive technique that attempts to influence user behavior by activating individual motivations through game design elements. Thus, the focus here is no longer only on the components of the PBL system; it is also on the factors that influence the participant and make him or her decide whether or not to continue his or her progress toward the final goal.

Drawing on the above definitions and considering a marketing perspective, gamification can be defined as a process that can be implemented by companies to meet certain objectives. The means to achieve these objectives, as well as the gamification mechanism to be implemented, will be different depending on the target. According to Huotari and Hamari (2017), gamification in marketing refers to a process that reinforces a service with suggestive capabilities for gamified experiences to support overall user value creation. Unlike the definitions provided in game studies, this definition emphasizes the purpose of gamification rather than the method, strategy, and outcome for the company implementing gamification.

2.2   Three Key Characteristics of Gamification

Gamification can be characterized by three main elements: game features/ mechanics, benefits, and player profile. It is thus the combination of these elements that creates engaging and immersive gamification experiences.

2.2.1   Game features
This refers to the use of elements such as points, badges, leaderboards, and so forth, and is common to most games. Depending on their implementation, such features build a path for players and provide feedback on the actions they perform. Several categories of elements constituting game mechanics can be considered by companies when designing the ultimate gamification experience, as stated by Dale (2014). These include rewards (points, bonuses); tasks in the form of challenges; community through ranking and collaboration; transparency of results by incorporating a progress bar or feedback; time should include a countdown or speed of execution; and luck (e.g., lottery). The way these elements are used, that is, their implementation within a unified system, will enhance the game experience, which should be playful, interesting, exciting, and fulfilling for the players, who will feel involved and thus be more eager for long-term participation and commitment.

2.2.2 Benefits

This is considered an integral part of gamification design and experience. Research indicates two types of expected benefit: benefits for the editor of the game or the company, and benefits for the user. The benefits of gamification are closely related to the objectives to be achieved. On the one hand, a company that implements gamification does so for a precise reason (e.g., to increase sales, improve its reputation or productivity, or to enhance customer loyalty). By defining clear objectives, the company can then design a suitable gamification experience that will encourage certain behaviors and actions from participants, whether employees or customers. On the other hand, the benefits to the players should also be considered. Indeed, earning points is not enough in itself to encourage actions, especially in the long term. Other user benefits companies should consider in their gamification experience include aesthetics, a feeling of learning something, fulfillment, and socialization, among others. As a result, identification of user benefits is related to the player profiles that companies need to capture to implement suitable and efficient actions to target them.

2.2.3 Player profile

Bartle (1996) identified four main player profiles: socializer, achiever, explorer, and killer. Socializers are more interested in relationships within the game than in the game itself. They have less interest in winning the game, but they like being part of a team and participating in the collective effort. Achievers, even if they want to win, are more oriented toward mastering the game mechanics. They follow the rules, learn from their mistakes, and work out ways to get to the top of the leaderboard. They are determined, aim for excellence, and like to show their expertise. Explorers are focused on discovery. They aspire to know every element of the game, and pride themselves on showing other players what they have discovered or understood. As such, they are good team players even though they tend to go it alone. Finally, killers are interested in competing: their objective is to be the best, and they consider the other players as the opposition; they aim to demonstrate their superiority and impose themselves as masters of the game. They are calculators and only collaborate with other players if it helps them achieve their goals. Therefore, when designing gamified experiences from the player perspective, companies need to imagine a system that can address all types of player. The use of varied game mechanics allowing players to progress according to their own mode of functioning, aspirations, and level is thus a requirement and a condition for long-term involvement.

3 HOW CAN COMPANIES IMPLEMENT GAMIFICATION TO DESIGN ENGAGING CUSTOMER EXPERIENCES?

Companies can implement gamification at different levels to cover the various stages of customer experience, ranging from the lowest level, such as a series of actions and decisions taken by the consumer to obtain bonuses, to the highest where customers are fully engaged in the game experience. At the lowest level, gamification is seen as a benefit that will be added to a global strategy to engage consumers in a particular issue (Batat, 2019b).

At the highest level, companies can integrate the game mechanics into existing platforms, services, and products. They can, for instance, incorporate mechanics from a video game into a website, thereby pushing users to comment more on the different product series and associated articles. This mechanism leads to the integration of a system through the accumulation of points: the more users post comments, the more points they get. To generate value for the content posted, the points also depend on the number of people who like these comments. In another level of gamification, geolocation, the objective is to develop dialogue and engagement that can be achieved rapidly. This example shows that gamification, which requires a low level of commitment very quickly, is effective in changing user behavior.

Therefore, companies operating in different sectors should approach gamification to create playful customer experiences within a non-game setting. To design immersive and entertaining experiences that can engage customers, linking physical and digital settings, companies can implement gamification strategies by considering three main components related to games that are employed in a business context: ingredients, design, and a non-game context. The following section explains and discusses these three gamification components.

3.1 Gamification Elements and Design

Studies show that successful gamification should consider two main elements: artifactual and social aspects of games. The artifactual elements should be considered more as a means of gameful interpretation rather than elements that are themselves gameful (e.g., Taylor, 2009). Indeed, the characteristic of gamified apps, compared to games, should provide more subtle experiences that combine playful and gameful elements along with more instrumental and functional aspects. Reeves and Read (2009) suggest ten critical elements for designing good games:

1. personal representation through avatars;

2. 3-D environment;
3. narrative context;
4. feedback;
5. rewards;
6. marketplaces;
7. explicit rules defining the competition;
8. teams;
9. parallel communication systems;
10. pressure generated by a time limit.

Each of these elements taken individually could not define the game; it is their amalgamation that makes the game and enables it to be classified as such. For example, an avatar is necessary for role-playing, whereas in a game of cards it does not contribute anything to the mechanics. While the design of a game should be positioned in relation to these elements, the design of a gamified app will rely on some of them without building a complete game (Batat, 2019b).

Thus, gamification uses the mechanisms of the game to divert consumers to a different goal: to act on their behaviors. Thus, the game becomes an environment in which brands come closer to users as they notice the positive impact this creates between the brand and the consumer. Besides, while the play component refers to an entertainment function, gamification refers to a customer engagement function (Batat, 2019b). Gamification also suggests that companies should enhance the aesthetic aspects of the experience while offering customers the opportunity to develop their knowledge and challenge themselves in a non-game context in which different values are assigned to various outcomes. Customers as players can then exert effort to influence the outcome of the gamification experience. In addition, to create suitable and immersive gamification experiences, companies should consider different levels in the design process, which are more or less abstract (e.g., Taylor, 2009). In game studies, authors refer to five key levels requiring different design patterns:

- The interface of game design patterns. This refers to common and recognized digital design elements and solutions tailored to a particular issue in a given context (e.g., rankings, levels).
- Game design mechanism. This consists of the current reworking of game design elements that relate to gameplay (e.g., time restriction, limited resources).
- Design principles and heuristics. These include evaluation principles to address a design problem or analyze a given design solution (e.g., specific objectives, diversity of playing styles).

- Game design model. This encompasses game components or the game experience, such as aesthetics, challenge, or fantasy.
- Game design method. This refers to specific game design practices and processes (e.g., testing).

A further vital ingredient, namely user engagement, contributes to the success of a gamification strategy. In this sense, by proposing an ecosystem based on game mechanics, gamification is an environment where the player/user becomes involved. Companies should consider three components to enhance user engagement within the gamified experience: vigor, dedication, and absorption. Indeed, playfulness is inseparable from the notion of motivation, and we can consider gamification as a non-game version of play designed to foster motivation, encouraging participants to spend time on the challenges they are offered and concentrate on completing the task at hand. Thanks to gamification, companies can foster different forms of user motivation, ranging from personal achievement, empowerment, and ownership to social influence, scarcity, chance, and avoidance (Chou, 2015).

User motivation to engage in gamification can also be either intrinsic or extrinsic. Intrinsic motivations are related to the will and enthusiasm to perform an action, while extrinsic motivations are related to rewards. It is generally accepted in the field of gamification that extrinsic motivations are useful in the short term since once the reward has been earned, there is no need to continue, while intrinsic motivations favor actions over the long term. Likewise, Batat (2019b) suggests that a set of common characteristics emerges in a highly immersive gamification experience:

- Challenges that promote self-motivation of the player, whether an enigma to solve or elements to discover.
- Rewards to recompense the player for his/her commitment and encourage him/her to continue. These can be real (gifts, prizes, etc.) or virtual (access to higher status, badges, and medals/trophies).
- Captivating scenarios through a story unfolding around a theme. Storytelling is therefore at the heart of the gameplay. The story can be based on real characters and facts (historical or not) or fictitious (imagined for the game or inspired by films, comics, or novels).
- A blurring of the borders between fiction (game) and reality (a physical place), a mix between the real world and the virtual realm. This immersion in the world of play favors the emergence of the experience of "flow" specific to the game experience—defined by Csikszentmihalyi (1990) as a mental state in which individuals are totally immersed in the action they are engaging in.

- Strong interactivity of the player as an active participant. Indeed, the player is asked to produce real work of personal reflection to solve the riddle.
- Collaboration between players who form a community at the time of the resolution of the enigma. They combine individual and collective competence and collaborate either virtually or in the real world.

BOX 7.1   TRIPADVISOR USES GAMIFICATION VIA REVIEWS TO ENGAGE ITS COMMUNITY

TripAdvisor, a leading actor in online customer reviews and tourist advice, used a gamification system to engage its community. Since the website functions mainly through activity and content posted by its users, it is essential to encourage members to frequently post reviews on the platform. To do so, TripAdvisor decided to use compliments directed to its most active reviewers by sending an email congratulating them for their contributions and giving them a ranking compared to other members. Those in the top ten even receive a personalized message encouraging them to write even more to become number one.

This is a good example of gamification through the mechanism of competition: the user, stimulated by his/her desire to reach first place, will be even more inclined to post new reviews. With these campaigns, TripAdvisor observed a 185 percent increase in click rates on its emails compared to previous campaigns. The results are just as satisfying: almost half of users wrote a review after opening the email, and the number of reviews submitted increased by 354 percent in the week the email was sent. The platform also introduced a badge system, which is awarded following reviews of the different categories of places visited (hotels, restaurants, etc.). Each user moves up one level in these categories, motivated by collecting all the available badges: a supplementary way for TripAdvisor to enrich its data collection.

3.2   The Non-Game Context of Gamification

Gamification uses game elements for purposes other than the non-play use that would be expected in the context of an entertainment game. Gamification can be applied in several contexts mixing entertainment and seriousness along with commercial and educational purposes, covering different domains, such as serious games, training games, or health games. Considering a business perspective, gamification is one of the techniques used by various companies to encourage employee involvement or boost sales by engaging customers in gamified shopping experiences. Thus, gamification in a business context uses game design elements without necessarily relying on games, or necessarily on elements related to professional skills. Thus, organizations can implement internal (involving employees) or external (targeting customers) gamification levels.

BOX 7.2   HERMÈS' *H-PITCHHH* APP OFFERS A GAMIFIED EXPERIENCE LINKING REAL AND VIRTUAL SETTINGS

To celebrate its 2018 theme, "Let's Play!", Hermès, the luxury perfume and leather goods brand, launched *H-pitchhh* – a horseshoe-throwing mobile game app. Horseshoe pitching is one of the oldest games and is still very popular in the United States. Throughout three days of competition, participants were invited to play in the galleries of the Grand Palais in Paris, on a real playground with stakes and horseshoes. The virtual player has five horseshoes, and, with the tip of his/her finger or a movement of the arm, the player directs and throws the iron toward the stake. In order to immerse participants in an interactive, playful, luxury gaming experience, the game guides the player through five different realms, including immersion in an aquatic and fun space, climbing the stairs of the Hermès store at 24 Faubourg Saint-Honoré, and a walk in a garden. Each world is illustrated by a musical theme, from hip-hop to calypso, electro or rock.

H-pitchhh is also a live game where users can challenge their connected friends. Hermès designed a trailer to the Western-inspired promotional video to promote the app (downloadable from the App Store and Google Play), where players dressed in the company's new collection clash in a desert landscape. For the luxury brand, this event app perfectly matched its equestrian activity and its values of tradition and respect. However, the gamification experience within both real and virtual spheres also emphasizes another vital aspect of the luxury house: its creativity. Furthermore, the Hermès *H-pitchhh* app shows the ability of the brand to adapt to new mobile uses and gamification.

Gamification implemented in an organizational setting can take different forms. Werbach and Hunter (2012) distinguish three forms of organizational gamification, namely in the external environment, in the internal environment, and to foster behavioral change. While gamification in the external environment is aimed at people who are not part of the organization, it can nevertheless act as a catalyst and attract profiles and talents who would like to join the organization.

The internal environment addresses employees to encourage them to carry out specific actions and thus improve their performance or participate in the collective effort. Gamification targeting behavioral change aims to bring about changes in use for the benefit of the employee. An excellent example of this organizational gamification occurring in a non-game context is *My Marriott Hotel*, a game in which participants had to manage a hotel. To attract qualified talent, the Marriott group used an external environment. Depending on the player's performance, he or she could be invited to apply for a position within the group that matched his or her personality.

Gamification can also be used in the education context. The study conducted by Hakulinen and colleagues (2013) shows that gamification improves engagement in learning tasks and the motivation to learn. The activity is at the same time considered pleasant and entertaining. However, the study also points out that some aspects of gamification can be evaluated as poor: the difficulty of the tasks, the competition between the players, and the game's design.

When it comes to applying external gamification to attract customers, studies reveal that its effects on consumer engagement are mostly positive. Also, research highlights the moderating factors of gamification efficiency, and thus its ability to engage the user. These are essentially the motivation of the user, the type of service in which the game is implemented (e.g., gamification might not be appropriate for purely utilitarian services), and, finally, gratification (points, levels, etc.).

A study conducted by Hamari and Koivisto (2013) also highlights the role of player age and gender on the perceived benefits of gamification. These authors state that women perceive more social benefits than men and that the older the players, the more difficulties they perceive in interacting with gamified devices. Other studies highlighted an effect of gamification on different dimensions of the lived customer experience: cognitive (learning, willingness to learn), commitment, and pleasure. They also revealed the importance of the type of service/product being gamified as well as the elements of gameplay (e.g., grades, difficulty) in the effectiveness of the device.

If the device is too complex or misunderstood, gamification could also reduce the customer's shopping experience and limit his/her commitment. Furthermore, gamification is not an end in itself. Other devices and strategies whose purpose is to contribute to the improvement of the customer experience and, more generally, to customer satisfaction have to be taken into account by companies to improve the overall customer experience.

BOX 7.3   SPOTIFY'S PERSONALIZED
"DISCOVERIES OF THE WEEK"
PLAYLISTS: DISCOVERY GAMIFICATION

The music streaming platform Spotify has set up a fully personalized weekly track selection for each user. The playlist, called "Discoveries of the Week," allows members to discover a compilation of tracks that match their musical tastes each week. Based on the user's listening history, it cross-references this information with that of other members with similar musical preferences thanks to a recommendation algorithm. The result is a unique selection of tracks, allowing people to discover new songs in a very intuitive way.

Spotify's promise with this feature is to offer a playlist as relevant to the user's tastes as possible as they use the platform. This way, the more they use Spotify, the more likely they are to like the selection. They will then browse the selection and discover its tracks and artists, exploring and sharing their new discoveries with their friends. This gamification through discovery is a good way for the service to build loyalty among its members and allow them to discover the depth of the catalog.

4   OPPORTUNITIES AND CHALLENGES OF GAMIFICATION IN CREATING SEAMLESS CUSTOMER EXPERIENCES

For companies, implementing gamification to create and enhance experiences represents a valuable source of value creation throughout the customer journey. Because of the potential of using game elements in a non-entertainment context, companies can utilize gamification to improve customer experiences, especially in relation to pain points in the customer journey, ranging from waiting in line and filling in data to exchanging a defective product— experiences that are necessary moments in the life of a brand but unpleasant from a customer perspective. All these moments represent a great opportunity for companies to transform the experience they offer by using gamification to make the customer journey fun and enjoyable while fixing a problem.

Nevertheless, although companies have been quick and efficient in integrating gaming mechanisms into the upstream phase related to the development of new products and services, they often limit themselves to points systems or badges awarded to users. In reality, gamification is much more complex. Firms can consider several levels and aspects to improve the customer experience and the overall journey. For instance, narrative design is also part of gamification and, above all, is the easiest element to implement. By creating a story with the selection of specific words, tone, look, and feel, companies can transform the actual functional experience into a playful and engaging journey by, for example, using humor or an emotional story, both online and offline.

Companies can also implement the highest level of gamification by creating an entire universe around the brand, in which playing and gaming (including the mechanics of a game device) are combined. Yet, the decision to set up a gamification system usually depends on the company's objective and the outcome sought, such as improving its visibility, targeting actual and prospective customers, increasing customer engagement, improving the shopping experience, or enhancing customer loyalty, among others.

These objectives refer to moments in the customer journey that lend themselves to gamification. It is from a precise objective and a moment in the customer journey that reflections on the gamification system begin. Thus, by implementing a gamification strategy, companies can improve the overall customer experience, both online and offline, by focusing on different elements. Below are some examples that illustrate how gamification can create engaging and enjoyable customer experiences while solving problems:

- *Gamification to promote products and increase sales.* The famous coffee chain Starbucks used gamification through My Starbucks Rewards as a promotional action. This involved the use of a points card: the more products customers consume, the more stars they accumulate, and the more levels they reach to finally get rewards. A good idea that relies on successfully passing levels and a reward system is a fundamental aspect of game dynamics.
- *Gamification to create and enhance commitment among community members.* The sports brand Nike used its Nike+ app to create a gamified sports experience. Many running enthusiasts are familiar with this app, which makes running a little more than a simple exercise to burn calories. With Nike+ users measure themselves and compare their results among the Nike community as this tool records speed, distance covered, and calories burned during physical activity. Runners share their results with other runners, whose participation and interaction within the community contribute to improving and spreading Nike's image and enhancing the commitment of members within the community. The sharing of athletic performance strengthens the community's identity and the individual's commitment to a common goal: work out and get healthy.
- *Gamifying customer experience to cope with pain points.* Kenzo, the French luxury ready-to-wear brand, decided to address customer frustration during limited-edition sales. A key moment is when its young and connected target consumers indirectly fight to purchase new products. The most disappointed among them did not hesitate to let it be known on

social media by challenging the brand. Kenzo therefore launched *Shopping League* in 2018, inviting Internet users to compete via online mini-games to catch and buy exclusive pieces during express sales. This feature brought together 20,000 players in 24 hours and created a strong buzz around the new Kenzo Sonic Sneakers: 100 pairs were sold in a few hours, six times more than in previous private online sales. This action game was selected because of the target users' profiles, their emotional state, and the moment of the journey. This operation was a real success on several levels: marking the brand's differentiation, creating customer proximity, increasing sales, and of course, handling the pain point.

- *Gamification to build bridges between various services.* Amazon implemented gamification to build bridges within its ecosystem of digital services. To keep attracting subscribers, Amazon Prime Video is betting on its original productions and turning its release into immersive events. For example, for the release of Season 2 of *Jack Ryan*, the platform paired the TV show with its powerful e-commerce platform. Viewers could take a screenshot of an object from a scene in the series and post it on Twitter for a chance to win that object on the e-commerce platform. This action resulted in 30 million exchanges and feedback on social media in 24 hours, and an increase of more than 160 percent in views of the show.

- *Gamification to educate customers while improving the company's image.* To test adults' knowledge of vegetables, a supermarket chain used gamification to "trick" its online customers with captchas—automated tests to differentiate human users from a computer by asking them to identify images of cars or houses—based on vegetables to see if customers could recognize them. As a result, 95 percent of "trapped" users could not recognize chard, 63 percent did not recognize fennel, and 94 percent did not recognize salsify. Conversely, if customers passed the test, they received a 10 percent discount on their next fruit and vegetable order through their loyalty card. This gamification approach reinforced the educational dimension, which aligns with the brand's previous campaigns on consumer food well-being.

- *Gamification to enhance a social media campaign.* The confectionery brand M&M's developed its game *Eye-Spy Pretzel* via a social media launch. The app has its origins in the concept of hidden object games in that users have to find a small pretzel hidden among a mass of M&M's. This example of successful gamification managed to generate 25,000 new likes on the company's Facebook page, 6,000 shares, and more than 10,000 comments—enough to reach the campaign's goals.

These examples, among many others, underline the impact of well-thought-out gamification experiences thanks to detailed knowledge of the targets and their consumption habits beyond traditional points systems. Thus, gamification remains an infinite field of expression for companies. Also, unexpected partnerships and brand initiatives are even entering existing video games. For example, luxury brand Louis Vuitton created virtual clothes for avatars in the game *Fortnite*, and luxury sports car manufacturer Porsche promoted its 99X electric car live in a video game through online streaming platform Twitch.

Yet, although gamification can help companies solve problems and improve the customer experience, there are some challenges that companies should consider when engaging in gamification strategies. Batat states that one of the most significant challenges of gamification is related to limits to gamification by companies that use it to make a simple copy-and-paste of the mechanics that have already proved effective in video games. This practice is the subject of criticism by video game professionals as being too reductive and an appropriation of the concept by brands, as stated by Batat (2019b, p. 147):

> Gaming is not a question of integrating a badge, an avatar, a system of accumulation of points, or even a progress bar. The real gamification is upstream: it should result from a strategic reflection on the company's target, its needs, and the reasons for it. Gamification, in that it borrows the mechanics of the game, should be designed as a real game: based on powerful storytelling and an engaging user experience.

Besides, the literature shows that most gamification successes in business are related to large corporations; in small and medium-sized companies (SMEs) the results are more mixed (Woźniak, 2017). Why? The reason is that SMEs have less formalized procedures than large corporations. In the latter, employees are used to a system in which every action is calibrated, while SMEs operate more flexibly. Thus, the adoption of a gamification system is closer to employees' work habits in a large company.

Furthermore, analysis of the literature on other challenges for companies in their implementation of gamification shows the most common challenges are related to three aspects: "pointification," hacking, and exploitationware. Pointification refers to a system based on earning points. By using a points system, companies can lead their customers or employees to only focus on their ranking or the number of points earned, losing sight of the main objective, such as productivity or increasing sales. Also, if participants (both employees and customers) realize that the points have no value and that their efforts do not lead to anything concrete, they may end up losing interest in the system, and thus in the gamified experience.

Another drift is related to hacking or willingness to circumvent the game's rules, as stated by Van Roy and colleagues (2018). Some participants may then no longer play to win by following the rules but by cheating. In this case the main objective is shifted, and the whole point of gamification disappears in favor of a form of system manipulation. For this reason it is commonly accepted that gamification should be thought of not in terms of design skills or technical abilities but in terms of players and their motivation to engage in a gamification experience.

The last challenge related to the implementation of gamification to engage customers and employees is reflected by its exploitationware aspect— exploiting employees and customers by asking them for more under the pretext of gamification (Werbach and Hunter, 2012). This consequence arose from the idea that an involved employee or customer who will make an extra effort can generate rejections. Therefore, the design of the system should also consider the limits to be imposed on participants and safeguards to prevent this type of drift.

KEY TAKEAWAYS

This chapter underlined the importance of gamification to create playful and satisfying phygital experiences. Companies should consider gamification as a powerful tool to enhance their marketing and communication actions. Companies should also incorporate the fundamentals of the game in their customer experience design strategies, namely, the triptych of challenge–fulfillment–satisfaction. Each accomplished challenge generates in customers a sense of pleasure that drives them to continue playing in the entertaining universe created by the brand. What explains the trend for gamification is its impact in terms of consumer engagement. This chapter therefore explained how gamification could boost customer and employee engagement because it associates in users' minds the ability of the product or brand to challenge and be fulfilling.

8. Phygital customer experience strategy enabled by online 3-D printing platforms

CHAPTER OVERVIEW

This chapter presents online 3-D printing as a relevant device that allows companies to create customized and on-demand phygital customer experiences by shifting from online creations to tangible and physical objects. Although it is still too early to precisely determine where this digital technology will be adopted across industries and sectors, it appears to hold great potential, driven by continual progress in both the performance of the machines and the variety of materials that can be used. Thus, this chapter first sheds light on the progress of 3-D printing technology and its role in engaging customers in a co-creation process where they can produce their own consumption items, ranging from food to furniture, by using different 3-D printing platforms. Second, the chapter explains the challenges and opportunities related to 3-D printing platforms that companies need to consider in designing experiences, both online and offline, to offer highly customized and on-demand phygital experiences to their customers.

1   3-D PRINTING: FROM INDUSTRY TO CONSUMER SOCIETY

Three-dimensional (3-D) printing is a technology that allows, with the help of a machine called a 3-D printer, the manufacture of a physical object from a digital model. This technology, which breaks with traditional manufacturing techniques, was born in industry. The history and development of 3-D printing technology followed the following stages:

- In the early 1980s, French and American engineers experimented with manufacturing by adding successive layers of material.
- In 1984, a patent application was filed for a machine intended for rapid prototyping and operating according to a process called stereolithography (SL or SLA), not yet called 3-D printing.

- In 1986, this new type of printer was commercialized after the development of Standard Tessellation Language (STL), a digital file format that became the reference for 3-D printing.
- The term "3-D printing" first appeared in 1996. It covered various additive manufacturing techniques distinguished from each other by the technology used: filament deposition, powder bonding, powder laser sintering/fusion, stereolithography, digital light processing, and material projection.

Additive manufacturing technologies have been used in large-scale industries for almost 30 years. Although 3-D printing has existed since the 1980s (and uses technologies that were mostly patented during this time), it is only in the last decade that it has been highlighted as a valuable production asset for companies across different sectors. It is only since the 2010s that additive manufacturing has appeared and been developed in the marketplace by commercializing machines, thus shifting from the world of industrial manufacturing to that of communities of end-users. Since then, 3-D printer models available to the general public have been developing and accompany the rise of the "maker movement," which defends a particular conception of the adoption of manufacturing technologies and embodies, as Anderson (2012) states, a fertile ground for a new industrial revolution. The values of this movement—which brings together hobbyists, designers, artists, and users—intersect with both challenges and opportunities of on-demand manufacturing, the sharing of completed projects, and the opening up of technologies.

Recent technological advances have transformed the relationship between end-users viewed as "ordinary makers" and the design, development, manufacturing, and distribution stages of product creation. Nowadays, companies are increasingly aware of the opportunities offered by 3-D printing technology and its online platforms that allow customers/end-users to create, design, or co-create products. As a result, with standardized production lines, the traditional industry is shifting to more customized offerings made possible thanks to the democratization of 3-D printing technologies and platforms accessible to end-users and final customers (Batat, 2019b). This allows end-users to create or self-manufacture their own items by using external 3-D printing services; alternatively, they can buy entry-level 3-D printers.

This new technology, which advocates mass customization along with customer emancipation and empowerment, is regularly described as the Third Industrial Revolution. However, in the face of this great variety, there is often a lack of knowledge in defining it, capturing its value to enrich customer experiences, and identifying appropriate applications and uses according to each sector. The next sections therefore provide an overview of 3-D printing technology along with analysis of its online types and platforms that companies and/or end-users can use to enhance experiences.

2   OVERVIEW OF 3-D PRINTING TECHNOLOGIES

While there are many 3-D printing technologies, what they all have in common is that they build an object layer by layer. This process is called "additive" manufacturing because it works by adding material. This distinguishes 3-D printing from other traditional manufacturing technologies, known as "subtractive," characterized by subtraction of material until the final object is obtained. 3-D printing equipment also differs in the materials used, the way the layers are created, and how they are bonded. Such differences determine how quickly the part is made, the size of the object produced, the cost of production, and the amount of post-printing labor required.

All 3-D printing technology forms an object by successive deposits (layers) of material, following a predefined prototype. What will differ from one process to another are the materials used and how the layers are added. According to the American Society for Testing and Materials (ASTM, 2013), there are seven main categories: photopolymerization, fused deposition modeling, material jetting, binder jetting, powder bed fusion, laminated object manufacturing, and directed energy deposition.

2.1   Photopolymerization

This printing technology refers to a process that uses liquid polymers that solidify upon contact with light. It features an ultraviolet (UV) laser beam that selectively cures UV-sensitive liquid polymers to create a layer of solid material. Each time a layer is formed, the platform lowers and the laser performs its pattern on a new liquid surface, curing and bonding the resin to the previous layer (Gao et al., 2015). While this process has certain advantages—such as precision, speed of printing, and an excellent surface finish—it suffers from some limitations. These include process errors resulting from, for instance, the need for solidification after printing, and the high cost of the equipment and materials.

2.2   Fused Deposition Modeling

This refers to a material extrusion process characterized by successive deposition of molten plastic filament onto a printing plate following a path defined by a computer-aided design (CAD) file. This material deposition is done via an extrusion nozzle whereby each layer gradually hardens and bonds to the next, creating the object from bottom to top. The advantages of this process are that no chemical post-treatment is required and the equipment is inexpensive, making it a cost-effective 3-D printing system that is popular among end-users.

However, a disadvantage is that it requires high operating temperatures, which implies a significant amount of finishing work.

2.3   Material Jetting

Similar to the inkjet technology of 2-D printers, this process selectively deposits droplets of material onto a construction platform. This technology also allows the use of several materials simultaneously, which makes it possible to produce multi-material and multi-color parts. However, this process only works with UV-reactive photopolymers. Also, the parts produced with this technology are less resistant than those produced by the other processes, so it is often necessary to use support materials during construction.

2.4   Binder Jetting

In this process, a liquid bonding agent is deposited on a powder bed to join particles together. Once the first layer has solidified, the building platform is lowered and a new layer of powder is spread. By repeating this process, the various layers build up until the final object is complete. Any material that can be reduced to powder and moistened with a binder can be processed by this technology. Advantages of this process are low costs and the ability to easily add a color palette directly during printing. However, this process often involves post-printing work that can be time-consuming, and thus costly. Besides, the parts produced are essentially glued powder particles, which are fragile and of relatively low quality.

2.5   Powder Bed Fusion

This technique uses a thermal energy source, such as a laser, to selectively fuse powder particles in a process that is repeated until the final part is obtained. This 3-D printing process involves four technologies:

- Selective laser sintering or SLS is a process that heats the powder to the point when the particles can fuse at molecular level, thus allowing the production of complex shapes that could not be produced otherwise.
- Direct metal laser sintering or DMLS is also a sintering technology, but applied to metal alloys. Its advantage is that it produces objects free of internal defects.
- Selective laser melting or SLM is a melting process that uses a laser to obtain complete fusion, with the advantage of producing denser and more resistant objects.

- Electron beam melting or EBM, a process similar to SLM, produces dense patterns but the final parts involve finishing work to obtain a smooth surface.

2.6   Laminated Object Manufacturing

This refers to a process that combines additive and subtractive techniques to create objects (Gao et al., 2015). The materials are in the form of sheets, and the layers are bonded by a thermal adhesive coating and by applying heat. Once the first sheet is bonded, a laser or blade cuts each layer vertically to achieve the desired object contour. Advantages include printing on paper sheets and other materials, and obtaining multi-colored parts, large sizes, and good resolution. Yet, the final result is not perfect and often requires intensive finishing work.

2.7   Directed Energy Deposition

This uses focused thermal energy to fuse materials by melting them as they are deposited. This technology can be used with a wide variety of metals and alloys, including stainless steel, nickel-based alloys, copper alloys, and aluminum. Its drawback is residual stress from irregular alternations between heating and cooling, affecting the quality of the final printed object.

In addition to using the seven technologies outlined above, companies can consider different types of material in 3-D printing, which we can classify into three main categories: plastics, metals, and hybrids (e.g., food). Each type of material will be developed and used for one or more specific 3-D printing processes. The popularity of a 3-D printing technology also depends on the profile of the user (company vs. end-user) and the purpose it serves. For companies, we can note that stereolithography is widely used in industry due to its advantages related to high-quality products with a good finish. However, from an end-user perspective, fused deposition modeling is the most popular process, mainly due to its low cost and ease of use.

3   THE MAIN BENEFITS AND CHALLENGES OF 3-D PRINTING

Nowadays, additive manufacturing using 3-D printing technologies is leading companies to rethink their production processes and redefine their strategies and relationships with customers. On the one hand, integrating this technology opens the door to new ways of conceiving industrial production, allowing companies to expand their opportunities and improve performance.

On the other hand, 3-D printing allows companies to involve customers in co-creation processes, high levels of customization, and home fabrication. Although 3-D printing can have positive consequences on both companies and end-users/customers, this technology might create some challenges firms have to face while implementing 3-D printing processes. The benefits and challenges of 3-D printing technology are discussed in the following sections.

3.1   The Benefits of 3-D Printing

3-D printing technologies have multiple advantages for both companies and customers. These include economies of scale, mass customization and flexibility, home fabrication, and freedom of design, as well as environmental benefits and upcycling.

3.1.1   Economies of scale and flexibility

Traditional production techniques are characterized by objects being produced quickly, in a standardized way, and in large quantities, leading to risks of overproduction and waste. 3-D printing impacts this principle by eliminating the need to produce in large quantities to be profitable. With this technology, the minimum unit cost can be achieved at shallow volumes, and each production unit will have almost the same cost. However, this cost is initially lower, making 3-D printing an effective solution when it comes to low-volume production. Also, as technologies evolve, equipment costs will continue to fall, further intensifying the competitive advantage of this technology. Also, since it does not require expensive dedicated tooling, additive manufacturing is perfectly suited to small series production. This flexibility makes it possible to consider Just-in-Time production, which eliminates, for example, the need for large amounts of stock.

3.1.2   Mass customization

This refers to the process by which a company/brand allows its customers to personalize a product or service, and thus make it as unique as possible. Coca-Cola, for example, recently invited its "fans" to participate in a contest that allowed them to create a digital avatar via an app. After being scanned in 3-D at the Coca-Cola factory, the winners left with a figurine in their likeness, accompanied by a bottle of the famous brand. Today, the Web has seen the emergence of 3-D printing digital players and start-ups that allow end-users to create an object in one click in the form of a 3-D file or to send it to a 3-D printing service. This mass customization responds to the customer's desire to acquire, for a reasonable cost, exactly the product he/she needs, and in a limited time frame. The emergence of many niche markets centered on made-to-order products is the first step toward mass customization. For such products, standardization imposed by mass production will no longer be the case. The advent of mass customization will allow everyone to own different objects, and thus feel special.

3.1.3   Home fabrication

Although 3-D printing is currently confined to the industrial world, the figures point to rapid democratization of personal/home printers. In fact, sales of 3-D printers to the general public have increased by more than 300 percent since the 2010s as six-figure prices have fallen to more accessible prices (around $300). Advances in printing processes and falling prices for individual 3-D printers are signs of this expanding billion-dollar market. Thus, 3-D printing allows end-users to engage in home fabrication in different domains. End-users can then print everyday objects. Many websites now offer models for free download. Users just have to download them and send them to their printer, which will take care of the rest. Studies show that buying a 3-D printer to create such objects is profitable for the consumer. This makes 3-D printing at home an alternative to making accessories and other everyday items. Consumers can also use 3-D printing to print replacement parts for their broken items. Many everyday items can break and, most of the time, parts are unavailable commercially because the manufacturer has a vested interest in replacing the whole item rather than repairing it. Thus, by giving a second life to some everyday objects, 3-D printing allows individuals to make substantial savings. With individual and personal 3-D printing, it is now possible to recreate spare parts and personalize items, not by a stimulated desire but by needs and uses, to fight against programmed obsolescence, and thus enter the era of what we could call the series of the unique object. 3-D printing at home, via personal printers for users, is the latest step toward the democratization of this technology. It attests to a real craze, leading to the mass adoption of this technology.

3.1.4   Freedom of design

Not limited by the use of tooling, parts/items produced by additive manufacturing can have difficult characteristics, very complex shapes, or even be impossible to achieve with a conventional manufacturing process. These characteristics can be related to the geometry of the part or the material it is made from, allowing, among other things, the development of multi-material items. These new options and functions made possible by 3-D printing technologies allow users and companies to review the design of products from a functional, economic, and environmental perspective. For example, the functionality of a product can be optimized through a complex structure specifically designed to best meet a given specification. This encourages product innovation thanks to the freedom of design spirit brought by 3-D printing processes.

3.1.5   Environmental benefits and upcycling

The process of manufacturing by adding material uses only the material con-stituting the final product. Thus, producing all kinds of parts locally in units or small series reduces transport, packaging, and storage, drastically reducing CO_2 emissions. As for production waste, the material lost during additive man-ufacturing can be recycled and reused in a new print. Therefore, 3-D printing is a sustainable alternative to some mass production because it reduces the waste associated with material loss during the manufacturing process. Besides, 3-D printing can extend the life of certain products through upcycling. By giving consumers the ability to print custom objects, they can also give new life to objects that would generally have been discarded for lack of use. Consumers can use their 3-D printer to help repair a broken object, printing a replacement part downloaded from the Internet, and reprinting a part of a broken object themselves.

3.2   The Challenges of 3-D Printing

Although 3-D printing technologies are still in their infancy, their vocation is to accelerate innovation and the production of complex or customized parts, and they are constantly evolving (e.g., bio-printing) to extend their fields of application (e.g., the food industry). However these technologies present some constraints that make their implementation across businesses complex. The challenges of 3-D printing technologies companies should consider are outlined below.

3.2.1   Cost and accessibility

This refers to the purchase cost of 3-D printers, including choice and cost of materials. The cost of manufacturing remains relatively high compared to conventional processes. This is mainly due to the high cost of the machine coupled, in some cases, with a long manufacturing time. However, equipment and raw material costs are expected to drop significantly as additive manufac-turing develops.

3.2.2   Materials

Today, 3-D printing at home is restricted to plastic, which considerably limits the field of possibilities. Also, the materials available for 3-D printing are limited. Complex materials processing is not yet possible, and multi-color 3-D printing is still in its infancy, with professional 3-D printers capable of printing in color scarce and expensive. The price of materials for home users is still high since they must be adapted to the machine and the printing process. Thus, the development of new materials and the reduction in their price are the main challenges facing the technology's progress. Regarding accessibility, we can note that starting up a 3-D printer for an end-user is still a complex process. In addition, the creation of 3-D models and the complexity of export formats are barriers to the mass adoption of the technology. Consequently, the success of 3-D printing also depends on improved software for 3-D file design, 3-D scanners, and other technology-related tools.

3.2.3   Performance

This is related to multiple factors, including the speed and quality of printing and limited templates for parts. 3-D printing is still a very slow process compared to traditional manufacturing methods. Even for small objects, the process can take several hours, not to mention that the printing is not always of high quality and may require a finishing phase (e.g., polishing). In addition, 3-D printed objects, especially thin and/or elongated objects, are sometimes unstable and deform over time. Also, the reproducibility of 3-D printed objects is not reliable: from one print to the next, materials can react differently, depending on the printing conditions, and show slight differences in shape. This is particularly problematic in industrial environments where precision in the finish of the desired parts is one of the primary quality criteria. On the other hand, templates for parts that can be created by additive production are limited to 1 meter for industry; for individual usage this varies according to the materials used.

3.2.4   Ethics and copyright

Ethical issues refer to the need for control over 3-D printing technologies and printed objects. If 3-D printers can produce anything, including harmful or even deadly objects, control and regulation are needed to protect consumers. For example, in the United States, an individual printed a working firearm using the website Thingiverse.com, which contains many freely downloadable 3-D files. Thus, there is a need for a restrictive legislative framework to prevent all potential abuses and protect consumers. Regarding intellectual property (IP), issues of ownership and the protection of works arise when it comes to respecting patents and copyright. Thus, 3-D printing should not allow items to be reproduced, modified, or sold without the original author/creator's consent. Some solutions proposed to counteract the production of counterfeits might include measures that aim to insert a particular marking into the object without damaging it or verifying the authenticity of a file before printing it. However, tracking down all users who do not respect intellectual property rights or who use a 3-D scanner to create their own digital copy is a huge challenge for regulators and companies. It is therefore in the interest of companies to consider new economic strategies to evolve their business model.

3.2.5   Energy consumption

Although 3-D printers are energy-intensive, studies have shown that energy consumption in stand-by, preheating, and printing is less than two lamps lit. This means that the longer the printing time, the lower the average energy consumption. Companies should therefore consider continuous printing that can significantly reduce this average consumption.

4   TOWARD NEW BUSINESS MODELS

Nowadays, companies are clearly showing their willingness to benefit from the advantages of 3-D printing technologies to improve their competitiveness and develop new business models. Thus, 3-D printing can be used by companies across different sectors to develop new products while transforming manufacturing processes and customer service. At this level of transformation, product innovations regularly imply changes in the distribution and supply chain. The advent of this technology will therefore serve as a growth lever not only to disrupt the current competition for companies but also to access new markets and create new sources of value for customers.

Consequently, additive manufacturing will lead companies to explore new markets, which may have an impact on current activities. One area that could be developed is the economy of functionality, where, for example, companies could offer a solution integrating the sale of a product and a repair service. 3-D printing could extend the life of products by facilitating the production of spare parts locally, along with the emergence of companies providing the necessary equipment to create prototypes or finished products. These companies rent their manufacturing services to other companies that need them and that only focus on the design and marketing stage. For example, Hubs (formerly 3-D Hubs) is one company that offers access to a 3-D printing service without clients having to invest in the necessary equipment. This business model allows companies to outsource the printing stage, and facilitates access to both professionals and individuals.

A result of the simplification of the production stage is that the value of the product is now related to its design and not to the object itself. In other words, 3-D printing leads to a change in the value chain, ranging from the physical object to the information that enables its production. Factors such as the complexity of an object, its importance, its legal protection, and its degree of innovation will directly impact its digital value. As a result, new business models where revenues come from the sale of designs and their protection, rather than from the sale of finished goods or components, will emerge and change the dynamics in the marketplace.

BOX 8.1   STAPLES INCORPORATES 3-D PRINTING TO ENHANCE THE CUSTOMER EXPERIENCE

The American office supplies retailer Staples launched a space dedicated to 3-D printing in its stores and online. This service, called "Staples Easy 3-D," offers customers the opportunity to customize small objects using 3-D printers from a range of on-site offerings or by bringing their own files to be printed. For example, customers can create small figurines in their own image or create personalized phone shells.

Staples Easy 3-D is aimed at various targets, including consumers, product designers, architects, medical professionals, educators, and students. Customers can send electronic files to the Staples Office Center and pick up the models at the nearest Staples store or have them shipped to their home. Other examples of products that could be produced at Staples include custom parts, prototypes, art, models, medical models, and 3-D cards. The company also announced that it would be the first major US retailer to distribute 3-D printers: since 2013 it has rolled out 3-D printing equipment and accessories to a limited number of stores in the US, and has expanded its catalog to include other 3-D printing actors.

A company's ability to benefit from the opportunities offered by 3-D printing technologies depends on how it integrates them within its internal functioning. Some large established companies, although innovative, may be constrained by the need to satisfy their existing customers and investors. They are constrained by their current market position. Therefore, the integration of 3-D printing will be achieved gradually, by slight modifications to products or by the development of new services, such as the supply of spare parts. Conversely, new market actors or start-ups will be more flexible in their use of this technology. They will be able to use 3-D printing to offer new products and services in new markets, leading to a more remarkable change in the system.

According to Cotteleer (2014), a company's integration of 3-D printing technologies can follow four situations depending on the changes that additive manufacturing brings to the products and the production chain:

- Situation 1. The possibility of adopting 3-D printing does not involve a fundamental change within the company. The products offered and the production line remain the same. The technology is then used in small proportions compared to traditional methods for exploratory purposes, such as rapid prototyping.

- Situation 2. The use of 3-D printing does not generate changes in the products but rather in the production chain. The company uses the technology to reduce its costs and limit the stock necessary for on-demand production, which adds flexibility and reactivity.
- Situation 3. The company seizes the opportunities provided by additive manufacturing to change its production line without changing its product offering. Greater performance can be unleashed through the use of 3-D printers to customize the product according to customer expectations.
- Situation 4. The company uses 3-D printing technologies to make changes to both the products and the production chain. The changes here are radical, and ultimately disrupt the business model in place.

Thus, for companies, 3-D printing offers simultaneous product innovation possibilities combined with a transformation of production, distribution, and customer service. This makes the technology a vector for growth and innovation, which will allow the company to surpass the competition and access new markets by responding to new emerging customers' needs.

For consumers and end-users, 3-D printing can allow companies to engage in the on-demand design of customer experiences. On the one hand, 3-D printing technology allows companies to add other practices to their traditional manufacturing techniques by bringing a form of personalization in different high-end sectors where uniqueness of the piece is important (Batat, 2019b). This uniqueness in terms of tooling considerably reduces the production time and allows great freedom in terms of creativity. For example, in luxury fashion, designers have taken the lead and are now creating 3-D printed pieces. The objective of haute couture designers is to unleash creativity as 3-D printing technology is offering increasingly innovative creations in terms of design or materials. For example, Dutch designer Iris van Herpen is positioned today as an ambassador of 3-D printing in the luxury and haute couture sector by making 3-D printed clothes. Thus, 3-D printing can be regarded as a future movement in the fashion industry as it allows the design of unexpected/ unusual creations.

On the other hand, 3-D printing allows companies to create packaging or other wrapping products that can be customized by customers. By equipping themselves with cutting-edge technology, they also succeed in revitalizing their image and offer consumers innovative and engaging communication tools. According to Batat (2019b), companies, especially in high-end sectors, can benefit from 3-D printing technology and offer their customers new products and experiences through various means:

- *Reinforcing the feeling of exclusivity.* Many brands find in additive manufacturing the opportunity of limited series, capsule collections, or even unique objects.
- *Reducing manufacturing time.* For parts or finished products, manufacturing cycles are shorter, and customers have come to expect speed.
- *Embracing responsible production.* Additive manufacturing techniques are practiced locally. In addition to reduced deadlines, they support local employment.
- *Reducing manufacturing costs.* The technique of adding layers, rather than subtracting material, avoids the loss of expensive materials.

BOX 8.2   HOW IS 3-D PRINTING USED TO DESIGN HIGHLY CUSTOMIZED AND HEALTHY FOOD EXPERIENCES?

As a new technology, 3-D printing opens doors to many industries, including the food sector. The prowess of 3-D printing continues to seduce businesses, and the food industry is no exception. Many foods are already printable, as long as they can be reduced to raw materials fine enough to be processed (e.g., chocolate, meat). Consumers of 3-D printed foods are vital, and the greatest potential lies in food customization. Additionally, 3-D food printing has many advantages both for customers and the food or restaurant industry:

- *Healthy and controlled nutrition.* Food printing quantifies not only the physical shape of products but also their calorific needs. Based on the precision of 3-D printers, it becomes possible for food actors to perfectly balance meals with controlled nutritional intake and adapt to particular consumer profiles, such as high-level athletes, people suffering from digestive problems, or for babies or the elderly.
- *Tasty and easy-to-swallow food.* Elderly consumers with chewing or swallowing problems are often forced to eat food in the form of purees. The purees are fed into the refills of the 3-D printers. The food then becomes softer but retains its shape thanks to a gelling agent. 3-D printer-made vegetables are currently being served in nursing homes in Europe.
- *Customized shapes and decorations.* 3-D printing can add decorations (e.g., a customer's photo on a birthday cake) or create a snowflake cake,

flowers, or personalized ravioli. The food can be printed in any shape and size. The possibilities of creation are thus multiple for individuals as well as for companies. For example, brands could create food with their logos during events, or candies in the image of customers.

- *Environmentally friendly food.* This technology offers the possibility of using alternative sources of protein, such as algae and insects, which could be transformed into foods with a pleasant texture, appreciated by consumers.

From a managerial perspective, food companies and chefs may take a dim view of this technology, especially regarding the taste quality of the products produced via 3-D printing. Moreover, they may fear a "devaluation" of their know-how. Therefore, this technology, whether adopted or not, will never replace traditional cooking; but it is a tremendous development lever for artisanal companies since it allows them to offer new products, shapes, and services. In terms of production, 3-D printing offers many advantages, including optimization of raw materials (used only where needed) and considerable savings for the realization of small batches as part of the mold is made directly by 3-D printing, thus avoiding expensive tooling.

KEY TAKEAWAYS

This chapter introduced the opportunities and challenges related to 3-D printing technologies to design highly customized and on-demand phygital customer experiences. As highlighted in this chapter, optimization of production processes, customization possibilities, cost control, creation of complex shapes, and so forth, are among the advantages of this innovation. The world of 3-D printing opens new creative fields and facilitates potentially incredible advances across different sectors when compared to traditional techniques. Despite its current constraints—such as limited materials, environmental issues, costs, and accessibility—3-D printing predicts interesting futures for companies to rethink their production processes and business models to create new sources of value to share with their customers, and thus define themselves.

PART III

Strategies for successful phygital customer experience design

9. The death of the traditional marketing mix (7Ps) and the rise of the experiential marketing mix (7Es)

CHAPTER OVERVIEW

This chapter emphasizes the importance for companies to consider a novel marketing strategy framework, namely the experiential marketing mix, which encompasses seven critical components (7Es). Starting from the limits of a traditional approach of the so-called marketing mix and its 4Ps or 7Ps, when it comes to designing customer experiences, both online and offline, the chapter shows how the new experiential marketing mix and its 7Es can help companies meet their strategic objectives and create a solid competitive advantage while creating engaging experiences for their customers. This chapter outlines the limits of the traditional marketing mix in the experiential and phygital era. It then introduces the 7Es of the experiential marketing mix as a novel tool that allows companies to design satisfying and profitable phygital customer experiences connecting physical and digital spheres.

1   THE DEATH OF THE TRADITIONAL MARKETING MIX

The first part of this chapter presents the foundations, perspectives, and tools of the traditional marketing mix and its development through time and across various sectors. The second part then discusses the limits of the traditional marketing mix, which is mainly focused on the product to offer a more customer-centric approach.

1.1   The Foundations and Expansion of the Marketing Mix: From 4Ps to 7Ps

The marketing mix comprising four components (4Ps)—namely product, price, place, and promotion—was introduced and theorized by US Professor of Marketing Edmund McCarthy (1964) and popularized by marketing consultant and scholar Philip Kotler (1972) through the publication of several success-ful books. However, although Kotler has widely disseminated the marketing mix approach, and thus contributed to the field of modern marketing, it is US Professor of Marketing James Culliton (1948) who first used the expression "the marketing mix" to describe the "mix" of the main elements that form marketing decisions.

According to Culliton's research, it was necessary to mix certain ingredients or elements to achieve a successful marketing strategy, including consumer behavior, the industry, competition, planning, pricing, distribution, promo-tion, customer service, and market research. Culliton's Harvard colleague, Advertising Professor Neil Borden, proposed a combination of a dozen or so variables to ensure the commercial success of a product, including brand, product plan, pricing, distribution channels, advertising, promotion, personal selling, presentation, packaging, handling, services, research, and data analysis (Borden, 1942; 1964).

Then, McCarthy, in his thesis defended in 1958 at the University of Chicago, proposed to synthesize and group these elements into four distinct categories beginning with the letter P, hence the abbreviation 4Ps, to help companies manage their resources while maximizing profits. Along with Kotler's works, the 4Ps model has become the canon and a practical tool used by companies across different sectors and taught in universities and business schools. The success of the marketing mix is due to its easy implementation to analyze the market by considering a marketing strategy based on the 4Ps.

1.1.1   Product

Designing products to meet market needs is critical for companies. They should consider all characteristics of the product or service, for example, functionality, packaging, range, among others. The company should ask the questions: What is being offered? What expectations is it likely to meet? And what will be the benefits for the person buying the product? To answer these questions, the company should focus on the aspects that differentiate its product from existing offers. Additional services can also be associated with the proposed product (e.g., after-sales service or delivery). Indeed, from the product policy, companies will be able to define the properties or the quality of their offerings.

Product design and development with regard to the needs expressed by the market will depend directly on this analysis. Thus, creating a product requires taking into account the different phases of its life cycle and following four significant steps to create or relaunch a commercial offering. Creating or relaunching a product is a challenge for companies, which should consider the offer in terms of its tangible (e.g., technical) and intangible (e.g., creating a brand, an image, services) characteristics. Each step in the process of product creation responds to a well-defined objective:

- Step 1. Setting up an exhaustive list of all the tangible and intangible characteristics of the product. Services are also to be taken into account in this step.
- Step 2. Transforming the tangible and intangible territorial capital as well as the services into promises for the different targets, and associating a benefit and a solution adapted to the profile of each target.
- Step 3. Placing the brand at the heart of reflection on its association with the product. Creating a new brand or relaunching the existing one involves asking several questions, such as: What identity should be given to the product? What should it represent in the minds of the different targets? What reactions should the brand generate? What relationships should the brand build with its different targets?
- Step 4. After the conception of the offer and the creation of the brand, the developed and associated services are a nascent element for the loyalty of the target consumers and the creation of solid competitive advantage. The services offered by the company allow it to create a strong relationship with the different target consumers, who, once satisfied, will no longer be attracted to competitors' offerings.

Thus, designing a satisfactory offering should follow a rigorous marketing logic starting from the life cycle of the product and then following the four steps above, ranging from identification of the product's tangible and intangible characteristics to proposing associated services through a brand that fits the expectations of the target consumers.

1.1.2 Price
It is then necessary to set a price for the product or service being designed. This will depend on the target (market segmentation), the volume produced (economy of scale), and the positioning the company wishes to give to the product (luxury or mass market). Pricing policy is based on analysis of internal and external factors of the offering to determine the final price of the product:

- *Internal factors.* The price should reflect the product's market position. If the product represents a strong competitive advantage and is perceived by customers as a unique offering, the price of accessibility and installation may be high compared to the competition. On the other hand, if the product is commonplace, its price will be aligned with or lower than the competition's. Internal factors include positioning, the cost of ownership, company objectives, and harmonization of offers.

- *External factors*. These are multiple and varied and can include elements such as the value perceived by the target consumers; competition through the study and comparison of living costs; price elasticity, which refers to setting the cost of living in relation to demand; and regulation where certain sectors are subject to regulation.

Companies can also define different prices, such as final customer price, distribution price, or psychological price. In addition, they can implement pricing strategies based on the positioning of their offering:

- *Penetration pricing strategy*. In a highly competitive market, some companies set a low price when launching a new product to gain a market share and attract price-sensitive consumers.
- *Alignment pricing strategy*. To avoid a price war, it is also possible to align with competitors' prices.
- *Price-skimming strategy*. To give their brands a high-end image and position, companies often set deliberately high prices to target high-income consumers. Later on, the price of a product can fall, especially if it is considered obsolete (as with old versions of smartphones or computers). Most companies in the technology sector use a price-skimming strategy.

Beyond these strategies, the main issue for companies when it comes to pricing is to define the right price for their products or services. This decision depends on three key elements: (1) being able to evaluate how much buyers are willing to pay for the products; (2) considering the profit margins and costs associated with production and marketing; and (3) considering the prices charged by competitors to define their positioning.

1.1.3   Place

Distribution policy consists of defining the distribution channels of the company's offerings. Multi-channel distribution is a primary concern of companies that seek to have distribution points. It is thus critical to offer potential target consumers many opportunities to access the company's products and services. Therefore, decisions will be made regarding the distribution mode to allow customers to access the company's products. This can be direct, with the installation of a website or other online store, or indirect via several partners to be defined (e.g., chain of stores, retailers). Thus, companies should ask: Where/how can target consumers find and buy their products? How can they get them delivered? It is essential, through a well-defined distribution strategy, to constantly seek to facilitate accessibility.

1.1.4   Promotion

Promoting a company's offer involves placing it in the spotlight by relaying a strong message via appropriate communication channels. There are five main steps companies should follow to implement an effective communication policy:

*   Defining the objectives and the strategy. This step aims at defining what the company wishes to convey as a message in the mind of the chosen target consumer.
*   Identifying and selecting the profile of the target consumer that the company wishes to reach and the type of message to be communicated.
*   Drafting the content and the key message the company wishes to convey to the chosen target consumer.
*   Choosing the communication paths, media, and support used to deliver the message.
*   Managing the operational follow-up of the company's promotional actions and setting up dashboards with appropriate performance indicators.

Thus, promotion is a vital element of the marketing mix, a component of this economic matrix, which includes several characteristics. It refers to how a company can best deliver its message to both prospective and existing customers. Promotion includes several tools that companies can use according to their objectives, target consumers, and the features of the products on offer. The first is advertising, which can be either through traditional displays or, even more effectively nowadays, through social networks. There is also sales promotion, a sales force, direct marketing, and public relations (PR). Also, when we refer to communication in the marketing mix, we also include everything that is part of the brand, everything that relates to its identity—not only, for example, the colors and shape of its packaging but also the logos. Logos can help deliver messages to customers because they characterize the company and create an identity for it within a particular sector. The same goes for various advertising and promotional campaigns.

Therefore, the marketing mix allows the company to create, modify, and adjust its products by dosing the content of the 4Ps and thus concentrating its efforts on a single P or the 4Ps, according to the stage of the product life cycle. Beyond the 4Ps used to operationalize strategic and creative thinking in marketing, other approaches can incorporate additional elements, depending on the problem and the sector (e.g., tourism, hospitality, services). For example, to create touristic offerings it is necessary to incorporate elements that cover all dimensions, both tangible and intangible, and that can be translated into an effective marketing strategy. For this reason, in 2009 the Chartered Institute of Marketing approved an expanded definition of the marketing mix with three additional "P" variables: people, process, and physical evidence. From then on, the 7Ps became popular and are now part of the new definition of the marketing mix that aims to meet the needs of the service sector and beyond. Indeed, the previous version, the 4Ps, was considered too succinct to be applied to selling services or online offers.

1.1.5 People

The fifth P in the marketing mix is people policy. It is essential in the service sector and for consumers who have difficulty assessing the value of services because they are not material (tangible). Consumers therefore look for key indicators that indicate the quality of the service. In the service sector, a high-quality workforce is one of these key indicators. For a company, it is thus important to employ excellent staff and deploy them effectively. Human resources (HR) policy is an important marketing tool because people often provide services, and customer satisfaction depends mainly on these people.

1.1.6 Process

Process management is not only about purely technical processes, such as manufacturing a product. It is also critical to ensure that a service can be experienced. To achieve this, the business processes should be customer-oriented, and the customer should be made as comfortable as possible. This process should include the entire sales journey: from the first contact between the product and the consumer to the final purchase. This requires implementing a reflection on the consumer's journey on a website or in-store to promote a high retention and purchase rate: for example, setting up pleasant queuing systems or using sensory marketing to create a universe specific to the brand.

1.1.7 Physical evidence

The seventh P in the new marketing mix is about optimizing the physical environment of a product or service. Physical evidence plays an important role, especially in the service sector, because perception of a service cannot be influenced as easily as, for example, a product with a high-quality design or material. Therefore, the objective is to positively influence the customer's subjective perception through the visible environment of service following the company's objectives.

Design, architecture, appearance, and materials are the principal tools here. Physical evidence also offers the opportunity to stand out from the competition: many providers offer similar services but differ considerably in terms of the atmosphere related to their physical evidence policy. Indeed, one of the main problems with selling services is that, unlike products, they are intangible. Some customers may be reluctant to buy something they cannot test beforehand, in which case the company should set up systems to reassure them. For instance, a company could give customers the opportunity to leave a review after the purchase, a satisfaction guarantee, reactive after-sales service, etc. For services, this can also be achieved through a well-defined and thought-out user experience, especially on the company website. Fluid navigation, a clear and easy interface, and personalization all let the consumer gain a positive image of the company and the service provided.

To sum up, while the 4Ps and the 7Ps are still the most common components of the marketing mix, when implementing product and service strategies, marketing scholars have proposed new definitions where more than 7Ps can be used. For instance, the 10Ps mix adds three extra Ps to the 7Ps presented above: partnership, permission, and persuasion. However, this latest definition of the marketing mix is not yet widely used and is somewhat contested. Some consider the 10Ps superfluous since the 4Ps, or even the 7Ps, should typically encompass these factors. Furthermore, scholars have called for a review of the foundations of the marketing mix because of its focus on the product. Recent developments in the marketing field underline the importance of focusing on customers and end-users instead of products, especially in the highly experiential and digital era.

1.2   Marketing Mix Limits in the Experiential and Phygital Era

The digital era has pushed some companies to reflect on their marketing strategies by initiating a shift from the 4Ps to the "4Cs" of the marketing mix tool, focused more on the customer: convenience of buying, customer need, cost to satisfy, and communication. Although the 4Cs have no scientific foundation and are only used by consultants and bloggers, the idea of focusing on the customers instead of the product is validated in the scientific marketing literature, and most marketing scholars have recently acknowledged the importance of shifting the company's thinking from a product-centric logic to more consumer-centric thinking.

In the evolution of marketing, we can clearly see the growing role of the consumer in the definition of marketing through six main phases, ranging from the economy of production to the current situation related to the experience economy:

- The economy of production—Unique Selling Proposition or Point (USP), product attributes, no competition.
- The economy of distribution—when supply catches up with demand— commerce and negotiation.
- The market economy—when supply exceeds demand, competition, differentiation, 4Ps of the marketing mix.

- The macroenvironment economy—when supply is much higher than demand.
- The economy of consumption—the rise of the consumer society and hyper-consumption.
- The experience economy—postmodern society, emotions, and subjectivity.

Therefore, the new marketing mix should be aligned with an economy of experience. I thus define contemporary experiential marketing as: a state of spirit, a set of tools, processes, sciences, and strategies focused on the market and the consumer. It helps companies, individuals, associations, institutions, governments, etc. define their uniqueness and share values with their customers by anticipating and capturing future trends, innovating, and disrupting the actual reality of their market.

This definition highlights the limits of the marketing mix tool (4Ps or 7Ps) when it comes to creating emotional and profitable customer experiences within a phygital era in which the starting point is the consumer who seeks to live enchanting experiences instead of merely purchasing a product to satisfy a basic need. Thus, the marketing mix, as we know it today, is not compatible with the focus on the consumer and his/her emotional needs, and thus does not allow companies to design engaging and profitable phygital experiences. To do so, I introduce in the next section a new tool of the experiential marketing mix, with 7Es.

2   THE RISE OF THE EXPERIENTIAL MARKETING MIX (7ES): A NOVEL TOOL TO DESIGN SUCCESSFUL PHYGITAL EXPERIENCES

In this section, I introduce the fundamental idea of the strategic framework of the new "experiential marketing mix." As Figure 9.1 illustrates, the framework highlights controllable components of the mix that companies can use to implement effective strategies and actions to design successful, satisfying, and profitable customer experiences in the phygital era, combining both physical and digital settings.

The 7Es of the experiential marketing mix are: Experience, Exchange, Extension, Emphasis, Empathy capital, Emotional touchpoints, and Emic/etic process. Companies should build up a combination of the 7Es, which can help them meet their organizational and strategic objectives. This will guarantee a strong and sustainable competitive advantage generated by value creation and sharing, the highest levels of customer satisfaction and loyalty, and a positive image offline and online. The 7Es of the experiential mix are outlined below.

Experiential marketing mix	Marketing mix
☐ Experience	☐ Product
☐ Exchange	☐ Price
☐ Extension	☐ Place
☐ Emphasis	☐ Promotion
☐ Empathy capital	☐ People
☐ Emotional touchpoints	☐ Physical
☐ Emic/etic process	☐ Process

Source: Adapted from Batat (2019a).

Figure 9.1   Experiential vs. traditional marketing mix

2.1   Experience

Companies can achieve a competitive advantage and differentiate themselves within a highly competitive market by producing experiences instead of products. In other words, experience should replace product in the traditional marketing mix. Experience is considered a new category of offer from the experiential perspective that can be marketed online and offline to consumers. This section presents the offer of "Experience" as the first component of the 7Es of the new experiential marketing mix, replacing the "P" of "Product" in the traditional marketing mix based on the 7Ps. Following this perspective, new tools (developed by Batat, 2019a) to measure and improve the quality of customer experiences, such as the Experience Territory Matrix (ETM) and the EXQUAL, can be used by companies to create and design practical, satisfying, and profitable phygital experiences.

2.1.1   The Experience Territory Matrix
Batat (2019a) introduced the Experience Territory Matrix (ETM) to help companies manage their portfolios based on experiences instead of products. The ETM is also a long-term strategic planning instrument that helps businesses consider opportunities by reviewing their portfolio of experiential offerings

and the way customers perceive them to decide where to invest in improving the quality of the customer experience, to renew the offer, and to develop new experiences (both physical and digital) to retain their customers.

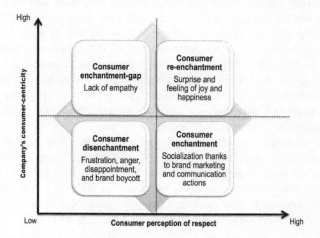

Source: Adapted from Batat (2019a).

Figure 9.2   The Experience Territory Matrix

The ETM includes four typologies of experience that consider a customer's perception of respect and the company's customer-centricity. Based on these two bipolar constructs, four "experiential territories" have been identified: enchantment, re-enchantment, disenchantment, and the enchantment gap (Figure 9.2). The consumer's perception of respect refers to the feeling of being respected from his/her own perspective, and suggests that respect is a core issue when considering relationships with a company. Meanwhile, the company's customer-centricity refers to the company's ability to develop a solid management commitment, organizational shift, schemes and process support, and revised financial metrics.

The ETM shows that the two concepts help explain the paradoxes related to the subjectivity of customers and the way they perceive their consumption and shopping experiences online and offline related to a specific territory.

- *Enchantment territory.* In the ETM, customer experience enchantment can be produced when a customer's perception of respect is high and the company's consumer-centricity is low. This situation means that the customer is enchanted in his/her relationships with other consumers, although the company's customer-orientation is low. Indeed, solid social interactions among customers in experiential settings when the company or the brand is present can help the company enchant its customers, even though its customer-centricity is low, since customers may show satisfaction because they network, meet, and connect with new people, build social bonds, develop their social capital and social network, and so forth.

- *Re-enchantment territory.* As shown in the ETM, experience re-enchantment can be produced when the customer's perception of respect is high and the company's consumer-centricity is also high. This means that the customer is re-enchanted and positively surprised by how the company treats him/her. In other words, customers might feel respected by the company as well as valued, considered, and unique.
- *Disenchantment territory.* Customer experience disenchantment can be produced when both the customer's perception of respect and the company's consumer-centricity are low. This means that the customer is frustrated, disappointed, and upset because of a feeling of being disrespected by the company, which does not employ a policy centered on its customers and their functional and emotional needs. This will produce a negative experience that leads customers to look for brands, products, and services offered by other companies that provide positive experiences and treat them with respect.
- *Enchantment-gap territory.* The enchantment-gap experience is produced when the customer's perception of respect is low and the company's consumer-centricity is high. This means that the customer does not feel respected by the company, even though the company's strategy is customer-oriented. This mismatch between the company's approach and the customer's perception can be explained by the lack of deep understanding of the meanings customers attribute to their experiences.

2.1.2   The EXQUAL tool

To measure the quality of customer experience in physical and digital settings from the perspectives of both consumer and company, Batat (2019a) proposed the conceptual "EXQUAL" tool to help companies improve the quality of their customer experiences online and offline. Drawing on prior exhaustive research in the service literature and the recent development of the SERVQUAL instrument, EXQUAL—which combines four main measurement components (human, offering, environment, and value)—is a tool that leads companies to consider various elements to measure the quality of the perceived customer experience, as it is estimated through the four dimensions that are believed to represent customer experience quality.

2.2   Exchange

A company will engage in the co-creation process if the participation of the consumer is considered a value that emerges from the "Exchange" between the customer and the company, which is the second component of the 7Es of the experiential marketing mix, replacing the "P" of "Price" in the traditional marketing mix approach. Value-in-exchange encompasses various elements (e.g., self-fulfillment, confidence in skills, joy, fun, belonging, accomplishment, relational attitude, self-respect, excitement, interpersonal dealings) that are dependent upon the context in which the co-creation process is implemented, the company's objectives, and the outcomes sought by customers.

Thus, creating shared values with consumers requires transparency and the sharing of information. Beyond products and services, companies should offer their consumers a real experience of co-creation. Value is no longer unilaterally created by the company but created together with the consumer. The exchange of the co-created value requires specific skills that are the fundamental sources for creating a sustainable competitive advantage by applying collaborative marketing tools.

Collaborative marketing is applied in the fields of innovation, services, and design in which users/consumers are involved in improving products through their opinions, ideas, and suggestions. Therefore, companies should consider their customers as partners and economic actors capable of carrying the values of the enterprise or the brand, communicating them, and proposing creative solutions to improve the quality of the experience, including products and services.

As a result, collaborative marketing allows companies to differentiate themselves from competitors and retain customers by involving them and sharing values with them. However, consumers' participation depends on the level of their creative potential and the intensity of their involvement. Hence, the exchange between a company and its consumers is rewarding to both parties as consumers feel invested with an important mission and companies can use the creative potential of their customers.

2.3   Extension

Phygital experience offerings should be considered an "Extension," the next "E" of the experiential marketing mix. This approach leads companies to broaden their vision by shifting the focus from the "P" of "Place" in the traditional marketing mix logic to a more extended consideration of customer experience that is dynamic, evolving, and goes beyond the physical environment. The challenge of the experience continuum is to provide customers with quality consumption experiences involving all the senses that will result in advanced and creative potential in their forthcoming experiences to create an experiential continuum.

Therefore, the phygital continuum of experience includes all cognitive (intellectual), affective (emotional), and behavioral changes during a life cycle as new experiences adjust and change existing models. Furthermore, the experience continuum integrates the idea that any experience that is high in indirect service provision is also one that generates more opportunities for co-creation, up to auto-creation.

2.4   Emphasis

In the traditional marketing mix, communication is applied with a push logic to deliver messages to the audience. However, due to the increase in traditional and digital communication platforms, and the rise of experiential expectations, this is less efficient, and brands have had to compete by using creative originality in terms of communication to get their message across. For this reason, companies need to shift the focus from a traditional communication policy focusing on brand content and the media to a more holistic approach based on a brand culture emphasis that humanizes the brand by bringing its personality to life to create a strong relationship with customers, and thus differentiate the brand from its competitors.

A brand culture emphasis refers to the way companies should use consumption culture elements to connect with their customers. Instead of using a brand promotion approach (as in the "P" of "Promotion" of the traditional marketing mix), the emphasis on brand cultural meaning provides a necessary complement to promotional strategies by including a focus on the meanings that are embedded and shaped by particular cultural settings and the meanings that the brand shares with its customers.

The shift from brand content to brand culture can be explained by the motivation of consumers to live experiences with the brands that are charged with meaning. Brand culture signifies that the cultural norms of brands affect brand significance and value in the marketplace. Consequently, brands that effectively achieve this cultural emplacement can make consumers produce unique and distinct identities and, surprisingly, resist conformist business influences. Brand culture is, then, a central element in building a strong brand since it is co-constructed by injecting cultural meanings embedded within different consumption experiences in the phygital era.

The brand community is an integral part of this cultural construction because brand culture can go beyond the company. To be able to influence this culture, the brand manager should understand the mechanisms of the emergence of cultural meanings in consumption experiences, both online and offline. To do so, companies have to identify the mechanisms behind brand culture in a community and the characteristics of these cultural elements to design suitable and meaningful customer experiences within a phygital setting.

2.5   Empathy Capital

Empathy capital replaces the "P" of "People" in the traditional marketing mix. It helps companies to design emotional and efficient phygital experiences with employees who can empathize with customers and professionally respond to their needs. A good experiential marketing mix is then based on the idea that, with substantial empathy capital, employees who are in contact with customers would think "customer first" at both the emotional level (how does he/she feel today?) and the cognitive level (what does he/she need according to his/her feeling today?). This can be achieved when employees develop an adaptive empathy capital that helps them use their social and interpersonal intelligence to identify the profile, moods, aspirations, and expectations of the client's experiential moment.

An empathic experiential setting can be created either through a controlled process or instinctively, leading to behavioral outcomes. Empathy in customer experience is, then, the ability of salespeople to perceive and be sensitive to the emotional states of their customers, often combined with a motivation to worry about their well-being. The empathy of people such as sales staff, waiters, and front desk staff, who have direct relationships with customers, refers to a complex mental state in which different perceptual, cognitive, motivational, and emotional processes interact with the "others."

An empathic experience includes two connected but different processes through which sellers (perceivers) relate to buyers (target customers). The empathy experience framework assembles a set of processes that generate empathy, which fits into three comprehensive categories: (1) experience sharing (vicarious sharing of customers'/target customers' internal conditions); (2) mentalizing (clearly seeing and possibly examining customers'/target customers' mental state and what underlies it); and (3) prosocial concern (conveying a stimulus to advance customers'/target customers' experiences, for instance by reducing their anxiety).

Therefore, empathy capital is important for companies, and particularly for customer experience design, because it allows marketers and brand managers to truly understand and decode the hidden needs and emotions of the customers for whom they are designing the experience, by developing the empathy capital of their employees. Marketing professionals who demonstrate empathy provide better customer experiences with higher customer satisfaction.

The best approach to training professionals in developing their empathy skills is to make sure that their professionalized empathy is customer-centric, focusing on customer well-being, helpful, intentional, self-conscious, self-inspiring, and sustainable.

2.6   Emotional Touchpoints

Touchpoints are the points of contact between the company (products and services) and the customers who will interact with these service encounters, and their experience might be affected in a positive or a negative way. Thus, touchpoints are an essential characteristic and one of the most important pillars of customer experience design, in both physical and digital settings. However, in the actual definition and practice of experience touchpoints, emotions and the way they are generated and expressed by customers are not considered in the process; the focus is more on the tool or platform of contact rather than the emotion generated by the tool.

We know that a successful contact that emotionally engages the customer is a fundamental part of successful customer experience design. Therefore, the starting point for identifying customer experience touchpoints is a focus more on emotions to define the touchpoint and not the other way around. Batat (2019a) proposed an approach to emotional touchpoints that could offer a tangible input to the customer experience design base and show how to support such customer emotional engagement in practice. Thus, "Emotional touchpoints" in the "7Es" of the experiential marketing mix replace the "P" of "Physical evidence" in the traditional mix.

Emotional touchpoints go beyond the idea of customer journey touchpoints in which customers might find a brand online or in an advertisement, see evaluations and reviews, ask friends who have already had experience with the brand, visit a company's website, shop at a retail store, or contact customer services before, during, or after their experience. Emotional touchpoints allow companies to develop a deeper understanding of the emotions related to the experience by focusing more on the moments where customers' memories are being activated. Were they touched in an emotional way (feelings) or in a cognitive way (profound and long-term memories)? This could happen independently or where there were profound moments in a customer's contact with the company (e.g., a dining experience or a hotel experience), or it could be a case of small, short-term interactions. All can have the same significance for the customer in terms of emotional and cognitive impact.

Thus, establishing contact and conversation with customers through emotional touchpoints is very helpful for companies to guarantee customer satisfaction and loyalty, and thus create a durable competitive advantage. Therefore, emotional touchpoints are fundamental facets of customer experience design and vital to the experiential marketing mix. They represent the connection between the service provider or the company's employees and the end-user or customer. In this way, emotional touchpoints first have to be considered in terms of the emotions they generate, followed by identification of the touchpoints that generate them—not the other way round, as in the traditional logic of customer touchpoints.

2.7   Emic/etic Process

As applied in the 7Ps of the traditional marketing mix, "Process" refers to the idea that the value delivered to the customer follows a top-down (etic) logic in which meanings are created and delivered by the firm throughout the customer journey. Using an emic/etic approach fundamentally involves the observation of a single cultural group of consumers. It offers structured and embedded observations about consumer behaviors that help the company in the design and adaptation of the customer experience, which matches different consumption cultures and subcultures.

The "Emic/etic process" component of the experiential marketing mix replaces the "P" of "Process" in the traditional marketing logic of the 7Ps. It extends the vision of the process from a one-way, top-down process to inject consumer value into an iterative process that considers both consumer and company visions embedded within a particular cultural setting. By using emic and etic perspectives in the understanding of consumer behaviors, attitudes, and cultural consumption schemes—as well as to generate consumption experiences that are both intellectual and perceptual—these two thoughts underline opposing standpoints as they analyze behaviors by considering the perspective of the insider (observed: consumer) or the outsider (observer: company). Therefore, the distinction between etic and emic can contrast the knowledge produced of the behavior of a community or social group (etic) and the knowledge produced by the community members (emic).

Assuming the subjectivity of customer experience, emic and etic viewpoints play important roles in defining the process that the company can use to deliver meaningful phygital experiences. Therefore, the process to understand and design meaningful customer experiences should incorporate the two perspectives—emic and etic—because they are complementary and valuable to studying a specific consumption culture in which the experience is shaped and embedded. The use of both emic and etic processes should be an advantage instead of a constraint or a source of confusion when it comes to customer experience design.

To sum up, it is relevant to note that by implementing this new experiential framework, companies can concentrate on the key decision domains related to the 7Es that constitute the experiential marketing mix when designing experience offers and forming their marketing plans in the phygital setting.

KEY TAKEAWAYS

This chapter highlighted the limits of the traditional approach to marketing mix strategies and the 4Ps and 7Ps when it comes to creating customer experiences in a phygital setting. It then introduced a new tool, the experiential marketing mix of 7Es, to help companies design successful and engaging phygital experiences that are customer-focused and allow the connection of physical and digital settings. Hence, for companies to design the ultimate phygital experience and offer their customers a satisfying, emotional as well as convenient experience online and offline, they should switch from a traditional vision of marketing based on the implementation of the 4Ps or 7Ps to a more holistic approach, through a phygital strategy that incorporates a balanced experiential mix of the 7Es.

10. Immersive research methods to study customer experience in the phygital era: from big data to "smart data"

CHAPTER OVERVIEW

In this chapter, I introduce "smart data," an immersive and exploratory tool with which companies should consider going beyond the limits of the "big data bang" when it comes to collecting insights about customer experiences in the phygital era. This chapter first presents the traditional methodologies, including quantitative and qualitative studies. This is followed by a discussion of the growth and decline of research methods based on the usage and analysis of big data. Immersive research methods to help companies study customer experience in the phygital by shifting their focus from a big data logic to a smart data approach are then presented and discussed.

1 TRADITIONAL RESEARCH METHODS IN MARKETING

Traditional research methods used in marketing to explore consumer behaviors include two main categories: quantitative and qualitative methodologies. Each study category encompasses a certain number of stages, which can be iterative and are mainly associated with the purpose of the study, its orientation, and the tools used. While quantitative research methods, mainly based on questionnaires and surveys, have been widely used in many areas of marketing, it is only since around 2000 that interest in qualitative research emerged among marketing scholars and companies.

Unlike quantitative research methodologies that aim to measure variables related to the purchasing process, qualitative methods provide immersive insights that help companies gain in-depth understanding of the driving forces of consumer behaviors as well as the main characteristics of customer experience occurring in the phygital setting. Given the limitations of quantitative studies, qualitative methods are the most appropriate for, if not fundamental to, capturing both tacit and explicit meanings consumers assign to their consumption activities and shopping experiences. In other words, qualitative methodologies such as focus groups and interviews allow companies to collect discursive data from the perspective of their customers.

In the qualitative logic, the investigator does not need to recruit large numbers of participants, as is the case in quantitative studies. However, representativeness and the reliability of the results are critical, and require careful thought in terms of participant selection: the more diverse the selection is of total participants, the more pertinent the insights obtained will be. Although the limitations of qualitative methods are mainly due to their subjective and interpretative nature, they are nevertheless essential in the study of consumer behavior patterns. However, with the integration and growth of digital technologies and activities such as online shopping, a new source of data has emerged—namely, big data. Thus, over a couple of years, big data became a reference in market research, used by companies across various industries, both small and large.

2   THE "BIG DATA BANG": WHY FIRMS NEED TO SHIFT TO SMART DATA IN THE PHYGITAL AND EXPERIENTIAL ERA

This section explores the emergence and growth of big data use by companies across various sectors. The objective is to define what we mean by big data and how they benefit the company's business. Big data's limitations and the need to shift to a smart data approach when it comes to examining customer experiences in the phygital era are also discussed.

2.1   The Growth and Questioning of Big Data's Relevance

Big data have become the most loyal allies of companies across different sectors. Businesses can use big data to predict and anticipate customer expectations and thus increase their innovation and attractiveness. However, big data are not enough to build substantial competitive advantage and differentiate the company's offers when designing emotional and profitable customer experiences within the phygital era, mixing both physical and digital settings. This can be explained by big data's shortcomings in terms of sociocultural contextualization and meaning embeddedness. But before delving into the critical questioning of big data (and even if we are all familiar with the term), let us first define what we mean by big data, how they work, and how they contribute to the study of consumer behaviors.

The term "big data" first appeared in the 2000s and was mainly used by the leading tech companies—Google, Amazon, Facebook, Apple, and Microsoft (GAFAM)—because of the amount of data generated from their activities on the Internet. These actors were then joined by social media platforms such as LinkedIn, Twitter, Instagram, and TikTok, among others. According to Batat (2019b), big data have several meanings that coexist, and there is no consensus on the definition due to the confusion in understanding the concept. We typically refer to big data as mass data production that companies should process to capture relevant insights to boost their businesses and sales. Big data have five main characteristics that differentiate them from traditional data collected by companies via customer relationship management (CRM), surveys, and billing processes. Thus, big data are considered a convenient source for *massive* insights, which are *varied* and *fast* (instant data generation). They are also characterized by their *unstructured* aspect and *velocity* because data need to be rapidly processed.

Nowadays, many companies across different sectors are using big data to remain relevant and competitive in the marketplace. Also, the majority of decisions in companies are based on big data, which are considered a reliable source of information that does not incur significant risk-taking in relation to intuitions and the analysis of human beings. With big data, the investigator has become an observer of the insights collected spontaneously and expressed easily on social media and other platforms without relying on traditional methodologies.

Consequently, human innovation is absent from the creative and problem-solving processes, especially when it comes to the analysis of customer experience in the phygital era. Therefore, a complementary approach should be considered by companies to implement phygital strategies combining both the efficiency of the data collected and the human elements of creativity and free thought. This approach allows companies to overcome the limits related to the use of big data as a unique source of insights to understand customer experience and consumer behaviors occurring in the phygital setting. Among the limitations of the use of big data when it comes to examining customer experience in the phygital context, Batat (2019b) identified the following issues that companies should consider in their market research:

- Gaps related to the knowledge of customers and their tangible and intangible needs. With the use of big data, consumers are no longer segmented by their actual behaviors; instead, they are segmented by their browsing patterns and click rates.
- Limits related to the perception of intrusion. The perception of intrusion linked to the use of retargeting techniques by companies can have a negative impact on the sharing of personal data.
- Legal constraints related to the collection and use of customers' personal data. Big data raise issues in terms of the protection of personal data;

therefore, regulations on data collected and used by companies have come into force.

- Constraints related to the anonymity of big data. The analysis of data from social networks is most often anonymous or attached to pseudonyms.
- Constraints related to the company's strategy and culture. The implementation of big data management, like any business project, requires commitment from corporate management, and especially the commitment of all staff to the overall project, which is not the case today in the majority of companies.

2.2   Why Do Companies Need to Shift to Smart Data?

"Smart data," a term I introduced in 2017 and then conceptualized in 2019 (Batat, 2019a), marks the limits of using big data to analyze and predict consumer behaviors with what I call the "big data bang." With a smart data approach, which refers to more immersive market research techniques, we can talk about the beginning of the end of the reign of big data as the only relevant tool for consumer analysis and the beginning of a new era. Yet, the rise of smart data depends on whether it is approached from an American or European perspective. In the American perspective, we talk about the big data bang by questioning the quality of the data analysis and its purpose; in other words, whether big data can provide companies with in-depth understanding of the real behaviors of consumers. However, in the European context, companies are still in the midst of discovery, enthusiasm, and total excitement about the big data realm.

Besides, the main issue with big data nowadays is not how to access insights and information about customers but rather how to analyze the data to develop business opportunities or solve problems when it comes to consumers' paradoxical and emotional behaviors online and offline. The aim is not to question whether big data is a valuable tool for companies or not. Instead, the purpose is to explore what other research methodologies can be put in place by companies to complement the wealth generated by the analysis of big data as this kind of information does not allow one to capture everything, especially when it comes to the "hidden obvious" aspects of consumption and purchase activities.

For instance, contextualization is one of the insights that big data cannot capture. Big data would not decode the meanings consumers assign to their consumption or contextualize users' or consumers' behaviors online and offline—for example, the use of a cell phone (mobile) or a computer. If a person uses a cell phone at home, on the train, or in the office with colleagues, the usage will differ depending on the setting; even with geolocation data, it is not easy to capture the types of use developed according to where they happen.

Thus, big data provide somewhat generalized information but do not allow companies to get closer to the actual usages embedded in various sociocultural contexts of consumers or users. This is where smart data come in as a primary or complementary tool to capture rich and relevant insights about customer experiences and consumer behaviors in both physical and digital settings. Smart data refer to highly immersive techniques, combining various exploratory research methodologies that allow companies to be as close as possible to their customers, simply spending time with them and observing them in a participatory manner and a natural context. It is about interacting with them, engaging in similar activities. For example, the investigator can join a group of consumers who are buying—using an app to purchase something online—and he or she starts buying, doing the same as participants involved in the study. Alternatively, the investigator could engage him/herself by simply observing participants in a non-participatory way. By so doing, the company can then capture the tacit meaning of the usage and all the paradoxes that will emerge from this observation, which are obviously contextualized and analyzed from the users' or consumers' perspective.

Thus, smart data are relevant because they adopt an immersive approach to collect rich data that will first solve a problem the company does not know how to solve. For example, a company that has installed a digital kiosk in its stores notices that consumers are paying no attention to it or using it for buying. So, there is a problem to solve by using different exploratory techniques to understand the "why" in this situation. Several tools can be used online, such as netnography (digital ethnography), or in the physical environment, using ethnographic methodologies to assess whether the problem comes from the digital device. Is it the consumer's profile, the location, or maybe the device's content?

Beyond identifying and solving specific problems, smart data can also be used for innovation purposes by using, for example, ethnography to predict and anticipate future trends and behaviors: How will we consume in the future? How will we shop? How will we pay for our shopping? Different insights generated will also be considered to assess whether consumers are ready to integrate novel innovations, mainly digital technologies, into their daily lives and shopping activities—not in a sporadic way, but in such a way that it is part of daily use, thus becoming part of their lifestyle. For example, you wake up in the morning and know you are going to buy something with your smartphone, that your credit card is on your phone, that is a given.

Smart data help companies anticipate and figure out innovations for the future to position themselves as pioneers that can disrupt their market by rethinking conventional business practices and consumer usages. Yet, although smart data allow companies to gain a profound understanding of their customers' behaviors both in physical and digital settings, the question is: Do companies really use smart data to gain marketing insights? The answer is not that common, and depends on the region. For example, some big companies in the US market are interested in ethnographic methodologies, such as innovating or solving sales or strategic problems. In Europe, however, companies are still following big data thinking because they are more eager to collect insights generated by big data. After all, they are immediate, fast, instantaneous, and, above all, available for reasonable fees.

It is thus interesting to note the significant drop in budgets for market research, especially exploratory and immersive methods based on field research, because the company should have the appropriate resources and adequate expertise to engage in immersive methodologies that allow the collection and transformation of smart data into innovations or solutions.

The adoption of smart data thinking in companies needs time because it can take about three months to one year, and even two years or more if the company is focusing on a complex problem or a novel technology. Consequently, companies should ask three main questions: Do we have time to engage in this process? Do we have the necessary resources to generate smart data to innovate and enhance customer loyalty? Can we create a solid and sustainable competitive advantage?

For instance, during collaboration with a company in the B2B sector that was interested in my expertise as an ethnographer, I used immersive methodologies to generate smart data and thus solve the company's problem regarding the accumulation of digital tools and platforms and their non-usage by employees. This situation is problematic because companies may spend enormous budgets on acquiring new tools and platforms, but the staff does not adopt these technologies. Each time a company offers its employees a platform to use in meetings, for example, they end up using external platforms such as Skype, WhatsApp, or Viber, which can have security and privacy issues for the company. In this case, I used organizational ethnography at the internal level, which allowed me to understand how these actors, depending on their function (e.g., marketing, sales, accounting), perceive digital technologies and how they would like them to be adapted to their needs. The insights generated by this ethnographic study show that employees need a scant number of tools that mix both personal and professional usages.

3   IMMERSIVE METHODOLOGIES APPLIED TO CUSTOMER EXPERIENCE

Immersive research methodologies include a range of qualitative and exploratory tools for advancing knowledge about consumer behaviors within highly experiential and phygital settings. To capture the paradoxes behind consumer behaviors and the meanings they assign to their consumption practices online and offline, traditional methodologies are not enough and do not allow us to capture the "hidden obvious." This is why, in 2019, I recommended a shift to more experiential and e-experiential research methodologies to thoroughly examine customer experiences in the phygital context.

This section introduces three main immersive research tools I employ both in my academic work and consultancy activities with companies across different sectors. These methodologies are projective, ethnographic and digital ethnographic, and introspective (as shown in Figure 10.1).

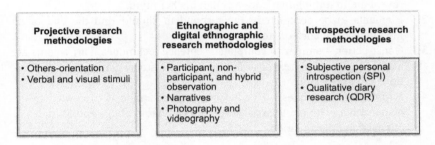

Figure 10.1   Immersive research methodologies

3.1   Projective Research Methodologies

In the marketing field, Haire's study (1950) of consumer perceptions of Nescafé instant coffee's new product image was the first that used projective methodologies to investigate consumer perceptions and attitudes toward a product. This research was conducted at a time when instant coffee was considered innovative and when most households still used traditional drip coffee.

Many marketing scholars duplicated and extended this methodology across diverse consumption domains, drawing on Haire's methodological approach. The strength of projective methodologies comes from their ability to lead individuals to express feelings that they would otherwise not express verbally. For example, to obtain a response from a respondent without asking a direct question, the investigator will create a situation where the respondent projects his/her feelings onto some other person or object. For instance, participants might be asked to comment on a situation represented as a cartoon.

Regarding consumer behavior studies, projective methodologies are used by scholars to overcome oral communication difficulties and uncover characteristics of the lived experience that informants may find challenging to voice out loud. This approach allows the investigator to capture participants' feelings, thoughts, and experiences. Besides, applying projective methodologies leads respondents to discuss personal issues or motives that the investigator may not be aware of, and without them feeling threatened by straightforward and open questioning. Respondents, whether deliberately or unintentionally, are motivated to deliver socially acceptable replies when positioned in the role of the subject in a research experiment. If this technique is used correctly, it will help researchers bypass the "common social barriers that inhibit the respondents' expression of attitudes and behaviors" (Steinman, 2009, p. 38). We can identify four main projective techniques:

1. Association—a stimulus is presented to a participant who is asked to reveal the first thing that goes through his/her mind.
2. Elements to be completed—the respondent should find the end of an incomplete sentence or story.
3. Construction—similar to completed sentence techniques. Participants are asked to construct a response in the form of history, dialogue, or description, and expression.
4. Expression techniques—a verbal or visual situation is presented to the respondents, who are then asked to describe the feelings and attitudes of others about the situation.

Projective methodologies can therefore offer verbal or visual stimuli through indirect methods and encourage respondents to disclose their unconscious feelings and attitudes without being aware that they are doing so. Consequently, as a tool to assess customer experience in a phygital setting, these methodologies are fundamental to companies and researchers studying customer experience both online and offline to apprehend the meanings and dimensions related to consumption practices. Projective methodologies are mainly used for answering the "how," "why," and "what" questions that arise in consumer behaviors. Thus, projective research tools provide in-depth comprehension of what consumers truly think and feel about their consumption and shopping experiences online and offline.

3.2   Ethnographic and Digital Ethnographic Research Methodologies

Ethnography is a research tool used in social sciences, consisting of descriptive and analytical investigations in the field of a given population's traditions, customs, and sociocultural practices. Thus, ethnography has been widely used by anthropologists and sociologists to decode individuals' behaviors in societies and thus understand society as a whole, considered as "a fundamental reality"—a metaphysical abstraction, a mystical entity. To understand the complexity of this society, ethnography is used as a tool and approach to the field in social science and humanities research.

According to Karl Popper (1959), it is necessary to start from the field, which gives a representation of the facts, phenomena, and behaviors that he qualifies as real worlds in his vision of academic scholarships. Thus, ethnography allows the understanding of phenomena that are difficult to quantify. For a long time limited to primitive populations, since the 1970s sociologists, anthropologists, and ethnologists have expanded the use of these methods to many other fields, including the study of our daily consumption practices and digital technology adoption, to better understand human experiences in their context.

Ethnography has also been implemented to study consumer behaviors online, in which case scholars refer to it as "digital ethnography" or "netnography," a method introduced by Robert Kozinets (2015). This section describes the ethnographic and netnographic research methodologies and their introduction into the marketing and customer experience field.

3.2.1 Ethnography to capture the "hidden obvious" of customer experiences

Ethnography is an exploratory, interactive, and immersive methodology that enables marketers, ethnographers, and companies to understand the social interactions between consumers and the marketplace (Batat, 2019b). It is a vital tool companies should use while analyzing customer experiences in new settings, such as the phygital context, because of its objectivity, accuracy, and completeness in recording and describing facts. Indeed, ethnographic studies do not seek only to describe facts; they go beyond collecting disparate and isolated facts by offering in-depth explanation of facts, phenomena, and behaviors in society, organizations, sectors, marketplaces, or work environments.

Companies and marketing scholars have used traditional research methods such as focus groups to understand consumer behaviors for several years now. However, today's consumer behaviors have become more complex, and focus group techniques are no longer relevant enough to analyze them. Indeed, with the focus group method, the investigator was no longer satisfied with interviewing individuals in rooms set up for this purpose, but there is a vital need to move into the field and immerse oneself in the consumers' natural environment to observe their actions, and thus decode the norms and codes of their consumption cultures. In so doing, consumer behaviors are much more natural and therefore closer to reality.

Moreover, these behaviors allow the ethnographer to react, discuss, and bounce back on new things. A simple example: a company that produces ovens can be interested in understanding how and under what conditions its product is used before putting it on the market. By implementing ethnography, the investigator visits people's homes to observe household practices and eating habits, and whether and how the oven is used.

This exploratory stage is essential in the upstream phase of the innovation process because it allows companies to design products centered on the consumer and his/her real, tangible and intangible needs; this means no longer only focusing on the supply side, but now also on the demand side. Therefore, ethnography's main objective is to analyze the symbolic and emotional aspects of consumers' consumption experiences, behaviors, and practices from their own perspective embedded in natural settings, whether physical or digital. As a result, to create a substantial competitive advantage, offer phygital experiences that fit with consumers' functional and emotional expectations, and differentiate themselves, companies should use ethnography because it is a source of innovation. It also provides companies with in-depth knowledge of their customers, which can help them identify, categorize, and analyze cultures, subcultures, countercultures, and micro-cultures of consumption. The benefits of using ethnography in exploring customer experiences in the phygital era are as follows:

- Ethnography helps firms go beyond the cognitive and rational vision of consumer behaviors by incorporating a symbolic and sociocultural perspective.
- It allows firms to decode how consumers build and develop attitudes toward brands and products in their consumption culture, and how the latter shapes their purchase patterns.
- It offers varied and immersive smart data. Thanks to ethnography, companies can collect both visual and verbal insights by recording behaviors occurring in their natural settings.
- Ethnography is a tool to use by the investigator because it allows him/her to "become invisible" and "essential" within the research group.
- Given the sociocultural dimension of consumption, ethnography appears to be the most appropriate tool in understanding the customer experience because it helps companies uncover, interpret, and understand the consumer's perspective shaped by his/her sociocultural environment.
- Ethnography allows companies to access customer experience dimensions imbued with social meaning that is otherwise tacit and made in day-to-day consumption practices; consequently, they can also gain a "thick description" of experiences.

Therefore, following the above discussion, the study of customer experience requires ethnographic tools, which include immersive and longitudinal methods for working with, rather than on, consumers, and for discovering meaning in, rather than imposing meaning on, consumer behaviors (Batat, 2019a). To better understand customer experiences occurring in the phygital context, companies need to familiarize themselves with various ethnographic techniques to collect smart data. I propose and discuss below five key ethno-graphic tools that companies can use individually or combined to examine the customer experience in the phygital setting: participant observation; non-participant observation; hybrid observation; narratives; and photography and videography.

a.   Participant observation

Observational research is traditionally associated with ethnographic and anthro-pological approaches. Participation observation occurs when a researcher joins a group for an extended period and observes the behaviors of the group members. In this case, the investigator is a "full member" when he/she partic-ipates as an actor and engages in the situation under study. The investigator does not inform the observed subjects of his/her actual role in the group. The objective of this approach is to share the experience of the individual in action. The observation is then concealed. For example, we can observe the shopping behaviors of a group of young consumers by going with them to the supermar-ket without revealing the investigator's identity while being one of them. This situation is conditioned by the group's acceptance of the outsider.

However, in participant observation in which the investigator does not reveal his/her real identity as a "hidden observer" there is a risk of being dis-covered; this raises ethical issues related to moral values, such as guaranteeing transparency toward participants in the field. That is why the investigator also chooses to disclose his/her identity and role in the group, and then ask for permission to integrate into the group and observe or study its members. In this case, the investigator clearly notifies the interview subjects of his or her status as a researcher and his or her membership of the organization and/ or company conducting the study. In this case, the investigator's position presents a trade-off. He/she has a greater degree of freedom to conduct the investigation.

In contrast to the "hidden observer" role, the "disclosed observer" role can supplement the investigator's observations with interviews. However, there are some limits to this approach. For instance, the investigator is exposed to the subjects' reactivity because he/she is mandated within the organization. He or she can be seen as not being in a neutral position with regard to the subjects, who activate defense mechanisms against the investigation or resist the disclo-sure of certain information.

Whether participant observation discloses or hides the investigator's role in observational research, Batat (2019a) suggests that the implementation of observations in the field can be guided by the use of a framework such as PERCEIVE:

P = Proximity (spatial)
E = Expressions (facial)
R = Relative orientation (in space)
C = Contact (physical)
E = Eyes
I = Individual gestures
V = Voice (vocal gestures)
E = Existence of adapters (small mood-accommodating behaviors).

Such a framework draws explicit attention to participants, interactions, routines, rituals, temporal elements, and the setting and elements of a small social organization.

b.   *Non-participant observation*

Non-participant observation is a fundamental step in the field approach, designed to collect preliminary data. It can also be a source of additional data collection, and should be considered a complementary technique where the investigator's work is confined to observing the field without interacting with the participants. He or she can then observe indicators (e.g., sociocultural context, current consumption practices, lifestyles) that he/she will include in the database. The investigator can also add non-verbal indicators produced by the subjects (e.g., facial expressions, gestures, tone, dress code).

Following non-participant observation, the investigator conducts observations by adopting the same data collection and analysis system throughout the data collection. The elements observed should be defined beforehand. This requires the development and validation of a standard framework of observations before collecting the data that will serve as the empirical basis for the research.

The non-participant observation framework can be developed based on three critical criteria. First, the categories selected should respect the rules of exclusive attribution, exhaustiveness, homogeneity, and relevance. Second, the investigator should select units of division and recording. Third, the investigator must determine a sampling plan and define a data analysis plan.

c.   *Hybrid observation*

Hybrid observational research includes both participant and non-participant observation modes as well as multi-site and "quick and dirty" techniques. Hybrid observation gives the investigator more flexibility to adapt to different situations across various settings where he/she can decide to switch from participant to non-participant observation, and vice versa.

To implement hybrid observations, in my previous research I identified three stages to navigate from one approach to another, whether from participant to non-participant or from multi-site to quick and dirty observations (Batat, 2019a). These three stages are socialization, collaboration, and auto-confrontation (Batat and Tanner, 2021).

- In the socialization stage, the investigator can use observation and informal conversations to work with participants. This stage can be extended for three or six months, and allows full immersion in the consumption culture of the informants. Participating in formal and informal conversations and social activities among consumers, observing their behaviors and reactions, and informally interviewing as many individuals as possible can help the investigator accomplish socialization.
- In the collaboration stage, the investigator can invite participants to engage in collective and individual in-depth interviews and workshops on consumption experiences. This phase can follow two modes to collect data: multi-site, and quick and dirty. Multi-site observation consists of following several groups of consumers in several parallel fields, several consumption practices in different consumption cultures. Quick and dirty observation refers to an accelerated method in step with the changes and rapid shifts in the contemporary society. It is more fragmented, faster, and more fluid.
- In auto-confrontation, the investigator can ask participants to comment on principal results, describing their own and others' consumption experiences.

These paths, combining various observational techniques, can lead companies to build a full picture of consumers' perceptions and definitions of their own experiences that are shaped by a particular consumption culture within a marketplace in which they interact with other market actors (e.g., institutions, industry, other consumers).

d.   Narratives

Narrative is an ethnographic technique that refers to the life stories and tales of people as a qualitative research method. It originated in the social sciences, and can be used in marketing to understand individuals, their consumption experiences, and socially constructed practices within a particular consumption culture. The narrative discourse of consumers provides knowledge about their sociocultural sphere and their interactions with other people, companies, parents, and other social agents.

However, reducing consumers' life stories and narratives to a simple tool for understanding social phenomena is reductive. Indeed, collecting and analyzing insights based on life stories allows companies and marketers to search for and construct meaning relative to individual temporal facts. They are then conceived as tools to orient the company's marketing and communication actions and make it think about future innovations. Sociologists have identified three main narrative tools: life trajectory, biography, and cognitive mapping. Companies can use these tools to explore and learn more about both explicit and tacit aspects of phygital customer experiences. The three narrative tools are presented below.

Life trajectory refers to an interweaving of multiple biographical lines that are more or less autonomous or dependent on one another: educational path, work–life balance, family life, social life, health, residential trajectory, political itinerary, among others. Each of these domains reflects a set of practices, roles, and social identities that unfold along three axes: places; periods, temporalities, networks; and structural frameworks. The trajectory as a whole is thus made up of a succession of situations experienced by individuals within different spheres and by the history of the various successive configurations or "identity forms" that structure the articulation between these spheres of social life.

Moreover, individual trajectories are not linear but composed of stages, punctuated by ruptures and "bifurcations," in which timing and outcome are unpredictable. Path or trajectory bifurcation refers to the idea of "turning points" used to analyze professional careers, marked by succeeding phases of transition, more or less predictable, more or less brief, more or less ritualized or institutionalized. A moment of doubt, of uncertainty, often marks the beginning of a bifurcation. This differs from biographical "transition," in which arrival is predictable (e.g., end of college), or from the "crossroads," where outcomes remain limited and structured (e.g., school orientation due to compulsory choice).

Therefore, life trajectory, including different paths, is an integral part of the narrative experience. Through it, the individual presents a multiplicity of spheres: some of these have sometimes allowed a bifurcation or a change in choosing to reject or adopt brands or consumption fields; and others have subsequently been affected by these changes. For example, the story of the process of becoming vegan is rarely limited to only the ideological and the health spheres. It evokes other spheres—such as a family sphere, an economic sphere, or, even, more subjectively, a "life project" in its entirety—which significantly influenced the decision to convert from mainstream eating behaviors to becoming vegan. A life trajectory thus highlights a life story that includes different ingredients consumers use to make a meaningful decision.

Biographical narratives are defined as a method that allows the collection of fact-based stories. American sociologists of the Chicago School introduced this form of collecting narratives in the 1920s. It is based on a comprehensive approach to phenomena, and considers the social actor under investigation as an absolute observatory of the social sphere, from which the interactions and actions of all are made and unmade. From there, companies need to understand the factors that motivate consumer actions from each actor's perspective. This objective is only achievable by giving each of them a voice. Biographical narratives represent therefore an opportunity for the investigator to uncover in detail how each person reacted, for example, to the launch of a new product, the knowledge accumulated, and the actions taken by asking a study participant to tell all or part of his or her lived experience. Using biographical narratives, the investigator can then articulate and mobilize arguments to justify the stages experienced to form an ideology of one's own life. One of the difficulties inherent in the study of biographical narrative paths is finding methodological solutions that can unify different paths into a unique journey and account for the intelligibility of biographical orders. To overcome these limitations we can also use cognitive mapping.

Cognitive mapping is a conceptual map, which includes the product of an approach that aims to graphically project the mental representations or the statements that an individual or a group of individuals make about a problem. It is therefore a graph that presents the links between concepts or nodes. The links most often represent causal relations, but also relations of proximity and influence. Concepts correspond to regularities perceived in events, and objects are delivered orally through descriptions, and formalized in the form of labels. It is thus a graphic representation of the mental picture that the investigator makes of a set of discursive representations stated by a participant, based on his or her own cognitive representations about a particular field of consumption or a brand.

e.   *Photography and videography*

Photography and videography are considered relevant ethnographic tools that companies can use to capture rich and deep insights by collecting and analyzing visual data. Visual data allow details to be discovered that could have escaped the investigator's sight at first glance. Visuals are usually used to describe points of sale, salespeople, and customers (e.g., clothing, behaviors, usages). However, photos or videos should not be the only basis for in-depth interpretation; notes from the field should supplement them.

Visuals can be collected through two approaches: generated by the investigator, and produced by participants involved in the study. In the first case, the investigator uses a camera to film participants' practices and behaviors (e.g., how they use online shopping, how they use delivery apps). In the second case, participants are given cameras to film themselves or take pictures. Taking photographs or shooting videos are ways of involving participants in the data collection process. Indeed, having participants in the field who are offered the possibility of expressing their consumption practices through photographs and videos produced by them—that represent the consumption objects and practices that constitute their universe—allows companies to gain access to a visual representation of their consumption cultures.

3.2.2 Digital ethnographic (netnographic) research methodologies

Digital ethnography or netnography appeared in the late 1990s and flourished in the early 2010s. This methodology takes the classic steps of ethnography and adapts them to the study of behaviors and online communities. It refers to an online immersion technique on social media and specialized blogs to analyze the discourses and exchanges between people on the Internet. In order to conduct a netnography study, the investigator/researcher should follow the four main stages described by its founder, Kozinets (2015):

1. *Entry.* The investigator should prepare the groundwork before selecting the community to study and beginning analysis. First, it is important to set clear goals and questions; then, identification is needed of the online communities that correspond to the defined objective.
2. *Data collection.* Data are available within the virtual community in the form of texts written by the members of the group and other data related to the external elements of communication with subjects, such as voice, silences, etc. Other data are also considered, such as that produced by the investigator (notes, reflections, written remarks, etc.).
3. *Data analysis and interpretation.* During this stage, data are encoded with variables that reflect the participants' behaviors. An ethical approach is then considered to conceptualize the results.
4. *Validation by participants and ethics of the process.* Here, the virtual community members can be contacted and the results of the netnography research presented to them to obtain their comments so that they are transparent. Feedback is essential because it allows members to qualify the results and improve their understanding.

Therefore, like ethnography, netnography is interested in the study of brand communities on the Internet. A netnography approach can employ several methodological tools, including online interviews, participant observation on the Internet, and a narrative account of consumer practices. Overall, netnography can be conducted through participant or non-participant observations applied online. This approach allows companies to collect richer and more personal insights because of the lack of physical maintenance.

3.3   Introspective Research Methodologies

Collecting data using introspective tools engages the investigator in an interactive dialogue with participants who share their private experiences and insider knowledge. Holbrook (1997) introduced subjective personal introspection (SPI) more than 25 years ago as a research methodology with an extreme form of participant observation. According to Gould (2012), there are two approaches that marketers can use to capture rich insights about customer experiences within physical and digital settings: (1) related to the use of introspection by considering multiple investigators' perspectives; (2) a personal perspective—in other words, how the investigator can tell a story in his/her own way. This latter state implies looking inward at oneself (Batat and Wohlfeil, 2009).

Holbrook (1997) argues that SPI is an experiential, private self-reflection on the joys and sorrows related to consumption found in one's own everyday participation in the human condition. Aligned with Holbrook's view, Gould (2012) states that, unlike other methodologies in qualitative research, with SPI the investigator often takes on the dual role of researcher and informant. One of the main benefits of this tool is that SPI methodologies allow companies to explore the subjective nature of human feelings—daydreams, sensations, and streams of consciousness related to consumption—which could not be identified with traditional research methods or big data analysis.

Wallendorf and Brucks (1993) identified four essential introspective techniques companies could use to generate rich insights about customer experiences: self-introspection, interactive introspection, guided introspection, and syncretic introspection. Table 10.1 provides a summary of the characteristics of each tool.

In addition to SPI, companies can also use Qualitative Diary Research (QDR), an innovative tool to capture rich insights into customer experiences, processes, relationships, settings, products, and rituals (e.g., Patterson, 2005) in physical and digital settings. QDR is defined as a personal diary reporting daily events, observations, and thoughts that inform about how individuals see and talk about their everyday lives.

For Arnould (1998), diaries could add previously unexplored experience dimensions to consumer research methods because they allow companies to capture a thick description of the complexities and the dynamics of the customer experience (Patterson, 2005). Thus, as an immersive research tool, QDR is suitable for revealing the experiences and thoughts of consumers which are often hidden since events are recorded in their natural environment.

Table 10.1   *Introspective research approaches*

Approach	Characteristics
Researcher self-introspection	This is an auto-ethnographic technique, and the most controversial introspective data collection approach. The context is the researcher's private life experiences; therefore, he/she acts as the expert and sole informant in a sample of one study
Interactive introspection	This technique has been used in recent works focusing on interactive introspection through a narrative transportation approach
Guided introspection	Informants are asked to write a detailed introspective essay on their personal lived experiences with regard to a phenomenon of interest
Syncretic introspection	This is essentially a mixed-method approach that involves a combination of the first three methods

KEY TAKEAWAYS

This chapter underlined the limits of methodologies based on traditional research techniques and big data as ways to learn more about customer experiences in the phygital setting. It then examined the need for companies to shift to a smart data approach to develop a better and deeper understanding of the tacit and hidden dimensions related to the customer experience. For companies, the transition from big data to smart data can be implemented by using various tools that include projective, ethnographic and netnographic, and introspective research methodologies.

11. Experiential Design Thinking (EXDT): a new tool to create innovative phygital experiences for consumer well-being

CHAPTER OVERVIEW

This chapter examines how the new model of Experiential Design Thinking (EXDT) can offer critical insights on approaches for designing innovative and ethical customer experiences in the phygital era. The chapter answers the following questions: What are the limits of traditional design thinking methods? And why should companies consider an "experiential approach" to their innovation process when it comes to creating satisfying, efficient, and profitable phygital experiences? The chapter first presents the emergence and development of design thinking models. It then discusses how the EXDT model works and what steps design thinkers and companies can follow to create innovative and pleasurable phygital experiences that help consumers achieve well-being.

1   FROM A TRADITIONAL APPROACH TO DESIGN THINKING

Across industries where traditional business models are being challenged, design thinking seems to have become one of the most promising sources of innovation. This section examines the emergence and development of design thinking as a tool and a way of thinking implemented by companies in the product innovation process. The objective here is to understand how design thinking can be integrated into an innovation process. I also introduce the limits of traditional design thinking when it comes to shifting the focus from designing products to designing phygital customer experiences.

1.1   The History and Development of Design Thinking

Beyond its fashionable effect, design thinking is a way of thinking with origins going back to the nineteenth century, as heir to industrial design. A designer named Tim Brown brought it to the forefront to understand the growing complexity of the contemporary world and help companies solve problems by considering design thinking to comprehend the vast quantities of information at their disposal.

The complexity also comes from the rapid change that characterizes today's technological, social, economic, and institutional macroenvironment. In these circumstances, the ability to innovate becomes a key success factor for organizations, which seek to industrialize the means to make innovation happen. Design thinking has emerged in this context, described as a method, as a set of practices, and as a philosophy.

At the heart of design thinking are the ways in which designers approach complex situations to produce viable solutions through the application of principles, methods, and tools that organizations could potentially benefit from. Figure 11.1 summarizes the major phases of design thinking development across different fields and disciplines.

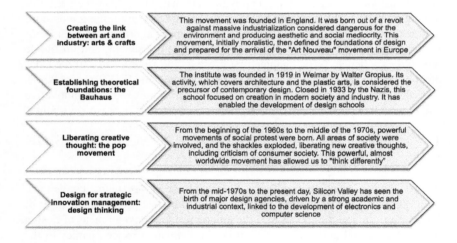

Figure 11.1   Key phases of design thinking development

From a historical perspective, the roots of design thinking go back to the 1960s and 1970s with the work of the first generation of researchers who tried to understand and describe the work of designers, thus developing a new field of research: design research.

- Herbert Simon, a cognitive scientist and winner of the Nobel Prize in Economics in 1978, is undoubtedly one of the concept's originators. In his book *The Sciences of the Artificial* (1969), Simon describes it as "a way of thinking" that refers to the works of designers as an abstract activity that allows them to solve "wicked problems."
- The second milestone in the history of design thinking came in the 1980s with a new approach focusing less on the idea of design as a science and more on the actual practice of designers. In a seminal article, Cross (1982) examined the specificity of designers' modes of knowledge by focusing on what he refers to as "designerly ways of knowing." The term "design thinking" only emerged as such a few years later.
- Rowe (1987), the first to use the term, defined design thinking as methods and approaches used by architects and planners to shape ideas for buildings and public spaces.
- Similarly, Norman (1988) introduced the notion of "user-centered design," which is one of the foundations of design thinking.
- Buchanan (1992) then defined design thinking as a concept that can be applied in all areas, tangible or intangible. He identified four main fields of application: visual communication; material objects; organizational activities and services; and complex or environmental systems. At the same time, Stanford University and the design agency IDEO (both located in California, in the heart of Silicon Valley) provided a conceptualization of design thinking as an innovation process with specific steps, methodology, and tools. Nowadays, design thinking is considered a new approach to innovation that extends well beyond the traditional sphere of industrial design.

Since the 2000s, design thinking has been spreading on a large scale, first in the United States and then in Europe, in the business world and in education and social innovation. Three key moments mark the progression of design thinking. First, an article published in *Businessweek* by Nussbaum (2004) refers to design thinking as a powerful lever for innovation, a tool that was part of the success of the design agency IDEO. The focus is on the agency's methodology and its five-phase process: observation, brainstorming, rapid prototyping, redesign, and implementation. Even if the term "design thinking" does not appear in the article, the method and the state of mind are there.

The second key moment is the conference by IDEO's executive chair, Tim Brown, at Stanford University in 2007, entitled "Strategy by Design: How Design Thinking Builds Opportunities." The third is the publication of his book *Change by Design* (Brown, 2009), which marked the founding of design thinking as an inevitable tool within business innovation. In it Brown offers one of the most widely used definitions of design thinking today. He defines it as a discipline that uses the sensibility, tools, and methods of designers to enable multidisciplinary teams to innovate by matching user expectations, feasibility, and economic viability. This definition underlines the importance of finding a harmonious balance between three criteria to validate an idea: desirability, feasibility, and viability. This is a complex approach that calls for different ways of thinking. The desirability criterion requires, for example, excellent observational skills, empathy, and intuition, whereas the feasibility and viability criteria mainly require technical, economic, and financial skills.

Later on, the first school dedicated to design thinking, Stanford University's d.school, was created to disseminate knowledge of the tool in the United States, and then expanded to Europe (including Germany, Finland, and France).

The IDEO conceptualization of design thinking—that, instead of asking how to solve a problem, we should ask ourselves why we have this problem—is now considered a recognized method of coming up with new ideas to solve problems. It is also one of the most effective methods for social action, disruptive innovation projects, and business development. Brown's contribution to design thinking confirms the effectiveness of this mode of thinking, particularly in terms of:

• the efficiency of the creative professions in the innovation process;
• the relevance of leadership in the project not only through design but also beyond the exercise of the project, in the company;
• the importance of considering subjective and intuitive elements, including identity and emotional values, in relation to a business strategy to differentiate the company's offerings.

Thus, this vision repositioned designers at the center of the innovation project, no longer just as specialists but also as mediators of interdisciplinary cultures or as liaisons in multidisciplinary teams. Since around 2015, with Brown's approach, the term design thinking has become more encompassing by placing the human being at the center of the problem-solving approach, in contrast to technology- or organization-centered approaches traditionally adopted until then. However, analysis of the literature shows that the IDEO/Brown definition has been challenged and is not the only approach to design thinking. Although Brown's approach has contributed to both business and academic spheres, it has two main weaknesses:

• The first is related to the lack of information or structuring that would allow design thinking to be used in a concrete way as a decision-making tool. For Brown, the decision is the result of the designer's reflections after integrating the context and all the data.

- The second is the absence of temporality in Brown's demonstration, whereas design thinking accompanies a process through successive phases in which, moreover, each sphere has a greater or lesser weighting according to the progress of the project.

Furthermore, scholars in different disciplines introduced multiple approaches, tools, and concepts that contrast, assess, or enrich IDEO's vision of design thinking. The following section summarizes the perspectives that contributed to the conceptualization of design thinking by expanding Brown's approach.

BOX 11.1 DESIGN THINKING IN PRACTICE: BANK OF AMERICA'S "KEEP THE CHANGE" PROGRAM

The Bank of America's "Keep the Change" program is interesting for understanding how design thinking can contribute to innovation processes in companies. In 2004, the bank noticed that few mothers aged between 40 and 55 were opening a savings account; so, in collaboration with IDEO, it decided to set up a project to resolve this issue. The project team undertook a multi-month trip across the United States to observe numerous mothers in their daily lives. This allowed the team to realize that these women tended to round up their spending to the nearest dollar (e.g., if they buy a sandwich for $5.70, including tip, most will give $6 and not get back the $0.30 in change). All these pennies left over add up to a certain amount that could save these women money.

The project members therefore created a special debit card for these women that automatically transferred the spare pennies to a savings account. Thus, without changing their lifestyle or consumption habits, they could now save money. The "Keep the Change" project has been a real success for the bank. It shows the importance of observation and empathy, especially in the early stages of a project. Thus, by looking at the product or service through the consumer's eyes, the design thinker identifies the problem more efficiently. The key to design thinking lies here: working more on understanding and redefining the initial problem than finding a solution. Consequently, the solution found is better adapted to the consumer's expectations, which improves the overall experience.

To sum up, we can note that design thinking is a practical tool that leads companies to design innovative products or services through the eyes of consumers. Design thinking allows everyone to develop a creative mindset while solving problems by changing the way of seeing things and considering a problem.

Although there is no consensus on the approaches to design thinking since each company can adapt it according to its needs and resources, IDEO has set up a three-step process that is widely used today:

1. The first phase is "Inspiration," when the problem, needs, and resources are identified.
2. Then comes the "Ideation" phase, which aims to generate, develop, and prototype as many ideas as possible.
3. The last phase, "Implementation," transforms the best idea into an actual product or service.

2 DESIGN THINKING PERSPECTIVES

Scholars of design thinking have offered numerous conceptualizations, which are used by both academics and practitioners. For instance, Kimbell (2011) defines design thinking as a cognitive style to resolve a problem, a theory to assess a thorny issue, and an organizational resource for companies seeking innovation. Design thinking has given rise to numerous perspectives to expand Brown's model, and thus solve the current challenges companies face across various businesses. These perspectives are classified into three main approaches to innovation: the silo approach, the sequenced approach, and the managerial approach.

2.1 The Silo Approach

The silo approach is grounded in the creation, innovation, and traditional development process introduced by Buxton (2007). The silo process encompasses four stages: step (−1), which is related to research and development (R&D) skills; step (0), which refers to design skills; step (1), engineering; and step (2), which includes sales and commerce. Buxton emphasized the need to mix the three fields of design, engineering, and marketing at the first stage of the innovation process to guarantee more efficiency and effectiveness.

However, although Buxton's model is practical and easy to implement, it is considered narrow because of its silo approach. It is thus necessary to overcome this traditional approach of compartments by combining various competencies as early as possible in the innovation process and incorporating human and social sciences at all product/service development stages. Undeniably, the contributions of the human sciences can be multiple. For example, anthropologists and ethnographers can enrich the innovation and design process via immersive observations that reveal the hidden obvious elements (Batat, 2019a). Thus, companies should develop a design thinking model that goes beyond the silo approach by considering other, more comprehensive methodologies, such as sequenced and managerial perspectives on innovation (Péché et al., 2016).

2.2 The Sequenced Approach

The sequenced approach emphasizes the idea that an innovation project is built through five phases, each of which has an objective and an outcome, and each of which requires certain cognitive patterns. These cognitive patterns (which often work in pairs) are as follows: analysis/synthesis; reflection-observation/ action-realization; convergence/divergence; and concrete/abstract. As a result, Péché and colleagues propose five phases of design thinking: (1) monitoring and exploration; (2) research and proposals; (3) development and evaluation; (4) experimentation and finalization; and (5) valorization and deployment. Table 11.1 summarizes the five steps of the sequential design thinking model.

This sequential design thinking approach allows businesses to incorporate multiple skills that are put into action during the innovation process. Kolb and Fry (1975) identified four major skills integrated into the process:

- the ability to reason about concrete experiences (feeling);
- the ability to reflect and observe (seeing);
- the ability to conceptualize in an abstract way (thinking);
- the ability to experiment (doing).

2.3 The Managerial Approach

Lastly, this perspective on design thinking models underlines the idea that the managerial approach to innovation is rooted in practices that originated in the First Industrial Revolution and have since been successfully developed. Particularly relevant in an era seeking a new management model, this thinking is beginning to find spaces to be developed, taught, and practiced.

A managerial approach to design thinking invites organizational actors to change their management and business practices in-depth, and to set up an innovation process that involves a diverse team considering different aspects: social, technical, functional, and cultural. This approach to design thinking is considered critical for companies to prevent the failure of innovation projects.

Table 11.1   The five steps of the sequential design thinking model

Step	Description
Monitoring and exploration	This step focuses on the problem statement, which must be examined from multiple perspectives, contextualized, and then confronted with multiple disciplinary and cultural fields
Research and proposals	This phase involves interpreting the results of the initial monitoring and exploration to extract design concepts
Development and evaluation	This phase synthesizes the coexisting solutions along with analysis of the technological and financial contexts
Experimentation and finalization	This phase provides the precise definition of the proposed solution in the form of a prototype and its validation in terms of usages, technologies, ethics, financial viability, and identity. The project presented at the end of this phase should be directly transposable into production
Valorization and deployment	This final phase includes production and commercial deployment. It ensures that the design chosen is indeed the one put into production or operation, and that the investments and technical choices for the product launch are respected

3   DESIGN THINKING TOOLS

Although the principles of design thinking are generally agreed upon by various practitioners and researchers, and several methods exist to guide their application, the tools used to design innovations are less documented. The following section briefly presents the main design thinking tools.

Among the current design thinking tools we can cite Gasparini and Chasanidou (2016), who associate each of the five phases of the Stanford method with several tools that allow innovation objectives to be achieved. These include observation, personnel, brainstorming, questionnaires, co-creation with users, interviews, workshops, customer journey mapping, prototyping, design scenarios, focus groups, interviews, storyboards, and stakeholder mapping. The authors refer to these tools as being capable of sparking innovation.

Of these tools, stakeholder mapping represents the project's actors and ecosystem, and the links between them. Customer journey mapping takes the customer's standpoint to describe the points of contact between the company and the customer during service delivery: the "service blueprint" highlights the stages of a service process and the associated actions on the organization's side and the customer's side; the "business plan canvas" is a visual way to take ownership of a business model and the related economic, operational, and managerial decisions; and rapid prototyping aims to improve the communication of ideas and the generation of feedback from stakeholders.

From research based on several professional sources, Alves and Nunes (2013) identified 164 design tools and techniques, which they classified by relevance to the service design activity, and note that about a third of them constitute a core set of techniques that are almost universally used. They labeled 25 tools they have selected because they are used by two or more professional sources in their sample. Also, IDEO has published a set of 51 cards briefly describing tools to be used during the design process.

3.1 The Limits of Design Thinking in the Experiential and Phygital Era

Although design thinking brings a fundamental change in the company's innovation process to solve problems while offering creative products and services, it has some limitations for designing customer experiences in the phygital realm. The main drawback of this approach seems to be its name.

On the one hand, emphasizing the word "design" diminishes the importance of the human aspect, especially when it comes to human intangible needs (e.g., emotional, social, symbolic). On the other hand, companies are commonly organized in silos, which is the opposite of the design thinking approach that encourages mixing skills and experiences within the project team. Also, the traditional approach to design thinking is mainly anchored in the present, including current needs, possibilities, and desires.

Bruce Nussbaum, one of the biggest advocates of design thinking, referred to it as a "failed experiment" and announced the death of design thinking (Nussbaum, 2011). He supports the idea that the tool in itself did not allow for the concept of disruptive innovations because it is sclerotic. By definition, consumers do not interact with products or services they do not know, and by observing them. Design thinkers can only analyze the problems of existing products, and so will not have clear solutions for designing new innovative and disruptive products or services that create opportunities for businesses.

Initially, design thinking allowed designers to increase their impact and liberate creativity in companies, which welcomed what they perceived as a well-defined process. There have been some successes, but also many failures. These failures can be explained by the fact that companies have integrated design thinking "too well" and have turned it into a linear and closed process capable of producing, at best, incremental innovation. Managers have sometimes made design thinking a linear process to improving company performance and organization. The consultants who promoted design thinking in companies hoped that implementing this new process alone would produce major cultural and organizational changes. However, we should keep in mind that, from the start, design thinking was only a technique, one among others, to achieve the real goal: creativity. The problem is that, to make it compatible with the procedural culture of companies, design thinking has been stripped of the disorder, conflict, failures, emotions, and the feedback loops that are part of creativity. Companies that have embraced the disorderliness inherent in the creative process are rare, and, in most cases, the success rate of implementing design thinking has been low.

Design thinking has had one great merit, however: it has played a fundamental role in completely rethinking the place of designers in society. Previously confined to a vision limited to products and their aesthetics, designers now occupy an increasingly central place because they include the human element in their reflections and systematically consider the social, economic, and environmental problems of our time.

Announcing the death of design thinking, Nussbaum (2011) believes that its future lies in abandoning it in companies as a fixed process from which an improved creative capacity would result. According to him, it is a matter of promoting creative intelligence; in other words, the company's ability to approach problems in a renewed way and to conceive original answers. It is a sociological rather than a psychological approach, where creativity emerges from the activities of a group rather than from a genius individual or from the implementation of a particular process.

Furthermore, in recent research by Batat (2021d), Batat and Addis (2021), and Addis et al. (2021), Brown's traditional design thinking approach has been questioned and revised in light of designing experiences instead of mere products. These studies emphasize the importance of rethinking design thinking by designing experiences that include both economic and ethical drivers and outcomes of the innovation process. In so doing, these scholars advance design thinking research by considering a holistic and systemic perspective, using multiple methodologies aimed at creating customer experiences that focus on consumers' well-being as an outcome of the innovation process.

Therefore, to fill the gap in the literature and go beyond the traditional approach that conceives design thinking as a linear process leading to innovation, I introduce here a new holistic tool: Experiential Design Thinking (EXDT), which can help companies design innovative, satisfying, and profitable experiences that are both ethical and focused on consumer well-being in phygital settings. The next section presents and explains the EXDT tool and its components.

4   TOWARD EXDT TO CREATE INNOVATIVE PHYGITAL EXPERIENCES FOR CONSUMER WELL-BEING

Based on my earlier work applying an experiential approach in the food industry to design innovation experiences aimed at promoting healthy eating among consumers (Batat, 2021d), I propose EXDT as a new holistic framework that defines design thinking from an experiential perspective. Here the focus is on well-being and business ethics as core values in the innovation process that designers and companies should integrate while creating innovative phygital experiences.

As discussed above, scholars of design thinking adopted a narrow perspective on customer experiences, restricting them to products. EXDT builds on prior research on business ethics, well-being, and design thinking to create innovative phygital experiences. Figure 11.2 illustrates EXDT's three phases (preparation, implementation, and outcomes) and components.

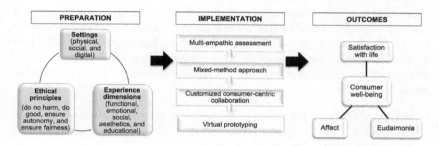

Figure 11.2   Experiential Design Thinking (EXDT) model

EXDT's holistic focus will help shed light on how designers and companies can solve problems and offer innovative and pleasurable phygital experiences by adopting a comprehensive and integral perspective rather than a one-sided approach to innovation. Accordingly, an integrated team of design thinkers, engineers, consumer behavior researchers, and community members—each bringing different areas of expertise and different sets of skills—has significantly more potential to address environmental, digital, and social issues than any one of these groups working alone.

The new EXDT tool follows an ethical logic and aims to deliver a comprehensive framework to examine how the experiential and phygital aspects of consumption modify the research agenda of scholars investigating the role of design thinking in innovation to help consumers achieve well-being. I define and explain the phases and components of this new tool in the subsections that follow.

4.1   The EXDT Preparation Phase

The preparation phase involves identifying the main drivers of innovation in the EXDT model, which should mainly be focused on an "experience-centric innovation" approach that considers a shift in the paradigm from "product design" to "experience design" (Batat, 2019a). By focusing on customer experiences and integrating an experience-centric innovation approach as a driver of innovation, companies can create suitable phygital experiences that can connect physical and digital settings to improve the individual and collective well-being of consumers.

In contrast to the traditional design thinking process, EXDT includes customer experience dimensions (functional, emotional, social, aesthetic, and educational) identified in prior work (Batat, 2019a) and physical and digital settings. Indeed, customer experiences are an integral part of social and cultural ties and evolve from digital to physical, and vice versa. Since customer experience is a multidimensional concept that should be assessed in a phygital realm, it is vital to consider the dimensions that should be integrated into the EXDT preparation stage. Drawing on research by Batat and Addis (2021) on the use of design thinking to create innovative experiences, three key settings that can affect the design of experience should be considered in the preparation phase:

- *Physical setting.* This refers to interactions between consumers and the consumption field environmental elements that can have positive or negative effects on the customer experience.
- *Social setting.* The social influences on consumption processes have long been recognized. The social environment to which consumers are introduced defines individuals' self-image and their role in society, which can refer to a real or a virtual society.
- *Digital setting.* Digital technologies allow designers to create environments that are flexible, adaptable, and even customizable. This provides many options to create immersive environments by including different touchpoints to enrich the phygital experiences and thus attract customers.

Furthermore, ethical thinking should be a guiding principle right from the earlier stages of the Experiential Design Thinking process. In their recent article, Addis and colleagues (2021) introduce a conceptual framework for designing experiences that enhance consumer well-being in the food service industry. The framework proposed employs a systemic rather than an endemic approach to the innovation process, and promotes prioritizing ethical decision-making alongside economic decision-making. The authors offer four fundamental ethical propositions that designers should consider to prevent unintended consequences of their innovations and thus design innovative experiences focusing on well-being:

1. Do no harm.
2. Do good.

3. Ensure autonomy.
4. Ensure fairness.

4.2   The EXDT Implementation Phase

This phase leads to the creation of phygital experiences following four key steps:

1. multi-empathic assessment;
2. a mixed-method approach;
3. customized consumer-centric collaboration;
4. virtual prototyping of the experience.

Companies and design thinkers can implement these steps to design innovative phygital experiences that incorporate consumers' individual and collective well-being.

4.2.1   Multi-empathic assessment

This refers to the use of empathy to understand consumers' functional and emotional needs. As in traditional design thinking, empathy has always been a critical factor that helps designers reveal and understand the tacit needs and emotions of the users they are designing solutions for (Olsen, 2014). Empathy has been defined by Cuff et al. (2016) as better care for well-being. A generic definition of empathy refers to the ability to take the perspective of others, to understand their reasoning and emotional state. However, a deep examination by Batat (2019a) of the concept of empathy emphasizes its multidimensional aspect, which should be considered in design thinking to create innovative experiences that fit with consumers' tangible and intangible needs in both physical and digital settings. Following an experiential perspective, empathy is the holistic perspective on design thinking, which should be assessed according to its type.

Batat (2019a) identifies six types of empathy that can be used to design experiential marketing policies to serve consumers and their employees optimally: (1) emotion contagion (feel and share emotions); (2) empathic accuracy (identify and understand emotional states); (3) emotion regulation (the ability to understand, regulate, and work with one's own emotions); (4) perspective taking (emotion projection); (5) concern for others (ability to care, compassion); and (6) perspective engagement (act in skillful ways based on empathy).

By adopting these six empathies companies can decode consumers' hidden needs and emotions and go beyond the concepts of attractiveness, viability, and sustainability of a product or service by becoming customer-centric with an eye on the customer's well-being. Thus, in contrast to the traditional conceptualization of design thinking, EXDT includes different types of empathy that evolve according to different stages of the lived experience, whether in a physical, digital, or phygital setting.

4.2.2   Mixed-method approach

This refers to problem identification and solving approaches. The traditional design thinking process identifies the problem as a result of initially observing consumers to try to increase an outcome variable, which is typically represented by sales. The EXDT framework, however, challenges both the start and end point, especially when designing innovative phygital experiences. Indeed, experiences are highly symbolic and need to be examined holistically from different methodological and disciplinary perspectives to improve the full range of experience results. While focus groups and surveys can be helpful, these methods simply ask consumers what they think they want or need.

Researchers can observe consumer behavior for clues about their range of unmet needs to gain even more precious insights. The EXDT process puts the individual—as well as cultural, environmental, and legal factors that shape healthy, responsible, pleasurable, and meaningful consumer behaviors—at the center of the innovation process (Batat, 2021d). Interpretative work from anthropology and sociology indicates that ethnicity, history, religion, and social status have shaped consumption experiences in both physical and digital settings. Thus, to understand both individual and societal factors and design innovative phygital experiences, EXDT integrates experimental and interpretative approaches while combining work based on qualitative or quantitative data on customer experience.

Furthermore, the iterative design process, especially experimental work, can be beneficial to improve the quality and functionality of innovative phygital experiences. Indeed, experimental work informs the iterative design process as it enables various testing variables that shape the phygital experience. Evaluative research processes are essential parts of the iterative design process, and experimental studies may provide the feedback necessary to adjust the system. Thus, findings from different methodologies (interpretative, data-based qualitative, or quantitative) inform the distinct levels and dimensions of the phygital experience. Each dimension calls for specific methodologies, whether experimental, interpretative, or immersive.

4.2.3   Customized consumer-centric collaboration

The next step of the EXDT model, customized consumer-centric collaboration, focuses on the consumer in the co-creation and innovation process. To create successful, fruitful, and innovative phygital experiences, involving, collaborating, and concentrating on the consumer are essential (Batat, 2021d).

In contrast to traditional design thinking that focuses on consumer usage for product innovation purposes, EXDT puts customers at the beginning of the innovation process to develop truly new experiences. Incorporating consumers into the design process can aid in understanding their unique problems, and enduring consumption experiences can be developed to enhance well-being. In the EXDT framework, the goal is to design experiences instead of products as a way to increase consumer well-being, both online and offline. Therefore, a customized consumer-centric collaboration goes beyond the traditional design thinking that focuses on value-in-use (Ramaswamy, 2008); EXDT adopts a co-creation logic that focuses on value-in-experience (Batat, 2019a). Focusing on the consumer shows that specific sustainability goals cannot be reached without consumer involvement. In reframing the issue from the consumers' standpoint, the company will grow the potential of its successful experiential offerings. Thus, EXDT, with its consumer-centric approach and its focus on value-in-experience, is an ideal tactic to create innovative phygital experiences to help consumers achieve well-being.

4.2.4 Virtual prototyping of the experience

The last step of the process revises and advances the critical final step of traditional design thinking: visualization and rapid prototyping. The latter focuses on the consumer's ability to visualize in order to create prototypes that can be changed quickly and cost-effectively. In traditional design thinking prototyping is devoted to visualization involving traditional charts and graphs, storytelling, experience journeys, business concept illustrations, and the use of metaphors and analogies. In contrast, EXDT uses immersive technologies, which focus on both tangible and intangible features of the experience to design innovative phygital experiences aimed at enhancing and improving consumer well-being.

By adopting immersive and virtual technologies, EXDT can leverage the vital resource of consumer imagery. Immersive technologies such as virtual reality (VR) and augmented reality (AR) can help designers make consumers feel the emotions of the experience they are designing within physical and digital settings. The literature provides evidence that immersive technologies and tools such as information acceleration (IA) and VR have been applied in the visualization and rapid prototyping of products (Urban et al., 1996). For example, IA enabled the recreation of a virtual car showroom where consumers could examine vehicles using tactile, olfactory, and visual senses and seek advice from a salesperson.

4.3   The EXDT Outcomes Phase

Innovation that centers on well-being is the first and core outcome of the Experiential Design Thinking process (Batat, 2021d). While traditional design thinking logic focuses on innovation as an outcome, EXDT follows an ethical logic centered on individuals' evolving experiences, well-being, and the meanings they assign to their consumption practices in physical and digital settings. In other words, in EXDT, ethical thinking is integrated from the start of the innovation process by focusing on individual and collective well-being. The only sustainable and advanced innovation method allows designers to include rather than exclude vulnerable populations (e.g., low-income consumers, people with disabilities) in designing products or experiences that help them achieve well-being while enjoying innovative phygital consumption experiences.

As stated by Batat and Addis (2021), well-being is a key concept that should be integrated while designing experiences and implementing new strategies and policies. Drawing on prior research, the two authors identified three key components of well-being that should be integrated into experiential design: (1) satisfaction with life (which refers to the cognitive assessment of a person's life or specific, more focused aspects of it, such as job, finances, housing, health, leisure, and environment); (2) affect (the emotions one experiences at specific points in time—not to memories later on); and (3) eudaimonia (reflects the individual's sense of purpose and meaning in one's life—in other words, the extent to which individuals realize their full potential).

Therefore, innovation that centers on well-being as an outcome of the EXDT process integrates ethical design methods and tools, and encourages designers to develop creativity based on users' vulnerability instead of product features. As a result, the ethical design of phygital customer experiences that can enhance well-being will become a top priority within both marketing and public policy fields.

KEY TAKEAWAYS

This chapter introduced a new tool, Experiential Design Thinking (EXDT), which can help companies create ethical, suitable, and innovative phygital experiences to enhance consumers' collective and individual well-being. In this chapter, I proposed a critical approach to the current literature and advance of traditional design thinking applied to the design of customer experiences in physical and digital settings. I also discussed how a holistic and experiential perspective on design thinking can contribute to rethinking innovation processes and strategies in companies through the EXDT model. This framework stimulates thinking about ethical design practices and beyond, prioritizing individuals, companies, and policymakers.

12. A holistic disruption strategy to create unique customer experiences in the phygital era

CHAPTER OVERVIEW

This chapter introduces "holistic disruption" (HD) as a strategy companies should implement to create innovative customer experiences in the phygital era. The theory of disruption is a strategic response companies can apply to generate change in the market while responding to unsolved functional and experiential customer needs that allow them to emerge as highly competitive market actors. Although this theory has been widely used in academic and business spheres, it is considered limited to introducing new technologies. This chapter goes beyond the idea of a disruptive strategy based on the launch of new technologies by introducing the holistic disruption framework, allowing the design of customer experiences that can disrupt the conventional market while creating new business opportunities. First, the chapter will explore the foundations, definition, and the different perspectives related to disruptive innovations. The holistic approach to disruptive innovation in customer experience design is then presented and discussed.

1   DISRUPTIVE INNOVATION: DEFINITION AND THEORETICAL FOUNDATIONS

One of the well-identified sources of the rapid transformation of an industry's environment is innovation, particularly disruptive innovation. Disruptive innovation, most often used by new entrants to a market, consists of disturbing current and established practices, leading to a shift in the marketplace's rules that redefine competition among market actors. Also, the rapid transformation of the industry induced by a disruptive innovation destabilizes the most successful companies for a long time in a given industry. It offers new entrants an opportunity to overhaul the standards of industrial performance and gain the assets needed to win market share (Batat, 2020b).

This section sheds light on the definition of the disruption theory that marked a shift from incremental to disruptive innovations. Different disruptive innovation perspectives will also be presented and discussed. A new approach is then presented, namely holistic disruption, which I recently introduced as a strategic path to creating innovative customer experiences in the phygital setting that can disrupt the marketplace while differentiating the company's offers and making it emerge as a competitive market actor.

1.1   What Is Disruption Theory?

From an academic perspective, disruption theory was introduced and conceptualized in the 1990s by Harvard Professor Clayton Christensen, an authority in the disruption field. Christensen uses the term "disruptive technology" in his book *The Innovator's Dilemma*, published in 1997. According to Christensen, few technologies are disruptive; it is instead the strategic use that has a disruptive effect. He refers to a "dilemma" because companies focus too much on satisfying current needs without worrying about future needs. Disruptive technologies then clash with technologies still in place and create a dilemma for companies in the sector—for example, downloading and sharing music digitally versus on static media, or digital books versus paper books. Christensen identifies two types of disruption:

- Lower disruption addresses customers who were not served by existing offerings from established companies. The performance of the products is such that they exceed the needs of specific customer segments. A company can then offer more basic, simple, and universal products. Marginal improvement will be possible through the volume effect, economies of scale, and a broader customer base.
- A market break occurs when the product is "inferior" in terms of performance but suits an emerging segment. For example, Airbnb offers rooms and rentals with few or no associated services, unlike the professional hotel industry, but it reaches a much wider segment.

Christensen also argues that disruptive innovation depends on the company's business model, which should be adapted to the disruption. For Christensen, the inability of the company to take advantage of disruptions in the environment is due to the outdated and rigid business model. He thus speaks of the "tragedy" of the business model. Indeed, the arrival of a new product linked to disruption can pose three key issues for a company:

- Its current customers are not interested in the new product, leaving the company to believe that there is no market.
- The company does not know who might be interested in the new product.

- The new disruptive product does not make sense for the company.

Consequently, this state requires deep reflection on the business model, which Christensen redefines into three components:

- the value proposition (what it offers the customer);
- the profit logic (how the company makes money with this value proposition);
- the structure of the company through its resources, processes, and values (RPV), which is the company's ability to mobilize and combine to achieve its value proposition.

It is therefore the fundamental business model that determines whether an opportunity is attractive or not. Thus, it is easier for a start-up to reinvent itself by implementing disruptive innovations than for a long-established company to seize the opportunity linked to this innovation. This is also what led to the idea that only start-ups could be disruptive.

On the other hand, disruption "from below" implies a widening of the market linked to a reduction in costs and an essential product proposal. This is not an obvious process for large established companies, which sometimes forces them to create specific brands for this segment. Another rigidity of the classic business model is related to the customer approach. Many companies think that they have to be "customer-oriented," whereas analysis of disruption implies a more refined and segmented analysis of customer types. There are three types of customer that imply different orientation strategies:

- Existing customers must continue to be served by incremental innovations.
- Over-served customers are overwhelmed by the company's offer and no longer wish to pay any extra costs linked to useless functions. A low-cost offer can quickly capture them.
- Non-customers are those the company does not know and for whom it considers there is no market. They are the ones who can become the customers of new disruptive innovations.

Thus, according to the disruption theory logic, we can say that new entrants in an industry are the most likely to use this strategy (Bower and Christensen, 1995). This is because they suffer from a structural competitive disadvantage compared to the most successful established groups, facing significant barriers to entry.

Conversely, the most successful established firms are reluctant to implement disruptive innovation strategies that might destroy some of the assets and sources of advantage that they have built up over time. Indeed, leading firms have acquired these resources through hard work: industrial experience, know-how, patents, work tools, among others. They have refined their knowledge of the market and built a reputation. These assets protect them; they constitute obstacles, barriers, and sources of disadvantage for new candidates who lack them.

Consequently, disruption as an innovation strategy opens an inflection point in this logic of accumulation: a particular moment where learning is no longer achieved through accumulation and continuity but, in contrast, through disruption and exploration of new avenues, neglected market segments, or niches (e.g., O'Reilly and Tushman, 2016). Therefore, new entrants are encouraged to favor this exploratory and disruptive approach to steer the game to their advantage. Aligned with this logic, disruption is then based on two complementary mechanisms. First, it changes the company's performance standards and criteria. Second, it modifies the skills and resources necessary for performance, rendering those operating until then obsolete, and thus transforming previous assets into liabilities. When successful, this strategy results in a radical inversion of the strengths and weaknesses of the market players involved:

- The assets of the established companies gradually become obsolete and constitute obstacles to their adaptation to the new standards.
- The elements that constituted barriers to entry become conversion costs and barriers to exit.
- The standards and practices of the new entrants impose themselves as the new performance standards to be acquired.

Everything depends on the reaction of the dominant firms. With their resources and reputation, they could imitate the newcomers or acquire them and, effectively, take over their market. Christensen and colleagues (2015) believe that this is usually not the choice they make. The phenomenon of standardization tends to encourage them to focus their investments on particular needs, those of their core customers, leaving aside underserved market niches because they initially yield low profitability or do not allow them to benefit from economies of scale.

On the other hand, new entrants focus on these niches to improve on definite competitive advantages that will later be difficult to catch up with. Table 12.1 provides a summary of disruption strategies implemented by companies and the types of innovation generated.

Table 12.1   Disruption strategy examples

Disruptive company	Disruptive idea	Disruption focus	Disruption outcome	Conventional market actors
TESLA	Build and sell sporty and luxury electric cars; design vehicles of the future	Market disruption	Technological mastery (electric vehicle) Design Skimming strategy (high prices)	Automotive manufacturers
AIRBNB	Connect travelers and hosts through paid community rental/ booking platform	Market disruption	Platform connecting users Customer experience Non-business hosts' profiles	Traditional hotel industry
ALIBABA	Internet sales platform and marketplace with online payment and cloud computing services	Entering the market by offering low prices and market disruption	Pricing policy E-commerce site selling all kinds of products Powerful algorithm for recognizing customers' buying habits Mobile apps	Physical stores Bricks and mortar
PAYPAL	Online payment for purchases; receive or send money; receive payment via secure transaction platform	Entering the market by offering low prices and market disruption	Security and buyer protection Free installation Low commission Simple registration service	Traditional banking sector

1.2   Innovation Strategies: Shifting from Incremental to Disruptive Innovations

Innovation can be defined as a result of the interaction of internal and external components. Internal components of innovation refer to the company's knowledge in terms of know-how, R&D capacities, financial situation, and structure. External components include elements that contribute to triggering innovation from outside the company, such as customers, suppliers, and consultants through the use of open innovation platforms. Analysis of the literature shows different approaches that define innovation and its types. For instance, Christensen (1997) distinguishes three types of innovation:

- *Incremental innovation* improves what already exists. This is the most noticeable type of innovation and the one that is sought through continuous improvement policies. Christensen finds it costly and hyper-competitive. It generates high costs in R&D, for sometimes marginal results.

- *Efficiency innovation* allows costs to be reduced to enter the market from below.
- *Empowering innovation* simplifies existing solutions by making the product/service accessible to the greatest number of people.

Furthermore, innovation strategies have been studied according to four forms of innovation:

- *Continuous innovation* improves a product or service already present in a mature market by optimizing its performance or use. This type of incremental innovation is achieved through stages.
- *Adjacent innovation* is one of the most used strategies to extend the life of a product/service or a market. The company that uses adjacent innovation uses an existing product or technology in a new market.
- *Disruptive innovation* promotes access to a certain product or service to make it available to a significant number of people in terms of cost and use. In the short term, the goal of a company that engages in disruptive innovation is to destabilize the competition to acquire market share rapidly. In the long term, the disruptive company aims at leadership in its sector of activity by acquiring a community of users who are committed to its cause.
- *Radical innovation* commercializes a brand new product and creates a new market that does not respond to any existing problem. This is, for example, the case of virtual reality shopping.

Although authors emphasized different forms of innovation, most innovation scholars' focus was related to the debate on the importance of distinguishing two types of innovation: incremental and disruptive. Incremental innovation is one that improves an already existing product year after year. While incremental innovation is part of a given competitive context within a given market, disruptive innovation profoundly changes what constitutes a substantial competitive advantage. In other words, once the disruptive innovation takes place, the nature of the competitive advantage is modified. For instance, in the early 2000s brands such as Nokia dominated the cell phone market. This market produced many incremental innovations, with phones constantly being enriched by new features. The problem was that, with so many incremental innovations, the phones were becoming more and more complex to use. A new need seemed to emerge among cell phone users, the need for simplification. However, it was not the market players who knew how to exploit and meet this new need through innovation, but a player from the computer world—Apple.

In 2007, Apple launched a brand new cell phone, the iPhone, whose main innovation was simplicity of use thanks to a touch screen, and the ergonomic and fun aspects of the device. Locked in their certainties, Apple's competitors did not see the tidal wave that was about to occur, considering that the iPhone was only an electronic gadget that did not even have 3G. As a result, in less than ten years Apple sold more than a billion phones. Meanwhile, Nokia and Ericsson almost disappeared from the market, leaving new players adopting a more disruptive approach to innovation.

However, incremental and disruptive innovations should not be opposed, but associated and approached as complementary strategies. A novel innovation can disrupt and open new markets thanks to its disruptive aspect, and then the company can exploit these new markets thanks to incremental innovation. To guarantee their progress, companies need to ensure the balance between incremental and disruptive innovation strategies. Indeed, innovation scholars have been interested in this topic by questioning how companies can balance incremental and radical innovations. They distinguish between incremental and radical innovation but, at the same time, insist on the need to balance these different types of innovation by considering three perspectives:

1. The first refers to the interrupted equilibrium model of Romanelli and Tushman (1994), according to which processes of organizational evolution alternate between two types of period: long periods of stability interrupted by short periods of radical change that establish the new foundations of the activity for the next period of stability. Building on this model, Brown and Eisenhardt (1997) proposed a model in which periods of incremental innovation deployment are interrupted by short periods of radical innovation introduction. While stabilized operations in formalized organizations characterize the first periods, the second periods are more informal, with more blurred roles and missions.
2. The second perspective emphasizes the need for large companies to maintain permanently and, in parallel, the possibility of developing radically innovative activities to protect the company from being locked into its acquired positions. These experimental activities, which are sources of disruptive innovations, are developed within structured divisions, with an evident market positioning and strategy, while being out of step with this strategy or positioning.
3. The third perspective refers to structuring entities specifically dedicated to exploratory activities and separated from the rest of the organization. This is the ambidextrous model of Tushman and O'Reilly (1997), who distinguished two types of entity: operating entities with routinized functioning, leaving room mainly for incremental innovations; and autonomous exploration entities that are less finalized and formalized than the former.

1.3   Disruptive Innovation Perspectives

According to Batat (2021e), disruptive innovation studies have followed three key perspectives: (1) a focus on the functional quality of innovation and its costs; (2) exploration of innovation's relativity and predictivity; and (3) consideration of disruptive innovation as a layered model and a framework for firms' strategic decisions.

In the first perspective, focusing on the functional quality and the cost of innovation, authors define disruptive innovation in terms of its "good enough quality" functionality and its related low cost. In other words, this perspective views innovation in terms of a company's ability to improve its product and lower its price, thereby enabling the organization to become a competitor capable of disrupting the market. Authors in this case believe that disruptive innovations can change the performance parameters of products and, in turn, guarantee a firm's success by aligning its market strategy with the real unsolved needs of customers and the market challenges they face.

The second set of works examined disruptive innovation in terms of its relative and predictive aspects (Sood and Tellis, 2011). These works emphasize the relative aspect of disruption. In other words, what is disrupting for some people might not be disrupting for other people. In the third perspective, disruptive innovation was defined as a layered model and a framework for firms' strategic decisions that show that disruptive innovations can be characterized by layers that can lead to important decisions at different levels (Kilkki et al., 2017). The six-layer disruptive innovation model includes technology, business, consumers, science, R&D, and firms.

2   HOLISTIC DISRUPTION TO DESIGN CUSTOMER EXPERIENCES

This section first presents the holistic approach applied in the marketing field to explore consumer behaviors. It then introduces the holistic disruption model as a framework that allows companies to design disruptive and successful customer experiences in the phygital setting.

2.1   A Holistic Approach to Consumer Behavior

Holism, introduced by Jan Smuts in 1926, comes from the Greek word holos, meaning "whole" (Morgan, 1927). Holism is a concept that emerged in philosophy but is now widely used in the medical world; however it is relatively new to the business sector. The holistic approach is considered a founding principle in the field of healthcare. It is based on the idea of considering the whole person rather than treating an organ, a disease, or symptoms.

In innovation management, holism has been used to examine sustainable approaches to problem-solving in companies across different sectors. Therefore, sustainable innovation thinking implies a holistic approach to problems, going beyond the immediate choice of technical manipulation and the spontaneity of human relations in groups. Consequently, the holistic innovation approach (e.g., Chen et al., 2018) consists of developing strategies that focus on all the fundamental elements that make up the business units involved. A global and integrated vision allows for a comprehensive understanding of the state of efficiency or deficiency, thus allowing for the restoration and maintenance of balance between the various components.

From a marketing and consumer behavior perspective, holism has been considered to examine both consumption practices and business practices in a globalized era, reflecting a situation where specialized skills (e.g., marketing, communication, human resources, sales) have been integrated by companies.

In contrast, customers have developed fragmented purchase and consumption behaviors. Therefore, in this context, companies should rethink their roles, missions, and relationships with their customers. For example, a company's mission to make a profit is not enough; it should rethink its marketing vocation and social role, and embrace business thinking and practices based on the idea of commerce for the common good, integrating a holistic approach to the consumer. Indeed, consumers do not separate their fundamental and emotional needs from their purchasing actions.

The holistic view of consumers underlines the importance of taking into account four dimensions of consumer behavior—physiological, emotional, spiritual, and social—that should be placed at the heart of companies' marketing strategy and innovation process:

- *Physiological*. Instead of focusing only on the functional attributes of goods, companies should consider consumer well-being and how their offerings can help improve and promote collective and individual well-being.
- *Emotional*. Emotions such as passion, sadness, and enthusiasm, among others, should not be neglected, and are even present in a purchase act.
- *Spiritual*. There is nothing more rational in the culture of a country than its spiritual history, which should be integrated into the company's offerings.
- *Social*. Consumption is by nature embedded in a social context where consumers interact with each other and with the company and its products and brands.

In addition to these four factors, to implement a holistic marketing approach to understand consumer behaviors and predict future consumption trends, and thus business opportunities, companies can follow holistic thinking based on the incorporation of seven main factors—covering individual, economic, social, experiential, and environmental aspects—that can positively or negatively influence the customer experience and decision-making process. These seven factors are as follows:

- *Macroenvironment.* Today's consumer society is characterized by a growing population and global warming challenges, forcing individuals to rethink their consumption habits by adopting eco-friendly behaviors. It is predicted that social tensions will only increase over the next decade as competition for resources intensifies. This situation could lead to greater social stratification and an inability to meet consumers' needs, such as food production and other consumption domains.
- *Digital technologies.* These will continue to blur the boundaries between time, space, and travel. Also, extended reality technologies (e.g., VR and AR) will revolutionize industries such as tourism and entertainment, while eSports will rival traditional sports in popularity. Companies should also consider that consumers might resist cashless payments and online stores in the future, demanding greater privacy and seeking more human and natural social interactions.
- *Collective and individual well-being.* Considering a holistic approach by refocusing on consumers' collective and individual well-being is key for companies to connect with their customers and help them achieve their well-being objectives.
- *Consumer empowerment.* This movement is gaining momentum as customers become collective and are more daring in criticizing companies, brands, and individuals they disagree with. Consumer activism will play a key role in raising public awareness of various causes and spur the legislative branch to develop and implement reforms that will bring about real change. At the same time, when it comes to personal data, we are seeing the emergence of a more human-centered approach that allows users to control how their information is collected and shared. Consumers are beginning to realize their actual value, and are demanding more from these data.
- *Economic value.* While consumers are looking for a more conscious approach to spending, they are also looking for something authentic and unique. Companies should therefore expect a shift toward slower, minimal consumerism that emphasizes sustainability and functionality while maintaining affordability.
- *Consumption is about self-identity.* As identities evolve, so do social relationships. Nowadays, consumers are increasingly interested in consumption to belong to a consumer culture that fits their own values and beliefs.
- *Experiential package.* Companies should shift their thinking from offering products to offering functional, engaging, and emotional experiences to enchant their customers and thus create a strong bond with them.

2.2 Holistic Disruption for Creating Innovative Phygital Customer Experiences

Holistic disruption is defined as a systemic approach involving emic and etic processes to engage in the company's innovation process following three stages, including the 3Ps framework introduced by Batat (2021e): purpose, people, and process. The 3Ps form the core pillars of the holistic disruption framework in marketing, and explain disruptive innovation by answering the following questions: What is the innovation's purpose? Who is involved with the innovation? How does it work? Thanks to the holistic approach, companies can rethink their innovation processes by placing the customer experience instead of the product at the center of the design process.

The first stage of the process refers to the company's ability to define the purpose of disruption. According to Batat (2021e), companies should define the purpose of their disruption based on two key elements: the firm's strategic vision and its pursued goals. Developing a clear definition and understanding of the strategic vision is fundamental to guide the aim of the disruption process and thus ensure the success of the innovation. Moreover, a clear strategic vision should be aligned with the company's corporate values (Hansen et al., 2008).

Corporate values are considered the markers of the company's identity, culture, and DNA, thus allowing firms to clearly define the purpose of their disruptions. Batat states that identifying corporate values is a critical step in clearly defining the purpose of the disruption. Indeed, companies that lack a clear definition of the purpose of their disruption strategies struggle to acquire a disruptive mindset that can help them create innovative customer experiences, which can disrupt the marketplace while responding to customers' unsolved needs.

The second element that helps companies define their disruption purpose is the pursued goal. For Batat (2021e), a firm's goal should be clearly stated and shared among the organization's actors. Defining the firm's goals before engaging in disruption is an important step to creating successful disruptive innovations. Thus, the goals pursued by firms should be a starting point in the disruption process because they allow companies to assess the value of their disruptive innovation processes.

The second stage underlines the importance for companies to identify and integrate legitimate stakeholders in the holistic disruption process. Batat (2021e) argues that disruption is not a solo process; it involves multiple stakeholders. Companies should thus adopt a comprehensive view of who the "legitimate actors" are while identifying complex, disruptive challenges and proposing disruptive innovations to solve them. These are actors who are not necessarily connected to the company and its business. Multiple actors with different profiles and backgrounds can be involved through collaborative platforms, with various selected recognized actors contributing to the process.

The last stage refers to the company's engagement in a *mise en place* process of disruptive innovation. Batat (2021e) suggests that companies should combine different tools to generate relevant insights, and therefore prepare the required ingredients to be set up before they engage in disruptive innovations. Companies should iteratively follow three main approaches in the *mise en place* of disruptive innovation: empiricality, transferability, and unconventionality.

- Empiricality emphasizes a firm's ability to generate novel and big ideas by following a trial-and-error principle that incorporates two elements: lived experiences and field-based experiences. While lived experiences are subjective, field-experience approaches are based on solid analytical studies.
- Transferability refers to the company's ability to transfer theoretical or practical knowledge from one field to another, from one individual to another, or from one field to an individual. Nevertheless, transferability is not a simple copy-and-paste process (Batat, 2019a). It requires creative skills as well as in-depth knowledge of the company's domain alongside the investigated field.
- Unconventionality reflects the company's ability to break the rules and offer the opposite of what is conventional, accepted, and expected in the marketplace and by its targets and competitors. Thus, a transgressive idea leading to market disruption emerges as a kind of saturation in uncertain situations.

Iteratively combined, these three modes of the *mise en place* disruption process can unlock the company's innovation potential and allow it to offer disruptive customer experiences that respond to tangible and intangible consumer needs expressed in both physical and digital settings.

KEY TAKEAWAYS

This chapter introduced the foundations and perspectives related to a disruptive innovation approach. It explained how companies can shift their strategic thinking toward a holistic and systemic approach to disruption to create more than just products, but customer experiences that can generate change in the marketplace while leading the firm to emerge as a highly competitive market actor. To do so, companies should implement a holistic disruption model to engage in the innovation process related to customer experience design within physical and digital settings. The holistic disruption model follows emic and etic thinking, and includes three key stages or 3Ps—purpose, people, and the *mise en place* process—to answer the following questions: What is the innovation's purpose? Who is involved with the innovation? And how does it work?

Concluding remarks

The objective of this book was to rethink traditional digital marketing thinking applied to the customer experience design by offering a novel framework—namely, phygital—as a holistic ecosystem that places the customer first and technology second. This critical framework provides a better understanding of the foundations, tools, and strategies regarding customer experiences that companies across different sectors and industries can implement to enhance the navigation experience between online and offline offerings.

This book is an analytical and practical guide that encompasses all aspects of customer experience design in the phygital age. It is based on up-to-date use of concepts and practices related to the digital transformation, the intensification of the use of digital technologies, and the erosion of the borders between the real and the virtual worlds. The ubiquity of smartphones is encouraging businesses to rethink their digital strategies and take a customer-centric approach that considers consumer experiences in a phygital environment, characterized by a continuum of offline and online behaviors. This book is intended for professionals, start-ups, engineers, and marketing, communication, and digital practitioners who wonder about the future of designing effective and seamless customer experiences that guarantee a continuum in the new phygital setting.

References

Abbott, L. (1955). *Quality and competition*. New York: Columbia University Press.

Addis, M., Batat, W., Atakan, S., Austin, C., Manika, D., Peter, P., & Peterson, L. (2021). Food experience design to prevent unintended consequences and improve well-being. *Journal of Service Research. 25*(2630), pp.143–159.

Alderson, W. (1957). *Marketing behavior and executive action*. Homewood, IL: Irwin.

Alves, R., & Nunes, N.J. (2013). Towards a taxonomy of service design methods and tools. In J. Falcão e Cunha, M. Snene, & H. Nóvoa (Eds.), *4th International Conference on Exploring Services Science* (pp. 215–229). Berlin: Springer.

AMA. (2020). Chatbots and customer experience in 2020. https://www.ama.org/marketing-news/chatbots-and-customer-experience-in-2020/, accessed August 2021.

Anderson, J.A., & Meyer, T.P. (1988). *Mediated communication: A social interaction perspective*. Newbury Park, CA: Sage.

Anderson, T.C. (2012). *Makers: The new industrial revolution*. New York: Crown Business.

Arnould, E.J. (1998). Daring consumer-orientated ethnography. In B.B. Stern (Ed.), *Representing consumers, voices, views and vision* (pp. 85–126). London: Routledge.

Arnould, E.J., & Price, L.L. (1993). River magic: Extraordinary experience and the extended service encounter. *Journal of Consumer Research, 20*(1), 24–45.

Arnould, E.J., & Thompson, C. (2005). Consumer Culture Theory (CCT): Twenty years of research. *Journal of Consumer Research, 31*(4), 868–882.

Ashton, K. (2009). That "Internet of Things" thing. *RFID Journal*. http://www.rfidjournal.com/articles/view?4986, accessed March 2021.

Askegaard, S., & Linnet, J.T. (2011). Towards an epistemology of consumer culture theory: Phenomenology, structure and the context of context. *Marketing Theory, 11*(4), 381–404.

ASTM International. (2013*). Standard terminology for additive manufacturing technologies: Designation F2792 – 12a*. West Conshohocken, PA: American Society for Testing and Materials.

Azwna, R.T. (1997). A survey of augmented reality. *Presence: Teleoperators and Virtual Environments, 6*(4), 355–385.

Bandura, A. (1980). Gauging the relationship between self-efficacy judgment and action. *Cognitive Therapy and Research, 4*, 263–268.

Bandura, A. (1986). The social learning perspective: Mechanisms of aggression. In H. Toch (Ed.), *Psychology of crime and criminal justice* (pp. 198–236). Prospect Heights, IL: Waveland.

Barba, E., MacIntyre, B., Rouse, R., & Boiter, J. (2010). Thinking inside the box: Making meaning in a handheld AR experience. In *2010 IEEE International Symposium on Mixed and Augmented Reality-Arts, Media, and Humanities (ISMAR-AMH)* (pp. 19–26). IEEE.

Bartle, R. (1996). Hearts, clubs, diamonds, spades: Players who suit MUDs. *Journal of MUD Research*, 1996, *1*(1). file:///Users/wbatat/Downloads/hcds.pdf, accessed March 2021.

Batat, W. (2011). An overview of postmodern research in the consumer behaviour field: Towards the "new consumer" paradigm. In Z. Yi, J.J. Xiao, J. Cotte, & L. Price (Eds.), *AP: Asia-Pacific advances in consumer research*, Vol. 9 (pp. 304–312). Duluth, MN: Association for Consumer Research.

Batat, W. (2018). *L'expérience client digitale*. Paris: Eyrolles.

Batat, W. (2019a). *Experiential marketing: Consumer behavior, customer experience, and the 7Es*. London: Routledge.

Batat, W. (2019b). *Digital luxury: Transforming brands and consumer experiences*. London: Sage.

Batat, W. (2020a). How can art museums develop new business opportunities? Exploring young visitors' experience. *Young Consumers*, *21*(1), 109–131.

Batat, W. (2020b). The business recovery. *Ivey Business Journal*, August/July. https://iveybusinessjournal.com/the-business-of-recovery/, accessed July 2021.

Batat, W. (2021a). Employee experience and well-being in the workplace: A new framework. *Employee Relations*.

Batat, W. (2021b). *Youth marketing to digital natives*. Cheltenham, UK and Northampton, MA, USA: Edward Elgar Publishing.

Batat, W. (2021c). Getting phygital with your customers. *Ivey Business Journal*, March/April. https://iveybusinessjournal.com/getting-phygital-with-consumers/, accessed July 2021.

Batat, W. (2021d). *Design thinking for food well-being: Creating innovative food experiences*. New York: Springer.

Batat, W. (2021e). Unveiling the black box of the disruption framework: An ethnographic case study approach (unpublished working paper).

Batat, W., & Addis, M. (2021). Design thinking approach for healthy food experiences and well-being: Contributions to theory and practice. *European Journal of Marketing*, Guest editorial, *55*(9), 2389–2391.

Batat, W., & Tanner, J. (2021). Unveiling (in)vulnerability in an adolescent's consumption subculture: A framework to understand adolescents' experienced (in)vulnerability and ethical implications. *Journal of Business Ethics*, *169*(4), 713–730.

Batat, W., & Wohlfeil, M. (2009). Getting lost "into the wild": Understanding consumers' movie enjoyment through a narrative transportation approach. *Advances in Consumer Research*, *36*, 372–377.

Baudrillard, J. (1970). *The consumer society: Myths and structures*. Theory, Culture & Society. New York: Nottingham University.

Belk, R.W. (1989). Extended self and extending paradigmatic perspective. *Journal of Consumer Research*, *16*(1), 129–132.

Belk, R.W., & Costa, J.A. (1998). The mountain man myth: A contemporary consuming fantasy. *Journal of Consumer Research*, *25*(3), 218–240.

Belk, R.W., Wallendorf, M., & Sherry, J.F. (1989). The sacred and the profane in consumer behavior: Theodicy on the Odyssey. *Journal of Consumer Research*, *16*(1), 1–38.

Berman, B., & Thelen, S. (2004). A guide to developing and managing a well-integrated multi-channel retail strategy. *International Journal of Retail and Distribution Management*, *32*(3), 147–156.

Berry, L. (2002). Relationship marketing of services: Perspectives from 1983 and 2000. *Journal of Relationship Marketing*, *1*(1), 59–77.

Bitner, M. J. (1992). Servicescapes: The impact of physical surroundings on customers and employees. *Journal of Marketing*, *56*(2), 57–71.

Bonetti, F., Warnaby, G., & Quinn, L. (2018). Augmented reality and virtual reality in physical and online retailing: A review, synthesis and research agenda. In T. Jung & M. Claudia tom Dieck (Eds.), *Augmented reality and virtual reality: Empowering human, place and business* (pp. 119–132). Cham: Springer.

Borden, N.H. (1942). *The economic effects of advertising*. Chicago: Irwin.

Borden, N.H. (1964). The concept of the marketing mix. *Journal of Advertising Research*, *4*, 2–7.

Bower, L.J., & Christensen, C.M. (1995). Disruptive technology: Catching the wave. Harvard Business Review, January–February, 43–53.

Bowman, D., Johnson, D., & Hodges, L. (1999). Testbed evaluation of VE interaction techniques. In *Proceedings of the ACM Symposium on Virtual Reality Software and Technology (VRST'99)* (pp. 26–33). New York: Association for Computing Machinery.

Brakus, J.J., Schmitt, B.H., & Zarantonello, L. (2009). Brand experience: What is it? How is it measured? Does it affect loyalty? *Journal of Marketing*, *73*(3), 52–68.

Brown, S.L., & Eisenhardt, K. (1997). The art of continuous change: Linking complexity theory and time-paced evolution in relentlessly shifting organizations. *Administrative Science Quarterly*, *42*, 1–34.

Brown, T. (2009). Change by design: How design thinking transforms organizations and inspires innovation. New York: Harper Business.

Brunswik, E. (1955). Representative design and probabilistic theory in a functional psychology. *Psychological Review*, *62*(3), 193–217.

Buchanan, R. (1992). Wicked problems in design thinking. *Design Issues*, *2*, 5–21.

Buxton, B. (2007). *Sketching user experiences: Getting the design right and the right design*. San Francisco, CA: Morgan Kaufmann.

Carpenter, J. (2013). *The quiet professional: An investigation of U.S. military explosive ordnance disposal personnel interactions with everyday field robots* (Doctoral dissertation, University of Washington).

Carù, A., & Cova, B. (2007). *Consuming experience*. London: Routledge.

Celsi, R.L., Rose, R.L., & Leigh, T.W. (1993). An exploration of high-risk leisure consumption through skydiving. *Journal of Consumer Research*, *20*(1), 1–23.

Chang, H.L., Chou, Y.C., Wu, D.Y., & Wu, S.C. (2018). Will firm's marketing efforts on owned social media payoff? A quasi-experimental analysis of tourism products. *Decision Support Systems*, *107*, 13–25.

Chen, J., Yin, X., & Mei, L. (2018). Holistic innovation: An emerging innovation paradigm. International Journal of Innovation Studies, 2, 1–13.

Chen, N., Mohanty, S., Jiao, J., & Fan, X. (2020). To err is human: Tolerate humans instead of machines in service failure. Journal of Retailing and Consumer Services, *59*(3), 102363.

Chen, T., Razzaq, A., Qing, P., & Cao, B. (2021). Do you bear to reject them? The effect of anthropomorphism on empathy and consumer preference for unattractive produce. Journal of Retailing and Consumer Services, *61*, 102556.

Chitturi, R., Raghunathan, R., & Mahajan, V. (2008). Delight by design: The role of hedonic versus utilitarian benefits. *Journal of Marketing*, *72*(3), 48–63.

Chou, Y. (2015). *Actionable gamification: Beyond points, badges and leader-boards*. CreateSpace Independent Publishing Platform.

Christensen, C.M. (1997). The innovator's dilemma: When new technologies cause great firms to fail. Boston, MA: Harvard Business School Press.

Christensen, C.M., Raynor, M.E., & McDonald, R. (2015). What is disruptive innovation? Harvard Business Review, December, 44–53.

Citrin, A.V., Stem, D.E., Spangenberg, E.R., & Clark, M.J. (2003). Consumer need for tactile input: An internet retailing challenge. *Journal of Business Research, 56*(11), 915–922.

Coll, S. (2013). Consumption as biopower: Governing bodies with loyalty cards. *Journal of Consumer Culture, 13*(3), 201–220.

Compeau, D.R., & Higgins, C.A. (1995). Application of social cognitive theory to training for computer skills. *Information Systems Research, 6*(2), 118–143.

Corcoran, S. (2009). Defining earned, owned, and paid media. *Forrester Research.* http://blogs.forrester.com, accessed April 2021.

Cotteleer, M. (2014). 3D opportunity: Additive manufacturing paths to performance, innovation, and growth. *Deloitte Review* (14), 18 January.

Crapanzano, V. (1991). The postmodern crisis: Discourse, parody, memory. *Cultural Anthropology, 6*(4), 431–446.

Cross, N. (1982). Designerly ways of knowing. *Design Studies, 4*, 221–227.

Csikszentmihalyi, M. (1990). Flow: The psychology of optimal experience. *Journal of Leisure Research, 24*(1), 93–94.

Csikszentmihalyi, M. (1991). *Flow: The psychology of optimal experience.* New York: Harper Perennial.

Csikszentmihalyi, M. (1997). *Creativity: Flow and the psychology of discovery and invention.* New York: Harper Perennial.

Cuff, B.M., Brown, S.D., Taylor, L.K., & Howat, D. (2016). Empathy: A review of the concept. Emotion Review, 8, 144–153.

Culliton, J.W. (1948). *The management of marketing costs.* Boston: Division of Research, Graduate School of Business Administration, Harvard University.

Curran, C.R., & Hales, G.D. (1995). Virtual reality. In M.J. Ball, K.J. Hannah, S.K. Newbold, & J.V. Douglas (Eds.), *Nursing informatics* (pp. 301–319). Health Informatics. New York: Springer.

Dale, S. (2014). Gamification: Making work fun or making fun of work. *Business Information Review, 1*(2), 82–90.

Daugherty, T., Li, H., & Biocca, F. (2008). Consumer learning and the effects of virtual experience relative to indirect and direct product experience. Psychology and Marketing, 25(7), 568–586.

Davis, F.D. (1989). Perceived usefulness, perceived ease of use, and user acceptance of information technology. *MIS Quarterly, 13*, 319–340.

de Graaf, M.M., & Allouch, S.B. (2013). Exploring influencing variables for the acceptance of social robots. *Robotics and Autonomous Systems, 61*(12), 1476–1486.

Decrop, A. (2008). Les paradoxes du consommateur postmoderne. *Reflets et Perspectives de la Vie Economique, 47*(2), 85–93.

Denegri-Knott, J., & Molesworth, M. (2010). Concepts and practices of digital virtual consumption. *Consumption, Markets and Culture, 13*(2), 109–132.

Denegri-Knott, J., Zwick, D., & Schroeder, J. (2006). Mapping consumer power: An integrative framework for marketing and consumer research. *European Journal of Marketing, 40*, 950–971.

Deterding, S. (2012). Playful technologies. In C. Wiedemann & S. Zehle (Eds.), *Depletion design: A glossary of network ecologies* (pp. 121–126). Amsterdam: Institute of Network Cultures.

Deterding, S., Dixon, D., Khaled, R., & Nacke, L. (2011). Gamification: Toward a definition. *Proceedings of CHI 2011 Gamification Workshop, 7–12 May, Vancouver.* New York: ACM.

Dey, A., Billinghurst, M., Lindeman, R.W., & Swan, J.E. (2018). A systematic review of 10 years of augmented reality usability studies: 2005 to 2014. *Frontiers in Robotic and AI, 5*(37). doi: 10.3389/frobt.2018.00037.

Dhebar, A. (2013). Toward a compelling customer touchpoint architecture. *Business Horizons, 56,* 199–205.

Dholakia, R.R., Zhao, M., & Dholakia, N.N. (2005). Multichannel retailing: A case study of early experiences. *Journal of Interactive Marketing, 19*(2), 63–74.

Dholakia, U.M., Kahn, B.E., Reeves, R., Rindfleisch, A., Stewart, D., & Taylor, E. (2010). Consumer behavior in a multichannel, multimedia retailing environment. *Journal of Interactive Marketing, 24*(2), 86–95.

Elliott, R., & Wattanasuwan, K. (1998). Brands as symbolic resources for the construction of identity. *International Journal of Advertising, 17,* 131–144.

Ellis, S.R. (1994). What are virtual environments? *IEEE Computer Graphics and Applications, 14*(1), 17–22.

Engel, J.F., Blackwell, R.D., & Miniard, P.W. (1990). *Consumer behavior* (8th ed.). Fort Worth, TX: Dryden Press.

Ferrey, A.E., Burleigh, T.J., & Fenske, M.J. (2015). Stimulus-category competition, inhibition, and affective devaluation: A novel account of the uncanny valley. *Frontiers in Psychology, 6,* 249.

Firat, A.F., & Dholakia, N. (2006). Theoretical and philosophical implications of postmodern debates: Some challenges to modern marketing. *Marketing Theory, 6*(2), 123–162.

Firat, A.F., & Venkatesh, A. (1995). Liberatory postmodernism and the re-enchantment of consumption. *Journal of Consumer Research, 22*(3), 239–267.

Fournier, S. (1998). Consumer resistance: Societal motivations, consumer manifestations, and implications in the marketing domain. In J.W. Alba & J.W. Hutchinson (Eds.), Advances in consumer research (pp. 88–90). Provo, UT: Association for Consumer Research.

Fournier, S., & Mick, D.G. (1999). Rediscovering satisfaction. *Journal of Marketing, 63*(4), 5–23.

Gao, W., Zhang, Y., Ramanujan, D., Ramani, K., Chen, Y., Williams, C., Wang, C., Shin, Y., Zhang, S., & Zavattieri, P. (2015). The status, challenges, and future of additive manufacturing in engineering. *Computer-Aided Design, 69,* 65–89.

Gasparini, A., & Chasanidou, D. (2016). Understanding the role of design thinking methods and tools in innovation process. In *The XXVII ISPIM Innovation Conference: Blending Tomorrow's Innovation Vintag*e. Porto, 19–22 June, 1–11.

Geller, T. (2008). Overcoming the uncanny valley. *IEEE Computer Graphics and Applications, 28*(4), 11–17.

Gentile, C., Spiller, N., & Noci, G. (2007). How to sustain the customer experience: An overview of experience components that co-create value with the customer. *European Management Journal, 25*(5), 395–410.

Gergen, K.J. (1991). The saturated self: Dilemmas of identity in contemporary life. New York: Basic Books.

Gnambs, T., & Appel, M. (2019). Are robots becoming unpopular? Changes in attitudes towards autonomous robotic systems in Europe. *Computers in Human Behavior, 93,* 53–61.

Gould, S.J. (2012). The emergence of consumer introspection theory (CIT): Introduction to a JBR special issue. *Journal of Business Research, 65*(4), 453–460.

Goulding, C., Shankar, A., & Elliott, R. (2002). Working weeks, rave weekends: Identity fragmentation and the emergence of new communities. *Consumption, Market and Culture, 5*(4), 261–284.

Grewal, D., Levy, M., & Kumar, V. (2009). Customer experience management in retailing: An organizing framework. *Journal of Retailing, 85*, 1–14.

Haire, M. (1950). Projective techniques in marketing research. *Journal of Marketing, 14*(5), 649–656.

Hakulinen, L., Auvinen, T., & Korhonen, A. (2013). Empirical study on the effect of achievement badges in TRAKLA2 online learning environment. In *Learning and Teaching in Computing and Engineering (LaTiCE): Proceedings* (pp. 47–54). Macau.

Hamari, J., & Koivisto, J. (2013). Social motivations to use gamification: An empirical study of gamifying exercise. In *Proceedings of the 21st European Conference on Information Systems, Association for Information Systems (ECIS)*. Utrecht, Netherlands.

Hamedani, M.H., Selvaggio, M., Rahimkhani, M., Ficuciello, F., Sadeghian, H., Zekri, M., & Sheikholeslam, F. (2019). Robust dynamic surface control of da Vinci robot manipulator considering uncertainties: A fuzzy based approach. In *7th International Conference on Robotics and Mechatronics (ICRoM)* (pp. 418–423). IEEE.

Hansen, H., Samuelsen, B.M., & Silseth, P.R. (2008). Customer perceived value in B-t-B service relationships: Investigating the importance of corporate reputation. Industrial Marketing Management, 37, 206–217.

Haring, K.S., Mougenot, C., Ono, F., & Watanabe, K. (2014). Cultural differences in perception and attitude towards robots. *International Journal of Affective Engineering, 13*(3), 149–157.

Hawkins, D., Best, R.J., & Coney, K.A. (1986). *Consumer behavior implications for marketing strategy* (3rd ed.). Plano, TX: Business Publications.

Heerink, M. (2011). Exploring the influence of age, gender, education and computer experience on robot acceptance by older adults. In *Proceedings of the 6th ACM/IEEE International Conference on Human-Robot Interaction (HRI)* (pp. 147–148). IEEE.

Heim, M. (1995). The design of virtual reality. In M. Featherstone & R. Burrows (Eds.), *Cyberspace/cyberbodies/cyberpunk: Cultures of technological embodiment* (pp. 65–78). London: Sage.

Hirschman, E.C., & Holbrook, M.B. (1986). Expanding the ontology and methodology of research on the consumption experience. In D. Brinberg & R.J. Lutz (Eds.), *Perspectives on methodology in consumer research* (pp. 213–251). New York: Springer.

Ho, C.C., MacDorman, K.F., & Pramono, Z.D. (2008). Human emotion and the uncanny valley: A GLM, MDS, and Isomap analysis of robot video ratings. In *3rd ACM/IEEE International Conference on Human–Robot Interaction (HRI)* (pp. 169–176). IEEE.

Hoffman, D.L., & Novak, T.P. (1996). Marketing in hypermedia computer-mediated environments: Conceptual foundations. *Journal of Marketing, 60*(3), 50–68.

Hoffman, D.L., & Novak, T.P. (2018). Consumer and object experience in the Internet of Things: An assemblage theory approach. *Journal of Consumer Research, 44*, 1178–1204.

Holbrook, M.B. (1997). Borders, creativity, and the state of the art at the leading edge. *Journal of Macromarketing, 17*(2), 96–112.

Holbrook, M.B. (1999). *Consumer value: A framework for analysis and research.* New York: Routledge.

Holbrook, M.B. (2000). The millennial consumer in the texts of our times: Experience and entertainment. *Journal of Macromarketing, 20*(2), 178–192.

Holbrook, M.B., & Hirschman, E.C. (1982). The experiential aspects of consumption: Consumer fantasies, feelings and fun. *Journal of Consumer Research, 9*(2), 132–140.

Holt, D.B. (1991). Rashomon visits consumer behavior: An interpretive critique of naturalistic inquiry. *Advances in Consumer Research, 18*(1), 57–62.

Holt, D.B. (1995). How consumers consume: A typology of consumption practices. *Journal of Consumer Research, 22*(1), 1–16.

Homburg, C., Koschate, N., & Hoyer, W.D. (2006). The role of cognition and affect in the formation of customer satisfaction: A dynamic perspective. *Journal of Marketing, 70,* 21–31.

Hoyer, W.D., Kroschke, M., Schmitt, B., Kraume, K., & Shankar, V. (2020). Transforming the customer experience through new technologies. Journal of Interactive Marketing, *51,* 57–71. https://doi.org/10.1016/j.intmar.2020.04.001.

Hsu, C.L., & Lin, C.C. (2016). An empirical examination of consumer adoption of Internet of Things services: Network externalities and concern for information privacy perspectives. Computers in Human Behavior, *62,* 516–527.

Huang, R., & Ha, S. (2020). The interplay of management response and individual power in digital service environments from a bystander's perspective. Journal of Service Management, 31, 373–396.

Hunicke, R., LeBlanc, M., & Zubek, R. (2004). MDA: A formal approach to game design and game research. In *Proceedings of the AAAI Workshop on Challenges in Game AI* (p. 2). 4 April, San Jose.

Hunter, G., & Garnefeld, I. (2008). When does consumer empowerment lead to satisfied customers? Some mediating and moderating effects of the empowerment–satisfaction link. *Journal of Research for Consumers,* 15. http://jrconsumers.com/academic_articles/issue_15/Epowerment_satisfaction_involvement__academic2.pdf.

Huotari, K., & Hamari, J. (2017). A definition for gamification: Anchoring gamification in the service marketing literature. *Electronic Markets, 27,* 21–31.

Hur, W.M., Yoo, J.J., & Chung, T.L. (2012). The consumption values and consumer innovativeness on convergence products. *Industrial Management and Data Systems, 112,* 688–706.

Juul, J. (2005). *Half-real: Video games between real rules and fictional worlds.* Cambridge, MA: MIT Press.

Juul, J. (2010). *A Casual revolution: Reinventing video games and their players.* Cambridge, MA: MIT Press.

Kalawsky, R. (1996). *Exploiting virtual reality techniques in education and training: Technological issues.* SIMA Report series, 26. Loughborough: Support Initiative for Multimedia Applications. http://www.agocg.ac.uk/reports/virtual/vrtech/intro.htm, accessed April 2021.

Keinan, A., & Kivetz, R. (2011). Productivity orientation and the consumption of collectable experiences. *Journal of Consumer Research, 37*(6), 935–950.

Kerr, G., Mortimer, K., Dickinson, S., & Waller, D.S. (2012). Buy, boycott or blog: Exploring online consumer power to share, discuss and distribute controversial advertising messages, European Journal of Marketing, *46*(3/4), 387–405.

Kilkki, K., Mäntylä, M., Karhu, K., Hämmäinen, H., & Ailisto, H. (2017). A disruption framework. Technological Forecasting and Social Change, 129, 275–284.

Kim, J., & Forsythe, S.M. (2007). Hedonic usage of product virtualization technologies in online apparel shopping. International Journal of Retail and Distribution Management, 35, 502–514.

Kimbell, L. (2011). Rethinking design thinking: Part 1. *Design and Culture*, *3*(3), 285–306.

Kleinginna, P.R., & Kleinginna, A.M. (1981). A categorized list of emotion definitions, with suggestions for a consensual definition. Motivation and Emotion, 5, 345–379.

Kolb, D.A., & Fry, R.E. (1975). Toward an applied theory of experiential learning. In C. Cooper (Ed.), *Theories of group processes*. New York: Wiley.

Kotler, P. (1972). A generic concept of marketing. *Journal of Marketing*, *36*(2), 46–54.

Kotler, P., Bowen, J.T., & Makens, J.C. (2010). *Marketing for hospitality and tourism* (5th ed.). Boston, MA: Pearson.

Kourouthanassis, P.E., Giaglis, G.M., & Vrechopoulos, A.P. (2007). Enhancing user experience through pervasive information systems: The case of pervasive retailing. *International Journal of Information Management*, *27*, 319–335.

Kozinets, R. (2015). *Netnography: Redefined*. London: Sage.

Latikka, R., Turja, T., & Oksanen, A. (2019). Self-efficacy and acceptance of robots. *Computers in Human Behavior*, *93*, 157–163.

Lee, H.H., Kim, J., & Fiore, A.M. (2010). Affective and cognitive online shopping experience effects of image interactivity technology and experimenting with appearance. *Clothing and Textiles Research Journal*, *28*(2), 140–154.

Lee, S.L., Lau, I.Y.M., Kiesler, S., & Chiu, C.Y. (2005). Human mental models of humanoid robots. In *Proceedings of the 2005 IEEE International Conference on Robotics and Automation* (pp. 2767–2772). IEEE.

Lemke, F., Clark, M., & Wilson, H. (2011). Customer experience quality: An exploration in business and consumer contexts using repertory grid technique. *Journal of the Academy of Marketing Science*, *39*, 846–869.

Lemon, K.N., & Verhoef, P.C. (2016). Understanding customer experience throughout the customer journey. *Journal of Marketing*, *80*(6), 69–96.

Levy, S.J. (1959). The status seekers. *Journal of Marketing*, *24*(2), 121–122.

Lippa, R.A., & Dietz, J.K. (2000). The relation of gender, personality, and intelligence to judges' accuracy in judging strangers' personality from brief video segments. *Journal of Nonverbal Behavior*, *24*(1), 25–43.

Long, C., & Wong, R.C. (2014). Viral marketing for dedicated customers. *Information Systems*, *46*, 1–23.

Lu, Y., & Smith, S.S. (2007). Augmented reality e-commerce assistant system: Trying while shopping. In J.A. Jacko (Ed.), *Human–Computer Interaction: Interaction Platforms and Techniques. 12th International Conference, HCI International 2007, Beijing, China, July 22–27, 2007, Proceedings, Part II* (pp. 643–652). Berlin: Springer.

Lusch, R., & Vargo, S.L. (2006). Service-dominant logic: Reactions, reflections and refinements. *Marketing Theory*, *6*, 281–288.

Macnamara, J., Lwin, M., Adi, A., & Zerfass, A. (2016). "PESO" media strategy shifts to "SOEP": Opportunities and ethical dilemmas. *Public Relations Review*, *42*(3), 377–385.

Markus, M.L., & Keil, M. (1994). If we build it, they will come: Designing information systems that people want to use, *Sloan Management Review, 35*(4), 11–25.

Mathwick, C., Malhotra, N.K., & Rigdon, E. (2002). The effect of dynamic retail experiences on experiential perceptions of value: An Internet and catalog comparison. *Journal of Retailing, 78*(1), 51–60.

McCarthy, E.J. (1964). *Basic marketing: A managerial approach.* Homewood, IL: Irwin.

McCracken, G. (1987). Advertising: Meaning or information? *Advances in Consumer Research, 14,* 121–124.

Mehrabian, A., & Russell, J.A. (1974). *An approach to environmental psychology.* Cambridge, MA: MIT Press.

Mende, M.W., Scott, M.L., van Doorn, J., Grewal, D., & Shanks, I. (2019). Service robots rising: How humanoid robots influence service experiences and elicit compensatory consumer responses. Journal of Marketing Research, 56, 535–556.

Meyer, C., & Schwager, A. (2007). Understanding customer experience. *Harvard Business Review, 85*(2), 116–157.

Mick, D.G., & Buhl, C. (1992). A meaning-based model of advertising experiences. *Journal of Consumer Research, 19*(3), 317–338.

Mickey, T.J. (1997). A postmodern view of public relations: Sign and reality. *Public Relations Review, 23,* 271–284.

Milgram, P., & Kishino, F. (1994). A taxonomy of mixed reality visual displays. *IEICE Transactions on Information and Systems, E77-D*(12), 1321–1329.

Mills, C.W. (1963). *Power, politics, and people: The collected essays of C. Wright Mills,* ed. Irving Louis Horowitz. New York: Ballantine.

Miorandi, D., Sicari, S., De Pellegrini, F., & Chlamtac, I. (2012). Internet of Things: Vision, applications and research challenges. *Ad Hoc Networks, 10*(7), 1497–1516.

Morgan, C. (1927). Holism and Evolution. By General The Right Honourable J.C. Smuts. (London: Macmillan & Co. 1926. Pp. 361 ix. Price, 18s.). *Philosophy, 2*(5), 93–97.

Mori, M. (1970). The uncanny valley. *Energy, 7*(4), 33–35.

Mossberg, L. (2008). Extraordinary experiences through storytelling. *Scandinavian Journal of Hospitality and Tourism, 8,* 195–210.

Nass, C., & Lee, K.M. (2000). Does computer-generated speech manifest personality? An experimental test of similarity-attraction. In *Proceedings of the SIGCHI conference on Human Factors in Computing Systems* (pp. 329–336).

Neslin, S.A., & Shankar, V. (2009). Key issues in multichannel customer management: Current knowledge and future directions. *Journal of Interactive Marketing, 23*(1), 70–81.

Ngai, E.W.T., Moon, K.K.L., Liu, J.N.K., Tsang, K.F., Law, R., Suk, F.F.C., & Wong, I.C.L. (2008). Extending CRM in the retail industry: An RFID-based personal shopping assistant system. *Communications of the Association for Information Systems, 23*(1), 16.

Norman, D.A. (1988). *The psychology of everyday things.* New York: Basic Books.

Norris, R.T. (1941). *The theory of consumer's demand.* New Haven, CT: Yale University Press.

Nussbaum, B. (2004). The power of design. *Businessweek.* https://www.ideo.com/post/ the-power-of-design-in-businessweek, accessed March 2021.

Nussbaum, B. (2011). Design thinking is a failed experiment: So what's next? http:// www.fastcodesign.com/1663558/design-thinking-is-a-failed-experiment-so-whats -next, accessed April 2021.

O'Brien, H.M. (2016). The Internet of Things. *Journal of Internet Law*, *19*(12), 1–20.

O'Reilly, C.A., & Tushman, M.L. (2016). Lead and disrupt: How to solve the innovator's dilemma. Stanford, CA: Stanford University Press.

Olsen, N.V. (2014). Design thinking and food innovation. In U. Rickert & G. Schiefer (Eds.), *Proceedings in food system dynamics and innovation in food networks* (pp. 135–143). Bonn: Universität Bonn-ILB.

Olsson, T., Lagerstan, E., Karkkainen, T., & Vaananen-Vainio-Mattila, K. (2013). Expected user experience of mobile augmented reality services: A user study in the context of shopping centres. *Personal and Ubiquitous Computing*, *17*(2), 287–304.

Pachoulakis, I., & Kapetanakis, K. (2012). Augmented reality platforms for virtual fitting rooms. International Journal of Multimedia and Its Applications, 4(4), 35–46.

Patterson, A. (2005). Processes, relationships, settings, products and consumers: The case for qualitative diary research. *Qualitative Market Research: An International Journal*, *8*(2), 142–156.

Payne, A., Storbacka, K., & Frow, P. (2008). Managing the co-creation of value. *Journal of the Academy of Marketing Science*, *36*, 83–96.

Péché, J.P., Mieyeville, F., & Gaultier, R. (2016). Design thinking: le design en tant que management de projet. *Entreprendre & Innover*, *1*(28), 83–94.

Pelling, N. (2011). The (short) prehistory of "gamification." The startup handbook: Funding startups (& other impossibilities) *blog*, 9 August. http://nanodome.wordpress .com/2011/08/09/the-short-prehistory-of-gamification/, accessed September, 2021.

Peñaloza, L., & Price, L.L. (1993). Consumer resistance: A conceptual overview. In L. McAlister & M.L. Rothschild (Eds.), Advances in consumer research, Vol. 20 (pp. 123–128). Provo, UT: Association for Consumer Research.

Petkov, P., Köbler, F., Foth, M., Medland, R., & Krcmar, H. (2011). Engaging energy saving through motivation-specific social comparison. In D. Tan, B. Begole, & W. Kellogg (Eds.), *Proceedings and extended abstracts for the 29th annual CHI conference on human factors in computing systems* (pp. 1945–1950). New York: ACM.

Pine, B.J., & Gilmore, J. (1998). Welcome to the experience economy. *Harvard Business Review*, *76*(4), 97–105.

Popper, K.R. (1959). *The logic of scientific discovery*. New York: Basic Books.

Porter, M.E., & Heppelmann, J.E. (2014). How smart, connected products are transforming competition. Harvard Business Review, *92*(11), 64–88.

Prahalad, C.K., & Ramaswamy, V. (2004). Co-creating unique value with customers. *Strategy and Leadership*, *32*(3), 4–9.

Quinn, A.J., & Bederson, B.B. (2011). Human computation: A survey and taxonomy of a growing field. In *Proceedings of the SIGCHI conference on human factors in computing systems (CHI'11), 07–12 May, Vancouver*. New York: ACM.

Ramaswamy, V. (2008). Co-creating value through customers' experiences: The Nike case. Strategy and Leadership, 36, 9–14.

Rauschnabel, P.A. (2018). Virtually enhancing the real world with holograms: An exploration of expected gratifications of using augmented reality smart glasses. *Psychology and Marketing*, *35*, 557–572.

Reeves, B., & Read, J.L. (2009). *Total engagement: Using games and virtual worlds to change the way people work and businesses compete*. Boston, MA: Harvard Business School Press.

Reis, J., Amorim, M., Melão, N., & Matos, P. (2018). Digital transformation: A literature review and guidelines for future research. In: Á Rocha., H. Adeli, L.P. Reis, & S. Costanzo (Eds.), *Trends and advances in information systems and technologies.*

WorldCIST '18 2018: Advances in Intelligent Systems and Computing, Vol. 745 (pp. 411–421). Cham: Springer.

Richins, M.L. (1994). Valuing things: The public and private meanings of possessions. *Journal of Consumer Research, 21*(3), 504–521.

Rigby, D. (2011). The future of shopping. *Harvard Business Review, 89*(12), 64–75.

Robert, L.P. (2018). Personality in the human robot interaction literature: A review and brief critique. In *Proceedings of the 24th Americas Conference on Information Systems*, 16–18 August, New Orleans.

Rogers, E.M. (1962). *Diffusion of innovations*. New York: Free Press.

Romanelli, E., & Tushman, M. (1994). Organizational transformation as punctuated equilibrium: An empirical test. *Academy of Management Journal, 37*(5), 1141–1166.

Rousseau, D. (2015). General systems theory: Its present and potential. *Systems Research and Behavioral Science, 32*, 522–533.

Rowe, P.G. (1987). *Design thinking*. Cambridge, MA: MIT Press.

Ryan, D., & Jones, C. (2012). *Understanding digital marketing: Marketing strategies for engaging the digital generation*. London: Kogan Page.

Salen, K., & Zimmerman, E. (2004). *Rules of play: Game design fundamentals*. Cambridge, MA: MIT Press.

Saravanakumar, M., & Lakshmi, T.S. (2012). Social media marketing. *Life Science Journal, 99*(44), 4444–4451.

Savela, N., Turja, T., & Oksanen, A. (2018). Social acceptance of robots in different occupational fields: A systematic literature review. *International Journal of Social Robotics, 10*(4), 493–502.

Saygin, A.P., Chaminade, T., Ishiguro, H., Driver, J., & Frith, C. (2012). The thing that should not be: Predictive coding and the uncanny valley in perceiving human and humanoid robot actions. *Social Cognitive and Affective Neuroscience, 7*(4), 413–422.

Schembri, S. (2006). Rationalizing service logic, or understanding services as experience. *Marketing Theory, 6*(3), 381–392.

Schlosser, A.E. (2003). Experiencing products in the virtual world: The role of goal and imagery in influencing attitudes versus purchase intentions. *Journal of Consumer Research, 30*(2), 184–198.

Schmitt, B.H. (1999). *Experiential marketing*. New York: Free Press.

Schmitt, B.H. (2003). *Customer experience management*. Hoboken, NJ: Wiley.

Schramm-Klein, H., Wagner, G., Steinmann, S., & Morschett, D. (2011). Cross-channel integration: Is it valued by customers? *International Review of Retail, Distribution and Consumer Research, 21*(5), 501–511.

Scopelliti, M., Giuliani, M.V., & Fornara, F. (2005). Robots in a domestic setting: A psychological approach. *Universal Access in the Information Society, 4*(2), 146–155.

Simon, H.A. (1969). *The sciences of the artificial*. Cambridge, MA: MIT Press.

Slater, M., Usoh, M., Benford, S., Snowdon, D., Brown, C., Rodden, T., Smith, G., & Wilbur, S. (1996). Distributed extensible virtual reality laboratory (DEVRL). In M. Göbel, J. David, P. Slavik, & J.J. van Wijk (Eds.), Virtual environments and scientific visualization (pp. 137–148). *Eurographics '96*. Vienna: Springer.

Smith, A.K., & Bolton, R.N. (1998). An experimental investigation of customer reactions to service failure and recovery encounters. *Journal of Service Research, 1*, 65–81.

Sood, A., & Tellis, G.J. (2011). Demystifying disruption: A new model for understanding and predicting disruptive technologies. *Marketing Science, 30*(2), 339–354.

Steinman, R.B. (2009). Projective techniques in consumer research. *International Bulletin of Business Administration, 5*, 37–45.

Stone, G.P. (1954). City shoppers and urban identification: Observation of the social psychology of city life. *American Journal of Sociology, 60*, 36–45.

Sung, E. (2020). Brand experience via mobile app marketing. *Augmented Reality and Virtual Reality, 1*, 3–9.

Taipale, S., de Luca, F., Sarrica, M., & Fortunati, L. (2015). Robot shift from industrial production to social reproduction. In J. Vincent, S. Taipale, B. Sapio, G. Lugano, & L. Fortunati (Eds.), *Social robots from a human perspective* (pp. 11–24). Cham: Springer.

Taylor, T.L. (2009). The assemblage of play. *Games and Culture, 4*(4), 331–339.

Thabit, M. (2015). How PESO makes sense in influencer marketing. *PR Week*, 8 June. https://www.prweek.com/article/1350303/peso-makes-sense-influencer-marketing, accessed July 2021.

The-VR-Headset (2018). Historical development of virtual reality, 12 November. https://thevrheadset.com/historical-development-of-virtual-reality-vr/#:~:text= Since%202016,%20virtual%20reality%20is%20finally%20accessible%20to,and %20venturing%20into%20imaginary%20worlds%20is%20not%20new, accessed July 2021.

Thompson, C.J., Locander, W.B., & Pollio, H.R. (1990). The lived meaning of free choice: An existential-phenomenological description of everyday consumer experiences of contemporary married women. *Journal of Consumer Research, 17*(3), 346–361.

Turner, B.S. (1990). *Theories of modernity and postmodernity*. London: Sage.

Tushman, M.L., & O'Reilly, C.A. (1997). *Winning through innovation: A practical guide to leading organizational change and renewal*. Boston, MA: Harvard Business School Press.

Urban, G.L., Weinberg, B.D., & Hauser, J.R. (1996). Premarket forecasting of really-new products. Journal of Marketing, 60, 47–60.

Van Roy, R., Deterding, S., & Zaman, B. (2018). Collecting Pokémon or receiving rewards? How people functionalise badges in gamified online learning environments in the wild. *International Journal of Human-Computer Studies, 127*, 62–80.

VanBoskirk, S. (2011). US interactive marketing forecast, 2011 to 2016. *Forrester*. https://www.forrester.com/report/US-Interactive-Marketing-Forecast-2011-To -2016/RES59379.

Verhoef, P., Lemon, K.N., Parasuraman, A., Roggeveen, A.L., Tsiros, M., & Schlesinger, L. (2009). Customer experience creation: Determinants, dynamics and management strategies. *Journal of Retailing, 85*, 31–41.

Von Ahn, L. (2006). Games with a purpose. Computer, *39*(6), 96–98. https://www.cs .cmu.edu/~biglou/ieee-gwap.pdf, accessed July 2021.

Voss, C., Roth, A.V., & Chase, R.B. (2008). Experience, service operations strategy, and services as destinations: Foundations and exploratory investigation. *Production and Operations Management, 17*, 247–266.

Wallendorf, M., & Brucks, M. (1993). Introspection in consumer research: Implementation and implications. *Journal of Consumer Research, 20*(3), 339–359.

Walters, M.L., Syrdal, D.S., Dautenhahn, K., Te Boekhorst, R., & Koay, K.L. (2008). Avoiding the uncanny valley: Robot appearance, personality and consistency of behavior in an attention-seeking home scenario for a robot companion. *Autonomous Robots, 24*(2), 159–178.

Werbach, K., & Hunter, D. (2012). *For the win: How game thinking can revolutionize your business*. Philadelphia: Wharton Digital Press.

Willman-Iivarinen, H. (2017). The future of consumer decision making. *European Journal of Futures Research, 5*, 1–12.

Woodworth, R.S. (1921). *Psychology: A study of mental life*. New York: Holt.

Woźniak, J. (2017). Some factors hindering acceptance of three gamification solutions in motivation systems, in small and medium enterprises. *Management Dynamics in the Knowledge Economy, 5*(4), 663–680.

Yang, S., Carlson, J.R., & Chen, S. (2020). How augmented reality affects advertising effectiveness: The mediating effects of curiosity and attention toward the ad. *Journal of Retailing and Consumer Services, 54*, 102020.

Yim, M., Chu, S., & Sauer, P. (2017). Is augmented reality technology an effective tool for e-commerce? An interactivity and vividness perspective. Journal of Interactive Marketing, 39, 89–103.

Zhang, J., Fan-is, P.W., Irvin, J.W., Kushwaha, T., Steenburgh, T.J., & Weitz, B.A. (2010). Crafting integrated multichannel retailing strategies. *Journal of Interactive Marketing, 24*(2), 168–180.

Index